Teacher Empowerment
through
Curriculum Development

Theory into Practice

Teacher Empowerment through Curriculum Development

Theory into Practice

Fourth edition

Arend E Carl

JUTA

Teacher Empowerment through Curriculum Development: Theory into Practice

First published 1995
Reprinted 2000
Second edition 2002
Reprinted 2005
Third edition 2009
Reprinted 2010
Fourth edition 2012
Reprinted 2014

Juta and Company Ltd
First Floor
Sunclare Building
21 Dreyer Street
Claremont
7708

PO Box 14373, Lansdowne, 7779, Cape Town, South Africa

ISBN 978-0-70218-912-8

Project Manager: Debbie Henry
Editor: Wendy Priilaid
Proofreader: Lee-Ann Ashcroft
Typesetter: ANdtp Services
Cover designer: Nicole de Swardt
Indexer: Sanet le Roux
Print Administration by DJE Flexible Print Solutions

Typeset in 10.5 pt on 13 pt Baskerville

Contents

About the Author

Professor Arend Carl is a curriculum specialist who has written a number of publications on the subject of Curriculum Studies. His main research focus is on curriculum theory and the role of the teacher as a key stakeholder in successful curriculum development. He is currently the Vice-Dean (Teaching) of the Faculty of Education at Stellenbosch University.

Dedication

Dedicated to Zoë and Megan, my grandchildren, who represent those who should be at the heart of the curriculum.

Preface

Someone once said that curriculum development is not something done **to** teachers but **through** and **with** them. This implies that teachers must be involved in curriculum development and that they should have the appropriate skills and knowledge to be able to make a contribution to relevant curriculum development. When one reflects on the role of the teacher as curriculum developer, the whole issue of teacher participation and freedom, as well as democracy in the classroom, comes to the fore. In order to optimise the teaching–learning situation in the classroom, teachers should be empowered with regard to the whole process of curriculum development. Empowerment does not mean unrestrained and unstructured actions, but rather increasing and developing teachers' autonomy, as well as the learning outcomes and other experiences which flow from it, thereby contributing towards the development of the learner's full potential. Everything about curriculum should be about the needs and interests of our children, and the development of teachers should lead to optimally unlocking and developing their potential. The future depends on how we succeed in doing this.

Teachers dare not stand on the periphery as onlookers or passengers with regard to what is done for them and what decisions are taken for them – they must be active participants in the process of relevant curriculum development. Success depends on their involvement – they must be at the heart of the process. Curriculum development must not be the jealously guarded domain of specialists and 'those who know', as teachers have a cardinal role to play in that they are directly involved in classroom practice. They must therefore be fully empowered in order to fulfil their role as empowered agents of curriculum development. As teachers grow and develop professionally, the process of empowerment should become one of self-empowerment.

This book is a synthesis of extensive research, not only on teacher empowerment but also on the link between this notion and the process of curriculum development. This book is thus intended to make a contribution not only to the field of curriculum studies as a research field, but also to the enablement and empowerment of teachers with regard to curriculum development. Success will finally depend on both the level and nature of each teacher's empowerment in the process of curriculum development as well as to the extent to which teachers accept their responsibility as curriculum agents.

Arend E Carl

Acknowledgements

Pearson for the use of the diagrams on pages 24, 68, 75 & 150; P Babin for the matrix on page 59; P Human for the diagrams on pages 61, 143, 144, 146, 153, 154, 156, 160 & 161; J Cawood for the diagrams on pages 98 & 147; the Institute for Social Research at the University of Michigan for the two diagrams on page 118; C Hattingh for the diagrams on pages 119 & 125.

1

The Issue of Empowerment of the Teacher as Curriculum Agent: Some Perspectives

At the end of this chapter you should be able to

- reflect on your own level and degree of empowerment
- understand and define the concept and the problems of empowerment
- identify the various manifestations of empowerment
- formulate a rationale for teacher empowerment and decide on a strategy for self-empowerment
- devise a strategy as to how you may make a contribution towards empowering others.

1.1 Introduction

When one reflects on the role of the teacher as curriculum agent, the whole question of teacher participation and teacher freedom with regard to curriculum development is also involved. Each teacher must be systematically empowered in curriculum development to optimise the teaching–learning events in the classroom. Empowerment does not mean unrestrained and unstructured actions, but rather increasing the learning outcomes and other experiences which may flow from it, thereby contributing towards developing learners' potential. A teaching environment within which teaching may occur optimally can only be created through effective empowerment.

According to Miller (1994), a teacher's adaptation and style determine the quality and standard of what takes place in the classroom. An empowered teacher is pre-eminently able to develop learners' potential optimally. Further, the whole nature of relationships within the classroom is determinative of development and a positive environment. Accordingly, the teacher's view (and handling) of the question of co-operative teaching as against a more individualistic approach is often determinative of the teaching environment. The role of the teacher is, of course, important, but to ignore the principle that every learner in the school is in fact part of a community and that this aspect can also be utilised within the class can be a disadvantage. By taking this aspect into consideration, learners can also develop a feeling of interdependence in the classroom.

The empowered teacher's view of the curriculum is just as important. Such a teacher will probably not regard the syllabus as a recipe from which one may not deviate, but rather as an opportunity to experiment and to make it relevant and meaningful. This requires specific knowledge, skills and proficiency, and this is where empowerment is such a cardinal process.

A third important aspect to which Miller (1994) refers is also the nature of supervision and control in the school's system. As an empowered person, the teacher will rather act as a facilitator and make learners realise that they have a share not only in their own learning process but also in the learning process of others. Learners must develop a feeling of autonomy and therefore opportunities for this purpose must be created. As opposed to this approach, the teacher would be the dominant authority figure who controls **how** and **what** is taught.

The difference between an empowered and unempowered teacher is already becoming evident from the above. It is therefore critical that the teacher be empowered in order to be a fully fledged and effective curriculum agent.

Teachers face tremendous challenges, several of which are related to the curriculum. These manifest themselves at various levels and in various areas, i.e. from national level to within the classroom, and there are various role players and interested parties who may make a contribution towards overcoming them. It is therefore essential that every role player is able to make a meaningful contribution.

One of the objectives of school reform efforts is to ensure that schools become places of excellence for all students (Clair & Adger, 1999). This creates certain challenges for teachers, and in turn demands a certain level of teacher empowerment in order to achieve this vision of excellence in a diverse society with diverse needs.

Especially now, it is essential that each teacher should not be just a receiver of curricula, but in fact a curriculum developer. Teachers must, however, be empowered to be curriculum agents in the true sense of the word. The crucial question which will be addressed in this book is: 'What does the concept of empowerment encompass and what does an empowered teacher look like?' This question could be further expanded, i.e.: 'What skills, knowledge and attitudes must teachers have at their disposal to be regarded as empowered?' In the final analysis, teachers themselves must also accept the responsibility of ensuring that they are adequately empowered. Self-empowerment is thus also vitally important.

This chapter will therefore endeavour to throw more light on the concept and process of empowerment by looking at the following:
- A notional and concept statement
- Various manifestations of empowerment
- Conditions and supporting factors
- The role of leadership in the empowerment process
- Strategies
- The teacher as empowered curriculum agent

Following on Chapter 1, the rest of the book will focus on the process of curriculum development and what the teacher's possible functions may be. It is very important to note that the underlying principle of this book is to enable the teacher, through exposure to this process, to grow into the process of empowerment and to acquire greater freedom with regard to curriculum development. There are no fixed requirements or recipes: teachers will, in the final analysis, have to decide for themselves to what extent they will make use of the opportunity.

However, teachers dare not stand on the periphery and be onlookers with regard to what is done for them and what decisions are taken for them: they must be active participants in the process of curriculum development. Successful design, dissemination, implementation and evaluation depend in the final analysis on the teachers and therefore they must be at the heart of the process. Curriculum development must not be the jealously guarded domain of specialists and 'those who know' (and who are quite often outside the classroom), as teachers have a cardinal role to play in that they are directly involved in classroom practice. Teachers must therefore be fully empowered to be able to fulfil their role as empowered curriculum agents.

1.2   A notional and concept statement

It should be stated right at the outset that some people view the term 'empowerment' as an emotive or loaded concept which may stir negative emotions. In this book this term is seen as a process of growth and development which enables teachers to optimise not only the teaching–learning situation but also their own potential as educators. Empowerment is therefore not seen as an external intervention whereby something is done **to** people, but rather as a process that generates growth and enablement and in which they are involved.

Terry (n.d. – see bibliography) states that the definition of empowerment has emerged from the corporate world and that the concept parallels that of employee empowerment in a business. According to Bogler and Somech (2004: 277), research on teacher empowerment began to appear in literature in the late 1980s.

When the concept of empowerment is investigated, it is clear that there are divergent and differing perspectives. The focus is often placed at different points and approached from varying points of departure, often from a political viewpoint. There are, however, also certain matters in common. When empowerment is involved, the question of authority is also present. 'Power', of course, implies authority; but the question is: 'Who has the authority; and how is that position of authority exercised?' Furthermore, does the privilege of empowering someone rest with an agent from outside, or are opportunities facilitated so that persons may also empower themselves? In answering these questions, various definitions will first be given and thereafter some of these commonalities will be further illustrated. Heller (1993: 95) alleges:

> The term teacher empowerment invokes different ideas, emotions, and concerns in people … [P]hilosophies are usually generated around the issues of authority, responsibility, job security, accountability, professional growth, and the ability to meet the needs of students.

Bolin (1989 in Terry, n.d.) confirms that it refers to the right of teachers to be involved because they are professionals.

Gore's (1989: 3) definition of this concept is particularly valuable and deserves mention. She states that the concept empowerment means 'to give authority and to enable'. She further says:

3

Empowerment embodies a notion of power as external, power which can be given, which can be provided, power as property. Power must be something which can be controlled. It implies some kind of vision.

The concept is also often defined according to the context within which it occurs. Singh's (2003) view is that empowerment means to allow participation and give equal power in decision making, especially to those who have been kept out. It means giving power to the teacher to decide what will be taught and how it will be taught. Empowerment has to do with things such as sharing of power, the right to participate, the right to articulate oneself and be heard, equality and accommodation. His view clearly is one where empowerment is seen as something external to the teacher which is given to the teacher.

Vavrus (1989: 2–4) describes empowerment as 'the overcoming of workplace alienation and gaining the freedom to participate more fully in public affairs as a teacher'. A more democratic environment is necessary according to him, otherwise alienated teachers are created and this in turn can adversely affect productivity. According to Lagana (1989: 52), empowerment is the

> ... process of providing people with the opportunity and necessary resources to enable them to believe and feel that they understand their world and have the power to change it; for example greater autonomy and independence in decision-making. It means loosening control over what people do but gaining a wider span of control over information and outcomes.

Empowerment therefore deals with change in that it focuses on the development of individual as well as collective potential. Empowered persons feel that they can take an active part in and contribute to making a real difference. This implies that risks will have to be taken. The above-mentioned writers also refer to the Japanese term *Kaizen*, which means continuing improvement and step-by-step growth through a willingness to take small risks. As empowerment is the key to enabling risk taking, without it there will be little risk taking and change in the school. Growth and development are thus the targets. Sleeter (1991: 4) states that empowerment includes empowering strategies that capitalise on people's ability to understand their own needs and that build on the energy and strengths people have. The teacher is in the centre here and empowerment is driven by the needs of the individual.

The idea of involvement in decision making is also a characteristic of most descriptions. Melenyzer (1990) believes that true empowerment leads to a growth in professionalism as teachers become involved with and take responsibility for their own decisions. The relevant environment must thus be conducive to teacher participation. In this connection, Browder (Browder & Singer, 1993: 3) says that empowerment in its broadest sense includes any activity which enhances the professional status of the teacher. This implies that the self-image of teachers must be promoted, as well as the prestige they enjoy from their colleagues, that they will be more subject proficient and that they will be able to work within a team context. This in fact means for him that if people have more authority over their own work, this can lead to improvement but that the existence of a strong group culture is just as important.

Zeichner (1991: 365) confirms this point of view, and states that teachers must be allowed to make their own decisions with regard to subject-related aspects and also to curricula and organisational aspects falling outside their particular classrooms. His statement refers to the question of teacher participation in decision making as well, and he also makes mention of the so-called democratisation of the school. There are various writers who in fact speak rather of democratisation than of empowerment. One such writer is Singer (Browder & Singer, 1993: 3, 6), who pleads for the extension of teacher participation in democratic decision making. His motivation is that if teachers wish to lead their learners into being good citizens in a democratic society, there must certainly also be a democratic dispensation in the school. He also warns that democracy is hard work, as people must learn to work with others, to understand others better, to respect differences, to take responsibility for decisions and to make a positive contribution in carrying them out. Democracy cannot be quickly learnt through a lecture or subject chart. He puts it very powerfully as follows (Browder & Singer, 1993: 6):

> We learn democracy by living it. They [students] are not going to experience democracy unless teachers are committed to democracy. Democracy is not a frill. It is what education is all about.

To a writer like Romanish (1991: 55–69), empowerment comes into its right if teachers can be involved in the restructuring of the school. Democracy cannot develop if the school is not also managed democratically, and teachers must at least have control over their own professional matters. There is strong support for the view of Stone (1995) when she states that empowerment grants an individual the ability to direct his or her own life.

Kavina and Tanaka (1991: 115) in turn accentuate greater professionalisation, calling it, most strikingly, as 'the power to exercise one's craft'. They further say:

> It is the extent to which teachers practice autonomous behaviour while maintaining collegial interaction, giving attention to … needs, accepting responsibility and accountability, … participating in group problem solving to determine collectively the goals and direction of the school.

To them this complex notion also contains the following:
- The degree of control over instructional aspects
- The type of organisational climate
- The availability of staff development programmes
- The views of leaders in the field of teaching
- Clarity in regard to the aims of the school
- The perception that teachers are professional persons

Bogler and Somech (2004: 286) also confirm the importance of acknowledging and enhancing teachers as professionals, because when teachers view themselves as professionals or utilise opportunities to grow professionally, this may be to the benefit of the school and the organisation itself. Teachers want to grow professionally and they want opportunities to enhance this process. A study undertaken by Bogler and Somech (2004) confirms that professional commitment is a key aspect in ensuring empowerment and growth. Ross (1990: 1–13) also debates the link between empowerment and professional development. He argues that to be 'truly autonomous professionals teachers will have to regain control over the curriculum as well as school issues and develop a much stronger voice in the production of knowledge about teaching'. These aspects accentuate the complexity of the notion.

Almost all the above stress the fact that teachers are empowered from external sources. This view does not enjoy support throughout, as teachers are then regarded as passive receivers who have little say in or input to their own development and empowerment. Cornett (1991), however, says that teachers are in any event decision makers and that they cannot be empowered by others. By implication he says that **other** persons cannot decide how teachers should look and then equip them accordingly from 'outside'.

Kruse and Louis (1998) are of the opinion that the isolation of teachers limits their professional growth and that school settings should be created which would produce the conditions for teacher empowerment. These include the fostering of caring relationships, the building of structural and social support, and the identification of shared instructional strengths. By developing these instructional skills, full advantage can be taken of the school's adult talent. Teachers would then have a shared engagement in the academic enterprise. Kruse and Louis also point out that teachers might experience discouragement when they feel their work is not respected or valued by their peers. By increasing their influence as social agents in the school, they may feel valued because they can make a difference.

Newman (1991, in Kruse & Louis, 1998) suggests that giving teachers more individual autonomy, discretion and control in conducting their work encourages a greater sense of ownership of and responsibility for quality student learning. This means that teachers will have to work together in what Kruse and Louis call 'the professional community'. Conditions such as shared norms and values, reflective dialogue, a collective focus on student learning and collaboration characterise a community in which teacher empowerment can thrive. As teachers become better able to create school environments that support their own learning, they can become more supportive of the emotional, social and academic needs of learners (Kruse & Louis, 1998). This increased sense of influence (and accountability) can lead to optimisation of student learning. It is therefore clear that empowerment does not only impact on teacher development but also on student learning.

In this regard, Stone (1995) states that empowerment is important for children as well, because if empowerment changes how teachers view their work, empowering learners should improve their view of learning. This clearly takes the notion of empowerment an important step further, as the impact on learners now becomes the centre of the process. Stone (1995) is of the view that individuals change as they become more empowered in that they tend to be more motivated, independent and responsible. They are also likely to become risk takers and to collaborate within the team context, and are willing to reflect on and assess themselves. Empowerment therefore strengthens the motivation of both teachers and learners.

Keiser and Shen (2000) stress that the advantages and benefits of teacher empowerment include increased teacher job performance and productivity, improved teacher morale, increased teacher knowledge of subject matter and pedagogy, and eventually also higher learner motivation and achievement.

It is perhaps useful to mention here what empowerment is **not**, i.e. it is not 'turning people loose and then hoping for the best'. There is still a high premium on output, outcomes and productivity. There is therefore no climate of carelessness and meaningless freedom, but rather of freedom with responsibility because a specific purpose is pursued. As DuFour and Eaker (1987: 89) state further:

> Schools must be both 'loose' and 'tight'. Principals must encourage innovation and insist on compliance. They must remember RM Kanter who wrote: 'Freedom is not the absence of structure – letting employees go off and do whatever they want, but rather a clear structure which enables people to work within established boundaries in a creative and autonomous way'.

Empowerment therefore takes place through a process and is not without structure. Even a bureaucratic system which is often strongly criticised offers a structure within which empowerment can take place. The key to empowerment is indeed teacher involvement. Carl (2005: 228) warns that if this input and 'voice of the teacher' is ignored, effective curriculum development can be thwarted.

From the above it is evident that there are clearly distinguishable views on empowerment. For the purpose of this book, the following working definition has been taken as a point of departure:

> Empowerment is that process of development and growth through which a person goes which enables him or her to take independent decisions and to act autonomously and independently with a view to making a contribution towards the development of his or her particular environment. This process is coupled with the development of applicable skills, attitudes and knowledge within a positive and democratic climate. These persons are therefore regarded as professionals in their own right, as they are able to make a contribution to change through their particular power.

1.3   Manifestations of empowerment

Although the concept has been explained in the previous paragraph, it is nevertheless also necessary to explain the various ways in which empowerment manifests itself. Gore (1989: 5–16) makes a useful contribution with her exposition of such manifestations. She divides them into three groups, referring to them as 'teacher empowerment in use'.

Gore avers that some practices, such as selecting the teacher of the year and giving teachers their own business cards, are not necessarily empowerment as they usually depend on outside agents and there is no access to joint decision making. The three groups are as follows:

a. Professionalisation

Empowerment is the development of greater 'professionalisation' which goes with the granting of more authority, status and individual growth. Teamwork and the acknowledgement of their work by colleagues is part thereof. According to Gore, this view also means that outside persons decide on behalf of teachers what they require. She puts it as follows: 'Empowerment is clearly to be defined by those who are already in positions of authority within the school system' (Gore, 1989: 5–16).

Gore quotes Maerhoff (1988), who states that there is no risk attached to giving teachers greater control over the curriculum, but 'the product ought to be carefully monitored'.

It is clear that there is a contradiction in this statement. It therefore takes place within defined school authority structures and can be a damper on initiative. Maerhoff also contends that there must be a specific vision and that if empowerment does not lead to more effective learning, it is of no value. 'The improvement of learning should be the goal of empowerment' (Maerhoff, 1988: 106, as quoted by Gore, 1989: 7).

To Gore this is a conservative view, as it does not really have to do with the interests of the teacher.

b. Liberal humanism

The second manifestation according to Gore (1989: 7–8) is that of 'liberal humanism'. A very strong emphasis is placed on freedom and emancipation in that the process during which persons have the right to design curricula and child studies is accentuated. Emancipation and individualism are strongly accentuated but do not always take into account specific institutional structures, which can be limiting.

c. Critical theory

The third manifestation mentioned by Gore (1989: 8–16) is that of 'critical theory'. This implies that there is a particular vision that persons must be able to change their particular social environment. She quotes McLaren (1988), who states:

> … [It is about] enabling students to do more than simply adapt to the social order but rather to be able to transform the social order in the interests of social justice, equality, and the development of a socialist democracy.

They must therefore be freed and their circumstances changed in order to be able to change the community. Following on this, Fay (1987, as quoted by Gore, 1989: 9) states that the whole purpose of critical theory is to address and rectify a situation within which a group suffers and their lives are regulated. The process of emancipation is therefore relevant here and it is also said by implication that there are particular oppressions, inequalities and injustices which must be rectified. This view is also, according to Gore (1989: 10), a political vision rather than a method which wishes to acquire true participation. The question is also put as to what oppression is to the teacher: whether it is caused throughout the structures or the manner in which schools are organised; what is meant by emancipation; and how much freedom there should be.

An interesting conclusion was made by Lichtenstein, McLaughlin and Knudsen (1991) after a research project, i.e. that greater decentralisation did not necessarily lead to greater empowerment, but rather that the development of professional relevant knowledge is necessary for true empowerment. To Peters *et al.* (1990, as quoted by Sidani-Tabbaa & Davis, 1991), empowerment is manifested in three areas, i.e. in the field of status, in knowledge and in the possibility of being able to make decisions for oneself. This clearly implies that, once empowered, teachers can empower their learners by no longer being transmission orientated as the mere transferor or transmitter of knowledge, but by rather being the facilitator of teaching (Sidani-Tabbaa & Davis, 1991).

Greene (1989) links up with this by mentioning that empowerment is manifested in the manner in which teachers reflect on their work and the freedom which they have to do so. She states that teachers' willingness to reflect on the contribution which they may make to improve the community and to what extent they allow themselves to be bound by bureaucracy and merely imitate it passively are an indication that they are not just going to accept the status quo. Such persons 'are more likely to become explorers and interpreters rather than transmitters of received ideas' (Greene, 1989).

Colyn (1991: 112) states that teachers must be active agents for change and must be in control of matters in their classes through being able to make decisions with self-confidence. This being 'in control' naturally takes place within a particular system, but it does not mean that initiative is now damped. As Colyn (1991: 112) puts it:

> ... [T]hey can take charge of what takes place within their classrooms although they may still operate within a rigid system. Teachers can take charge of transforming their practice in order for change to occur in their classes. ...
> [I]t is necessary that teachers start reflecting on their practices.

For some this would also be connected to the process of democratisation. These views naturally all have curriculum implications, but will be addressed in a later section. What is involved here is the question of teacher autonomy. For the sake of completeness, it may just be mentioned that to writers such as Ornstein and Hunkins (1988), Trousdale and Henkin (1991) and Prawat (1992), empowerment is manifested in the measure of consultation, freedom and involvement with curriculum development. Nihlen (1992) goes so far as to say that this even appears in the extent to which teachers act as researchers in their classes.

From the above it is clear that empowerment does not mean the same thing for everybody and is manifested in various ways. Empowerment is thus a broader concept than simply a definition, as it can be embodied in a particular manner.

1.4   Conditions and supporting factors

From the discussion above, it is already possible to infer specific factors which may be regarded either as supporting or limiting. These factors may come to the fore in various fields.

It is also clear that a democratic climate is conducive to the stimulation of empowerment. The particular organisational climate is of great importance according to Zeichner (1991), Short and Rinehart (1992), and Melenyzer (1990). Firestone and Wilson (1984: 7) state in this connection that the culture of the school is the key to greater effectiveness, because it asks questions such as:

- What are the acceptable standards?
- How can order and structure be maintained?
- How much freedom is there in the relevant curricula?
- What is the position with regard to personnel relationships?

Other than asking these questions, a culture also influences teachers' commitment to and assumption of the relevant values, their loyalty to the school and the standard of productivity.

The whole question of leadership will be more fully explained in the next subsection but is also regarded as being of cardinal importance. Stevens (1990: 66) avers that 'a strong leader who strives for an effective school climate and encourages staff involvement is on the road to success'.

McElrath (1988) points out that the manner in which schools are **organised** often works counter to empowerment rather than promoting it. Efficient structures which afford opportunities for consultation can lead to greater ownership and effectiveness. Another important factor is that the principle of empowerment must already begin during initial training.

Lagana (1989: 53–55) puts it clearly that school principals must realise that teachers are able to determine their own requirements with regard to professional development and that they are able to grow within this development if given the scope to do so. Sufficient support, time and scope must be allowed for this purpose. Access to sources which can stimulate development must be created. There must be a climate within which there are shared values with regard to the relevant mission. The school may then have a corps of empowered teachers who accept accountability for what takes place in the school. Other factors which play a role in the empowerment of teachers are the following:

- Educational leaders must themselves also be empowered.
- There must be a commitment to the process of empowerment.
- Empowerment must not be regarded as a threat to authority, but as an opportunity for development. It requires a particular adaptation.
- There must be clarity as to precisely what the process means so that misunderstandings cannot arise.
- Teachers must realise that they themselves have a specific role to play in a self-empowerment process. They must not be only passive receivers but must also play an active role in their self-development.

1.5   The role of leadership in the empowerment process

From the literature it is clear that leadership is of cardinal importance in enabling empowerment to come to its full right. There is a clear connection between the standard of leadership and the standard of empowerment. Without mentioning details, investigations by Martin (1990), Bredeson (1989) and Christensen (1991) confirmed this connection. This is not only valid in respect of the school principal as leader but also with regard to the measure in which teachers themselves are prepared to fulfil a leadership function. The school principal will in any event have to make a clear and conscious commitment with regard to the empowerment of staff. Lagana (1989: 54) says that enlightened school principals realise the necessity of empowering not only themselves but also their staff. They would also have to have gone through a process of empowerment in order to be able to function as educational leaders.

Terry (n.d.) states that the knowledge base of empowerment must be extended to enhance teachers to become effective leaders. The implication is that leadership is required to facilitate empowerment, but that teachers are also leaders and have a significant role to play. This can lead to putting teachers at the centre of reform and to using them as catalysts for change and renewal. He states that the most effective leaders are those whose teachers have ownership in the mission of the school and an interest in its effectiveness.

A very important aspect is that should school principals be prepared to play a role in the empowerment of teachers, it does not mean that they lose authority or are disempowered, but rather that teacher empowerment can be viewed 'as a more intensive professionalization of the teacher's role' (Kavina & Tanaka, 1991: 115). Lintner (2008: Abstract) also stresses the importance of principals needing to continuously evaluate and redefine their leadership roles.

What this implies is that should there be encouragement for decision taking and empowerment, this will require a particular leadership and management style other than the traditional. It requires a participating leadership style which gives opportunities for encouragement and joint decision making. Bernd (1992: 64) puts it very strongly, saying:

> Teacher empowerment loses its effectiveness if the teachers do not have an instructional leader to keep them on track, well-informed, and involved. The principal must fill this role.

A very interesting opinion is that of Peters and Waterman (1982), the writers of *In Search of Excellence*, who state that the role of the principal is not to be the best teacher or to be an expert, but rather to be a facilitator and an empowerer. As already mentioned, this requires school principals to break with the traditional and adopt other perceptions and attitudes. Houston (1993: 11–12) refers to this as **transformational** leadership. He says:

> The idea of taking one thing and making something else from it is a basic precept for the transformational leader. The leaders of the new world will be those who see a different world and realise they must also change to help others to get there.

Therefore there will have to be a particular vision as to what must be achieved and there must be a joint effort to do so. The eventual purpose is, according to Cunard (1990: 34), to prepare learners more effectively for the society within which they will live. The school principal as educational leader therefore has the task of empowering teachers in such a way that they will be able to make a contribution in this regard. In this way, not only is learner potential developed but teachers are also empowered. Cunard (1990: 33) says the following:

> The principal who shares power with teachers is still a leader. I believe this principal is a more effective instructional leader because empowered teachers are more likely to maximize their potential.

The team idea or the idea of participatory leadership is described by Grafft (1993: 18) as '[t]eaming for excellence'.

According to him, a very large measure of success depends on the standard of interaction between school principals and their staff. He suggests various steps that may be followed to promote this process and to stimulate empowerment:

- Building up confidence
- Promoting social interaction
- Maintaining and promoting good personnel relationships
- Maintaining good communication
- Carrying out effective conflict resolution
- Drawing and following up clear objectives
- Maintaining healthy working relationships

Huddlestone, Claspell and Killion (1991: 80–88) set out a motivation as to why it is desirable to promote teacher participation in decision making. They also suggest a procedure as to how it can possibly be done. There is a 'preparedness phase' which includes the following:

- Believing in the principle of participating in decision making
- Making an evaluation of the staff as to how receptive they will be for it
- Showing confidence and support
- Being patient and realistic
- Beginning on a small scale
- Building a basis of knowledge in order to be able to take informed decisions
- Developing the expertise of personnel
- Developing good communication channels

The following phases are those of 'experimentation', 'refinement and rounding off' and 'institutionalisation'. The message which, of course, comes strongly from this is that empowerment is not instantaneous but is a process which takes place over a long period.

Byham and Cox (1992, as quoted by Terry, n.d.) warn against a 'top-down' approach because it can demoralise people. It leads to a lack of responsibility, meaningless work, no challenges, the absence of trust and the presence of poor communication, rigid and bureaucratic policies, and no support, and 'people are treated exactly the same, like interchangeable parts'.

Terry (n.d.) stresses an important aspect when he says that outstanding principals 'go beyond merely involving teachers in decision-making'.

They can implement three strategies, i.e. provide a supportive environment, use specific behaviours to facilitate reflective practices and make it possible for teachers to implement ideas and programmes that result from these practices. Empowerment is thus a process that must go beyond the initial facilitation phase, as it should ensure further support and lead to self-empowerment.

Martin (1990) shows that educational leaders must be able to maintain good human relations, recognise potential and people's abilities, and maintain good interpersonal communication, and they must also show their teachers that they have enough confidence in them to give them the freedom to plan professional programmes for themselves and to take independent decisions. Following this view, Ornstein and Hunkins (1988: 69) believe that 'teachers are virtually an untapped source of energy and insight, capable of profoundly changing the schools'.

Levine (1987: 43) confirms this point of view, saying that one of the school principal's main objectives should be to democratise schools. This involves respecting all individuals and treating them with dignity, that the growth and development of those very people on whom reliance is to be placed will receive attention, that there will be opportunities for consultation in decision making, that every individual's expertise will be utilised, and that, if necessary, even restructuring of systems will take place. He says that preparation to take part in a democratic society requires the development of skills, attitudes and responsibilities, and that it will make particular demands on the school principal. According to McCoy and Shreve (1983: 102–103), this requires such school principals to be self-actualised, to be accessible to their staff, to have good communication skills, to build on the strengths and energies of their staff and utilise them, and to be prepared to take risks and to make provision for maximal growth and development on the part of both the staff and themselves. For this purpose, a special facilitating function is required.

From all this it would be possible to develop a feeling of ownership. This is only possible within a climate of shared decision making, according to Cherry (1991: 33). No restructuring is possible without it. Teachers should not feel threatened by school principals, but should develop the school as a team. This will mean, therefore, that school principals will have to 'share power' in order to attain the common goal. Goyne, Padgett, Rowicki and Triplitt (1999: 2) argue that a leader cannot 'give' power to people as it is innate. Leaders should rather use their power creatively and collaboratively for good, and should avoid giving teachers responsibility for decisions with no corresponding power to implement them.

A further question is, of course, what teachers must be empowered for. This matter has to some extent already been addressed but is illustrated further here. Specific areas in which teachers may be empowered are in respect of development of the curriculum, evaluation of students, the selection of instructional material, personnel development programmes, and the determination of instructional styles (DuFour & Eaker, 1987: 85–87).

The view of Sergiovanni in respect of 'value-orientated' leadership also deserves mention. He regards leadership as 'transactional (value)' and 'transformational (value-added)' (1990: 23–26). The first type is characterised by a style which he calls 'bartering'. This is, according to Franken's (1994) interpretation, the phase during which negotiation takes place between leader and follower. Reciprocal needs are addressed, with preference given to the need for improvement of the institution. Attention is given to both physical and social needs. Each knows what is expected of the other once this negotiation phase has been completed, and participation is consciously effected.

The second type, i.e. the 'value-added' type, is characterised by three phases. Leadership is now, after 'bartering', followed by 'building'. This support phase is often characterised by uncertainty, as it is the phase during which potential must be identified, expectations created and specific needs of different groups addressed. It is also the phase of symbolic leadership, as the leader begins to recede slightly into the background and, as facilitator, begins to pave the way for intrinsic participation. It is also the phase during which empowerment comes strongly to the fore. The aim is for a **commitment** to change.

The second phase is the so-called bonding phase during which greater clarity occurs (i.e. **transformation**) and one rises above the ordinary routine tasks. More is done than is expected, as a specific value system has begun to develop and persons now identify with these values. Objectives and vision are now shared, and leader and follower are now 'bonded' together. This phase is therefore characterised by the existence of a shared value system which strengthens the bond.

The last phase is 'banking' during which routinisation and institutionalisation take place. There is reciprocal confidence and the teachers have freedom, but in the process values are maintained. The school principal remains the facilitator, but the teachers are now in reality all leaders. Everybody's needs are now met.

From this view it is evident that to empower teachers can be a particular force. It is a good example of how external powers do not decide what teachers need, but that it is a team process. The focus then is on excellence, purposefulness and enabling teachers and the school; accountability is strongly in the foreground; intrinsic motivation is present; and good group relationships and shared leadership are part of the routine.

Rowley (1991: 28–31) also gives an example as to how schools may possibly be restructured. As already mentioned, this requires a particular aptitude on the part of the leader. The strategy of change may include the development of the applicable climate for participation, redefinition of roles, and experimentation and risk taking. Reep and Grier (1992: 90–96) confirm this *modus operandi* and particularly stress the willingness to take risks; they say in this connection:

> If you are dedicated to risk-taking efforts, you must provide a safety net for those testing new waters and communicate to your staff that failure is acceptable.

A new management philosophy is necessary, characterised by good communication; a suitable climate; the development of interpersonal relationships, participation in decision making; and acknowledgement of the professionalism of teachers. Foster (1990: 38–40) also describes a similar procedure to operationalise empowerment. Goyne *et al.* (1999: 5–6) argue that leaders want empowerment to succeed, but deep down they believe that people do not really want the responsibility that comes with empowerment. Leaders have to believe and work on the assumption that teachers will work on a higher level when given the opportunity. They do not need to fear that they 'will lose control' as giving up control might just enhance empowerment.

From the above it is clear that leadership is an essential determinant in allowing empowerment to come into its own. It is the presence of a particular view which leads to purposeful empowerment or the absence thereof which results in maintaining the status quo and not offering an opportunity for development. Perhaps Terry (n.d.) says it all with regard to the role of leadership in ensuring effective empowerment when he states:

> Without empowerment and teacher leadership, neither side wins. Principals and teachers are both faced with decision-making responsibilities.

1.6   The empowered teacher: A synthesis

It is clear that the question of teacher empowerment is not a simple matter. Carl (2009) refers to it as 'an elusive notion' as it is difficult to encapsulate in one definition. Teachers must have at their disposal specific curriculum skills and knowledge which enable them to be effectively involved in the classroom and outside it. Teachers must not only be able to do micro-curriculation within the classroom but preferably also become involved in curriculum development activities outside it. A detailed description of specific roles is set out later in the book, but at this stage some general remarks will suffice.

The process of teacher empowerment includes involvement in syllabus development (which, of course, can also take place inside the classroom), school curriculum development, fuller subject curriculation and even the development of the broad curriculum if possible. This involvement will in some instances be of a more direct nature and in others of a more indirect nature. To be involved in this way does require a certain aptitude, knowledge and skills. It will also be manifested in different ways. The core aspect which arises here is that the teacher must not be a mere implementer but a **development agent**, who is able to develop and apply the relevant curriculum **dynamically** and **creatively**. Effect can then be given to the working definition, i.e. the teacher can make a contribution to the development and the changing of the environment.

It is also most desirable that this process is a self-empowerment process (Carl, 1994: 192) and not only effected by outside agents (see Carl, 1986, for more detail). Teachers will therefore also have to be agents for change. They will be required to have a broad knowledge and understanding of educational views, a knowledge of children, a positive teaching aptitude and educational relationships, and knowledge and expertise in respect of both general curriculum studies and particular subject curriculum studies.

They will therefore not only have to be subject specialists but must also be able to consider and be involved in general curriculum aspects, such as the position and value of their particular subject within the broad curriculum.

What is the broad curriculum thinking with regard to relevant curriculation for South Africa? Practically speaking, it will not be possible for everyone to become involved in activities, but, where possible, there should nevertheless be an attempt to become an active role player. Creative thinking with regard to curriculum is therefore essential. Following on aspects previously mentioned, this will naturally imply that teachers will begin to have a say in decision making (not, as already stated, as threats to principals, but as partners). The question of teacher autonomy is also in issue here as it can assist in bringing about ownership and greater assumption.

According to Nihlen (1992), this involvement may come to the fore when, among other things, teachers also begin to function as researchers. In this way they are no longer civil slaves, but are seen rather as 'empowered practitioners'.

Fullan (1993: 16–17) follows this view, stressing that beginner teachers must not only be trained to teach well but they must also be able to bring about changes if necessary. This requires that teachers will always remain 'students' and active learners so as to develop in this manner to enable them to bring about these changes. In this way they may contribute to a better teaching environment within the classroom by also becoming involved outside it.

The debate about teacher empowerment is most certainly not over, but what it comes down to is that in the future, high demands will be made on teachers to play a greater role as curriculum agents than was the case in the past. To be able to do this requires that they be empowered to do so with a view to enabling them to make a contribution to the development and transformation of their environment. An environment should be constructed which will be conducive to teachers' eventually empowering themselves. Vaughn's opinion (1976: 24) gives direction. He states:

> All individuals have a role in developing, and sharing accountability for, the effective implementation of the educational goals developed. The result … will enhance the educational process and lead to the ultimate goal of quality education for all children.

Activities and questions

1. Are you clear as to what empowerment involves? What is the rationale for empowering the teacher?

2. Reflect on your own level and degree of empowerment as curriculum agent. How are you going to manage this profile you have just identified? Decide on a strategy for self-empowerment.

3. Formulate your own working definition of what you understand within your specific situation under the notion 'empowerment'.

4. Formulate a rationale for the phenomenon of empowerment.

5. Make a situation analysis as to how empowerment is manifested within your specific context. Please deal with this confidentially as it can be a sensitive matter.

6. What, according to you, are the five most important factors which
   - promote empowerment in your specific situation?
   - hinder empowerment in your specific situation?

7. Draw a profile as to how you think an empowered teacher will look.

2 Curriculum Studies as a Field of Study

At the end of this chapter you should be able to

- describe the necessity for the study of curriculum studies
- define the field of curriculum studies
- define some linked notions and utilise them within the curriculum context
- show an appreciation for the necessity of empowering the teacher with regard to curriculum development
- understand what is meant by 'curriculum' and contextualise it.

2.1 The necessity of relevant curriculum development for a developing South Africa

When education in southern Africa is placed under the spotlight from national to local level it is clear that many problems are directly related to the curriculum. To be able to solve these problems meaningfully and to ensure that dynamic and relevant curriculum development takes place, reflection on and study of the field of curriculum studies is essential. It is necessary to reflect theoretically on the subject of the curriculum with a view not only to understanding practice better but also to improving it. This reflection and acquisition of knowledge is very much in the service of teacher empowerment.

The curriculum problems of each country are unique, and each also has varying levels of locally available curriculum proficiency. In South Africa there is currently a greater awareness with regard to curriculum matters, but the question arises as to whether there are sufficient curriculum specialists locally who study both practice and theory, and who attempt to find a synergism between them and to ensure relevance.

As the ability to curriculate requires a great deal more than just a few actions and skills, this process must be understood.

Over the years, South Africa has had a number of factors which have detrimentally influenced effective curriculum development: a new curriculum and the accompanying challenges of implementing it; many uninformed teachers with regard to curriculum theory and practice; a tendency towards bureaucracy; a shortage in curriculum specialists; a lack of teacher contribution to curriculum development on meso- and macro-levels; and the frequent scepticism of teachers and principals towards curriculum research and experimentation (Carl, Volschenk, Franken, Ehlers, Kotze, Louw & Van der Merwe, 1988: 1–3; see also Human Sciences Research Council (HSRC), 1981: 116–124 for a fuller description). In the current (2012) period of transformation, many of these problems still exist.

In a changing and developing country such as South Africa, the stumbling blocks which are impeding development need to be removed. South Africa has a need for dynamic curriculum development so that relevant education may prepare learners for the world of work. Relevance is thus essential. There must be purposeful curriculum development to supply human capital and other requirements. This is only possible if the curriculum is thought through from the broad to the micro level within the classroom, and if appropriate development takes place. Van Rensburg (1992: 5) links up with this, stating:

> For South Africa to have any hope of competing in the same league as the global economic society, education will have to be more relevant to employment and the quality of both education and the work force will have to improve.

Focus must be placed on the development of relevant skills to meet needs and to deliver the necessary high-level human capital. These challenges accentuate the necessity to continue developing the field of curriculum studies.

There have been specific initiatives which have endeavoured to investigate curriculum development in South Africa and to propose a broad policy. Some examples of this are the HSRC's main investigation into education (1981); the document of the Committee of Education Department Heads (CEDH) – *'n Kurrikulummodel vir Onderwys in Suid-Afrika* (1991); the provisional report of the National Education Policy Investigation (NEPI) (1992); and the African National Congress's framework or discussion document entitled 'A Policy Framework for Education and Training' (1994). The last-mentioned did not propose a curriculum policy, but instituted an investigation into policies to identify key questions which may influence future policy and serve as a basis for discussion. In 1998, the so-called Curriculum 2005 was introduced, which, after an extensive review process in 2000, was replaced by the *Revised National Curriculum Statement for Grades R–9 (RNCS)*. The word 'Revised' was later dropped. The NCS was subsequently extended to the Further Education and Training (FET) band for Grades 10–12, with implementation in 2006 in Grade 10. In 2009 another review process was started, which led to the phasing in of the Curriculum Assessment Policy Statement (CAPS) from 2012 and onwards (South Africa, 2011; Department of Basic Education, 2011).

Relevant curriculum development is, however, not only assured on this broad front through national initiatives but also through the curriculum actions of those who are involved at other levels and in other fields (school and classroom).

At this stage it is perhaps appropriate to reflect on the actual curriculum practices which try to address this matter of ensuring a relevant curriculum.

Up until the early 1990s, South Africa's curriculum development practices and procedures were characterised by a process whereby curricula were normally designed at central level and then disseminated or distributed in a 'top-down' manner to the level of implementation. With the rise of greater democracy in South Africa after 1992, there was a greater emphasis on the democratisation of education.

The Constitution, which is the supreme law of the country, balances the rights of the state with the individual and the collective interests of the citizens by determining what powers the government has and what powers the citizens of the country have. All other laws are subordinate to the constitutional principles.

South Africa acquired a transitional Constitution on 27 April 1994, which remained in force until the new Constitution, finalised by the Constitutional Assembly, was signed by the state president in December 1996. One of the cornerstones of the Constitution is the guarantee of equality for all, and it is this provision which has been one of the major drivers of the transformation of the education system.

The *White Paper on Education and Training in a Democratic South Africa: First steps to develop a new system* (hereafter *White Paper*) (South Africa, 1995) sets out the envisaged process of transformation. One of the most fundamental changes is the emphasis on an integrated approach to education and training.

According to the *White Paper*, the rationale behind this integration is that it
* contributes towards the development of human resources
* bridges the rigid division between 'academic' and 'applied', and between 'theory' and 'practice'
* can contribute towards the recognition of learning and experience in more fields than only the formal educational sector.

Certain principles serve as points of departure for this process of transformation (South Africa, 1995: 15–18):
* Education and training are basic human rights.
* Parents and guardians have the primary responsibility for their children's education and have the right to be consulted by the state authorities on the form that this education should take and to participate in its management.
* The overarching aim must be to develop an appreciation of education and training among all individuals and to ensure access to education and training of a high quality.
* The system must increasingly ensure access to education and training opportunities for all children and adults.
* The inequalities of the past must be addressed.
* The principle of equality for all must be promoted by state sources, hence including education and training.
* The rehabilitation of schools and colleges must also lead to the establishment of representative management bodies and capacity building among such bodies.
* The realisation of equality, democracy, freedom, peace and justice are necessary elements for the successful implementation of lifelong learning.
* There must be mutual respect and regard for the diverse nature of the country's religious, cultural and language traditions.
* Education regarding the arts (music, dance, theatre and fine arts) must become increasingly available.
* The implementation of the new curriculum must promote independent and critical thinking.

- There must be curriculum choices to enable learners to acquire knowledge and skills that reflect the needs of the economy and for further career development.
- An appropriate Mathematics, Science and Technology teaching initiative is essential to supplement the shortages in these fields.
- Environmental education must be built in at all levels to develop environmentally aware and committed citizens.
- Education and training must meet the test of sustainability.
- Education and training must promote the principles of efficiency and productivity).

It is important to note that the *White Paper* (South Africa, 1995: 20–32) already makes reference to certain initiatives to operationalise these principles and to transform education. There are references to the South African Qualifications Authority (SAQA), the National Qualifications Framework (NQF) and the envisaged education and training certificates (South Africa, 1995: 20– 22). These principles were enacted between 1995 and 1998, which led to the implementation of a particular approach in school education that was carried through to the higher education sector.

This approach is known as the outcomes-based approach and it forms the foundation for the General Education and Training band, Further Education and Training band, and the Higher Education and Training band.

The South African Qualifications Authority was instituted by the South African Qualifications Authority Act, Act 58 of 1995, to certify all qualifications. SAQA's task is to establish and publish policy, structures and processes with regard to the criteria for standards and qualifications for institutions that wish to provide education and training, and to register these on the NQF. It also monitors the quality of education and training by continually assessing both the providers and learners in education and training. The National Qualifications Authority (NQA) was tasked with developing the NQF and ensuring that it was implemented successfully (Independent Examination Board, 1996: 7; SAQA, 1997: 5). This NQF is the curriculum framework within which qualifications may be obtained. It makes provision for the General Education and Training Certificate, Further Education and Training Certificate and the Higher Education and Training Certificate.

The NQF has adopted an integrated approach to education and training that attempts to give all South Africans access to equal educational opportunities of a high quality. Among other things the aims of the NQF are to do the following (Nasionale Opleidingsraad, 1994: 10–12):

- Institute a system to determine value that will assess performance against clearly defined standards.
- Create a dynamic structure that can adapt rapidly to new developments in the world of work, labour and education and training.
- Permit more people to enter education and training.
- Provide relevant education and training by addressing needs.
- Promote access to learning.
- Provide a variety of routes to qualifications.
- Simplify the qualifications structure.
- Ensure quality.

These initiatives are clearly focused on transforming the education dispensation to ensure that it realises the above-mentioned principles. This in itself creates major challenges for teachers, as they are the ones who are, in the final instance, having to implement the changes. This has vital implications regarding teacher empowerment in curriculum development.

What are the implications of these developments?

- There is a very clear shift of emphasis regarding the role of the teacher, who rather than simply being someone who conveys information, also has to be a curriculum agent and developer. There is a greater emphasis on the process, but it is necessary not to allow this to happen at the expense of the product. A balance between learning processes and learning outcomes is essential.
- There needs to be a close link between the classroom and the reality outside if the learner is to be prepared for the world of work. Taylor (1997: 2) says in this regard:

  ... [B]y linking classroom activities to the economic, political and social issues, the practical application of school knowledge is promoted.

- The traditional division of content in the form of school subjects has been replaced with a division in which contents are grouped into learning areas. (Note: With the new curriculum statements to be phased in from 2012 (CAPS: Curriculum Assessment Policy Statements), the notion of learning areas will be replaced with subjects.)
- Teachers will have to use a variety of methods which promote learner involvement and co-operative learning. Strategies will have to be devised and applied which will enable these methods to be used in classes with large numbers, in schools with few resources and facilities, in schools with no teaching and learning materials, and also in schools where teachers themselves have not been prepared to use these methods. They will also have to make adjustments in the classrooms depending on how learners react. This has certain implications for the in-service training of teachers in particular (Taylor, 1997: 2).
- Parents must also be kept fully informed during dissemination and implementation. 'Continuous' assessment now receives preference, and teachers need thorough preparation for this.

Teachers need be thoroughly prepared as curriculum developers seeing that they are expected to implement an extremely sophisticated system (Carl & Park, 1998: 29–30). (This information is available in greater detail in the discussion documents of the national Department of Education.)

Who then is responsible for relevant curriculum development? It can be stated that all persons involved in this process (from micro- to macro-level, i.e. the classroom up to national level) should have a high level of curriculum literacy. This involves not only skills but also a high level of knowledge. Various people are therefore involved at various levels or in various fields. A study of curriculum studies and in-depth curriculum inquiry are therefore essential, as a high level of mastery in both theory and practice is necessary in order to be able to curriculate effectively.

Theorisation is therefore essential. In this connection, Barrow (1984: 13) states quite clearly that 'it is the theory that provides the standards by which quality is judged'; and that 'there can be no doubt about what should be the essential influence on curriculum practice and that is sound curriculum theory'.

De Corte *et al.* (1981: 415) state that the curriculum gives a rational grasp of the instructional learning process and can help to bring about unity. For this reason, continuing curriculation is very important. It is essential firstly to study and develop curriculum theory. A unified point of view in regard to what is relevant for everyone will only be acquired with difficulty, but it still remains necessary to give an account of theory and practice on an ongoing basis.

The above is so much more necessary when one takes into account the enormous explosion of knowledge and changes with which South Africa is confronted. Curricula must be relevant and developed on an accountable basis in order to comply with the demands and needs of the country and the community. Defective curriculum competence and knowledge can lead to defective curriculation, which will eventually seriously prejudice the learners, as well as the country in the broad sense.

Pratt (1980: v) states: 'Curriculum is the major concern of the teacher. Curriculum thinking is … as old as education itself.'

In studying the curriculum, curriculum developers must understand in the first instance what curriculum studies as a study field includes.

2.2   Curriculum studies as a field of study

Curriculum theorising and inquiry

Why write about curriculum? The reason is because we have to understand the phenomenon we are dealing with. Much has been written about curriculum, and the idea is not to repeat everything here, but one has to admit that very little theorising has been done in the South African context – it is only since the 1970s and early 1980s that this really began. Considering the foreword of a book by Smith (1924), which starts by asking the question 'Why a new book on an old subject?', one realises the time it has taken to research curriculum in a contextualised way. At the time of the revision of this publication, research (funded by Stellenbosch University and the National Research Foundation) was being done into the state of curriculum studies in teacher training programmes in faculties of education (Carl, 2010–2011; 2011a; 2011b). Preliminary conclusions are that there is no real extensively developed theoretical field included in programmes; that there clearly are no typical South African curriculum studies; and that this field is fairly fragmented and underdeveloped (although there are a few centres where excellent work is being done).

What do we mean when we talk about curriculum theorising? Marsh (2009: 249–259) quotes Vallance (1982: 8) who avers that it is to shift the focus from the end product (i.e. the curriculum theory) to the process itself through which the theory is sought (the theorising process). Marsh (2009: 249) states that theorising is a general process where individuals are involved in three activities, namely being open and 'sensitive to emerging patterns in phenomena, attempting to identify common patterns and issues and relating patterns to one's own teaching context'. The implication is then, according to Marsh (2009: 249), that all stakeholders (including both teachers and academics) should be involved in theorising the curriculum. He then continues to unpack a number of proponents and approaches to curriculum theorising.

Description of the field: a study in its own right?

Authors agree that the field of curriculum studies is very broad and often vaguely defined. As it is complex, it is not easy to describe within a definition. Ornstein and Hunkins (2009: 1) claim that it 'has been characterised as elusive, fragmentary, and confusing'. The term 'curriculum' has so many possibilities of meaning, and the manner in which it is used by various people contributes to further confusion (Barrow, 1984: 3; Carl, 1986: 17). As a result of the many perspectives and approaches to curriculum development, Walters (1985: 6) quite rightly describes it as 'a field strewn with thorns'.

It was quite often the efforts to define the term 'curriculum' that led to this fogginess, as attempts were made to understand the **field** from descriptions of the **concept**. A description of the various attempts to define and describe the field can throw light on this statement, as they quite often mirror the approaches of the relevant writers.

Oliva (1988: 14) puts it clearly that for curriculum studies to qualify as a discipline or field of study there must be a clear set of theoretical constructs or principles directing it. Curriculum studies already have this strong theoretical basis and these principles. The relevant principles and criteria are described in Chapter 3, but the fact of the matter is that they already serve as guidelines. The concept 'curriculum' is, in itself, a construct. Oliva (1988) states that 'consecutive ordering of courses', 'career, education and behaviour goals' and 'systematic approach' are typical examples of constructs which are locked up in curriculum principles.

Oliva (1988: 15–17) puts as a further requirement for qualification as a field of study a pool of knowledge and specific applicable skills for that discipline. The field of curriculum studies complies with this requirement. A great deal of subject content has been taken from various pure and already established disciplines. The following (see Figure 2.1) is an example by Oliva of disciplines which may serve as sources.

The field of curriculum studies also continuously generates its own unique content and applicable skills. The latter are not necessarily unique to curriculum studies but may also be taken from other disciplines. This, however, does not detract from the importance and uniqueness of curriculum studies as a field of study, but rather accentuates its dynamics and challenges.

A third aspect of curriculum studies, according to Oliva (1988: 17–18), is the presence of its own theoreticians and practitioners. Curriculum specialists endeavour to develop the field by the application of their knowledge and skills, which generates new concepts and allows innovation to take place. A broad field description is possibly that curriculum studies is an inter-disciplinary field of studies, with the implication that various disciplines must work together in order to establish relevant curricula. It would therefore be a one-sided and narrow view to regard curriculum studies only as a field for didacticians and subject didacticians. On the contrary, there are too many

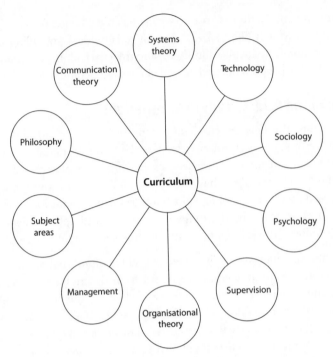

Figure 2.1: Possible disciplines which might act as sources (Oliva, 1988: 15)

psychological, educational, administrative and philosophical aspects involved to classify it under only one discipline.

Kelly (2009: 5–30) gives an extensive description of why curriculum studies is a field of study in its own right. He states that it 'is an academic and intellectual exploration of all of the factors we need to take account of in order to devise an educational curriculum' (2009: 6). This is an effort to analyse any aspect of the curriculum to determine how 'the different views and perspectives offered on them measure up to the educational principles and criteria we have identified as appropriate … to a democratic society'. Curriculum studies is thus a phenomenon which tries to investigate and understand the educational processes of society. Kelly (2009: 23–30) then continues to describe several unique features of curriculum studies, as follows:

- It is a study in its own right (i.e. not a sub-branch of other contributory disciplines) (2009: 23–24).
- It studies education as both a body of knowledge and practical activity (2009: 24–25).
- It is not an applied science (it studies human activities and 'does not lend itself to study of narrowly scientific kind' (2009: 25–26).
- It goes beyond methodology (the concern is not just on the how, but also on the why). It should not just focus on the 'mechanics of planning, development and innovation', because this is a narrow technicist view. Curriculum studies is much more than this. He puts it very eloquently when he says (2009: 28):

> Curriculum Studies … is a critical, analytical exploration of the curriculum as a totality, a theoretical/conceptual and practical/empirical examination of all of the dimensions of the curriculum debate and of curriculum planning, a critical evaluation of curriculum theories and practices, and a form of inquiry which goes beyond considerations of mere methodology and transcends both particular subject specialisms and particular age ranges.

- It is a conceptual analysis (i.e. it must concern itself with an analysis of curriculum concepts, views, range of theories and approaches, and insights with the view to providing conceptual clarity and coherence) (2008: 28–29).

The following is just one possible conceptual classification:

a. **Philosophical curriculum studies**
   - Philosophical perspectives on curriculum theory
   - The connection between philosophy and philosophies of life, educational views and curriculum
   - Formalisation of educational objectives and overall education objectives and legislation
   - Study of the influence of important educational views on curricula in the RSA
   - Operationalisation of the education ideal of Christian and other faiths in school curricula in the RSA
   - The accommodation of differing educational views in multi-cultural education
   - Structure models for curriculum content (e.g. Phenix, 1964)

b. **Sociological curriculum studies**
   - Community traditions
   - Community demands or expectations and the curriculum

c. **Historical curriculum studies**
   - Historical development of curriculum studies and thinking
   - Historical development of school curricula in certain/various countries (broad as well as specific curricula), with specific reference to curriculum paradigms

d. **Comparative curriculum studies**
   - Curriculation practices in certain countries
   - Study of curriculum innovation in these countries
   - Comparison of broad curricula
   - Comparison of specific curricula

e. **Psychological curriculum studies**
   - Child development phases and differentiated curricula
   - Learning psychology
   - Learning style differentiation

f. **Curriculum control**
   - Control and committee structures for curriculation

g. **Content curriculum theory**
   - Database/sources/foundations for content composition of educational objectives, including community needs, child development and culture content

h. 1. **Curriculum design: theoretical models and actual practices**
   - Criteria for curriculum design
   - Manifestations of curriculum (e.g. intended, delivered and received)
   - Curriculum models
   - Components of curriculum design
   - Curriculum levels and fields in which design can take place:
     - Community
     - Government level
     - School-phase and school-type planning
     - Syllabus development
     - School
     - Comprehensive subject curriculum development
     - Classroom/micro-curriculum development
   - Curriculum development procedures and practices in the RSA
     - Historical developments and trends
     - Curriculum functions and the roles of the persons and institutions involved
     - Teacher participation and involvement
     - Change in and renewal of school curricula

2. **Curriculum dissemination: theoretical models and actual practices**
   - Criteria
   - Strategies and models
   - Dissemination practices:
     - National
     - International

3. **Curriculum implementation: theoretical models and actual practices**
   - Criteria
   - Strategies for implementation and application
   - Strategies for effective feedback
   - Teacher involvement

4. **Curriculum evaluation: theoretical models and actual practices**
   - Criteria
   - Theoretical aspects:
     - Evaluation functions
     - Curriculum- and learner-orientated evaluation
     - Evaluation levels and fields
     - Evaluation methods
   - Evaluation practices:
     - Teacher involvement
     - Internal and external evaluation
     - Examination
   - Long-term feedback

i. **Didactics and subject didactics**
    - Particular connection between didactics, subject didactics and curriculum studies
    - Subject curriculum development
    - Micro-curriculation and the instructional–learning situation
    - Media education and the curriculum

Another conceptualisation is the one of Ornstein and Hunkins (2009: 31–149). They give an extensive description of what they refer to as 'foundations of curriculum'. They see foundations as the external borders of curriculum knowledge, and these provide valid sources from which theories, principles and ideas can be derived (Ornstein & Hunkins, 2009: 13). These foundations are (i) philosophical foundations, where the role of philosophy in curriculum is described (2009: 31–58); (ii) historical foundations, where the role of history in curriculum is described (2009: 63–102); (iii) psychological foundations, where the role of psychological aspects in curriculum is discussed (2009: 107–145); and (iv) social foundations, where the social setting is considered (2009: 149–177).

In reviewing Oliva's (1988) descriptions and the above-mentioned structure, it is clear that curriculum studies is a comprehensive field of study in its own right. This field has particular contents and constructs which are studied, as well as its own role players who are involved in various ways, either as theoreticians or practitioners during this process.

Barrow (1984: 6) argues that the field of curriculum studies eventually takes in the field of education from which it had its origin. He states: 'Curriculum studies boils down to describing, explaining and justifying curriculum practice'.

Furthermore, Brubaker (1982: 22–24) states that curriculum planners are interested in developing either curricula which would ensure control on the one hand, or enhance understanding on the other. This preference would colour one's view and influence the process of curriculum development.

Possible meanings and/or interpretations of 'curriculum'

It is essential that teachers have clarity about certain basic concepts. This is necessary in order to make the required distinctions as well as to identify and articulate their own involvement more clearly. A thorough knowledge and understanding of the most important concepts can also help in improving the understanding of the whole process of curriculum development.

There is a wide range of meanings of the term 'curriculum' and various ways in which this concept is interpreted. Smith (1984) writes in his article 'Taking Humpty Dumpty out of the curriculum' that educationalists should be very clear about what they mean when they use the term 'curriculum'. The title of the article is taken from a character that appears in Lewis Carroll's *Alice in Wonderland*. Smith refers to Alice's frustration when she is talking to Humpty Dumpty, who does not use words consistently to mean the same thing, but every now and again attaches a different meaning to a word. When Alice protests, he says: 'When I use a word, it means just what I choose it to mean – nothing more or less …' (Lewis Carroll, as quoted in Smith, 1984).

Posner and Rudnitsky (1982: 6) are also of the view that there are many different definitions but that it is necessary to consider what the conceptual distinctions between the various views are and to decide what the designer's understanding is of 'curriculum'. They distinguish between curriculum as a process and curriculum as a product.

Although there is no generally accepted interpretation of the term 'curriculum', it should always be explained in the context in which it is used. How you view curriculum and the context you ascribe to it is often influenced by your particular curriculum orientation and view of life (see Chapter 3). McKernan (2008: 13) has a valid point which one can agree with when he claims that the curriculum is not the final blueprint, as 'it is nothing more than an idea, and ideal in the form of a proposal that it represents some worthwhile plan for leading us out of ignorance and thereby resulting in further growth through education'.

Pinar, Reynoldts, Slattery and Taubman (1995: 1–65) provide an outstanding critique of the field of curriculum studies, and give valuable insights into the meaning of 'curriculum' for the curriculum student. They state (Pinar *et al.* 1995: xiii) that their book is **'a cacophony of voices'**, because it consists of the perspectives of a wide variety of authors – authors who each have their own specific view. Each reader is exposed not to **the** view of curriculum, but to a variety of views. Each individual is entitled to his or her view(s) and one has to provide for this space and freedom in their understanding of the concept.

The word *curro* (meaning 'I run' in Latin) from which the word 'curriculum' is derived, refers to a race, a track or a racetrack (Sönghe, 1977: 38; Brubaker, 1982: 2). When reference is made to the educational track on which learners move under the leadership of their teacher on the way to adulthood, it can be linked to the concept of *curro*. In terms of this, the curriculum serves as preparation for life.

Stenhouse (1976: 1–5) puts it clearly that definitions of the concept 'curriculum' do not solve curriculum problems, but rather offer perspectives from which the problems may be viewed. To him the curriculum is the way in which educational aims are realised in practice, and includes contents and methods and, in its broadest sense, a review of the implementation thereof, institutions and the accompanying problems. To him there are certain basic principles with regard to the planning phase (for the selection of content, methods, sequence and evaluation), principles for empirical studies and finally a clear aim for the curriculum. Marks, Stoops and King-Stoops (1978: 457) see the curriculum as:

> … the sum total of the means by which a student is guided in attaining the intellectual and moral discipline requisite to the role of an intelligent citizen in a free society. It is not merely a course of study, nor is it a listing of goals or objectives, rather, it encompasses all of the learning experiences that students have under the direction of the school.

Tunmer (1981a: 1; 1981b: 30) describes the curriculum as the whole spectrum of compulsory and optional activities which are formally planned for students. This view that it is always planned does not enjoy support overall. Attitudes and dispositions shown by students are not necessarily intentionally built into the original planning (Kelly, 1977: 2).

Where education must be effective and where learning must take place, there is unanimity that those activities which may promote learning must be well planned. An important contribution in this regard is from Tanner and Tanner (1975: 48–49), who see the curriculum as

> … the planned and guided learning experiences, formulated through the systematic reconstruction of knowledge and experience, under the auspices of the school, for the learner's continuous and willful growth in personal-social competence.

Greene (1989: 16) supports this view, but includes co-curricular activities. Barnett (2008) is of the view that curriculum is a 'pedagogic device for helping to fashion human beings of the highest kind'. Although his view focuses on higher education, it has merit in that it captures the ultimate aim of curriculum, which is to unlock the potential of learners.

Ornstein and Hunkins (2009: 10–12) are also of the view that the way people define 'curriculum' will also define their approach to it. They state that 'curriculum' may be defined in five ways, namely that it can, firstly, be a plan for achieving goals; secondly, it may broadly be described as a means of dealing with learners' experiences; thirdly, it can mean that it is a system which deals with people; fourthly, it may be defined as a field of study with its own foundations; and lastly, it can be defined in terms of subject matter.

The curriculum is therefore a broad concept which may include all planned activities and thus also subject courses which take place during the normal school day. It also includes after-school planned activities, such as societies and sport. This all takes place within a specific system, is continuously subject to evaluation, and aims to lead and to accompany the child to adulthood so that he or she can be a useful citizen within the community.

However, defining 'curriculum' is more complex than trying to put it in a box and capture one final definition and then claiming: 'This is what we understand by the concept "curriculum"!' Kieran Egan (1992, cited by Pinar *et al.*,1995: 867) says: 'Unlike the Grand Canyon, curriculum is not a thing of nature, but of culture'.

This statement touches on the complexity of the term itself, as it focuses on the dynamics, the complexity and the difficulty of trying to unravel such a dynamic and complex concept. It is through this process of trying to unravel it that one's understanding can grow.

From the above definitions, specific approaches may be deduced. It is also already clear that these approaches and thus also the definitions differ. When an attempt is made to define the concept 'curriculum', it is clear that writers have divergent opinions and that they may use the same notion within differing contexts. Schubert (1986: 26–34), for example, uses the term 'characterisation' rather than 'definition', as it gives a wider conceptualisation and offers a broad perspective as to what a curriculum can be. Without setting it out as fully as he does, his characterisation of curriculum as found in the literature is briefly as follows (in his work he examines the notions and critiques of each of these – see Schubert 1986: 26–34):

- The curriculum is content.
- The curriculum is a programme of planned activities.

- The curriculum is specific learning results.
- The curriculum is the cultural reproduction of a community reflecting the relevant culture.
- The curriculum is experience; in other words, specific activities and experiences leading to learning.
- The curriculum is seen as a set of tasks and concepts which must be achieved, or a predetermined purpose, which is the mastery of a new task or an improvement of a previous one.
- The curriculum is an agenda for social reconstruction whereby values and skills are acquired which may help to improve the community.
- The curriculum is *currere*. The focus is on the capacity and ability of individuals, so that self-discovery may take place through self-activity and they may get to know themselves – who, how and why they have developed in this way. Greater self-understanding is a crucial aspect in this regard. The crucial focus is autobiographical.

This contribution by Schubert is valuable as it prevents concentration on only one aspect of the curriculum and the loss of its totality. One cannot concentrate on only one facet, because then an understanding of broader perspectives may be lost.

Oliva (1988: 5–6) concurs with this, stating that the amorphous use of the term 'curriculum' has given rise to differing interpretations. Depending on what the writer's philosophies of life are, the following have arisen:

- Curriculum is that which is taught in a school.
- Curriculum is a set of subjects which are followed.
- Curriculum is content.
- Curriculum is a study programme followed by a learner.
- Curriculum is a package of material.
- Curriculum is a number of courses following on each other.
- Curriculum is a set of behavioural objectives.
- Curriculum is everything which takes place within a school, including co-curricular activities, guidance and interpersonal relationships.
- Curriculum is everything planned by the staff.
- Curriculum is the learning experiences of the learners in a school.
- Curriculum is what an individual learner experiences as a result of the school's involvement.

Oliva (1988: 6) therefore confirms Carl's (1986: 17) opinion that the notion 'curriculum' may have both a narrower (a set of subjects) and a wider (all the learning experiences offered by a school during and after school) meaning, depending on the context in which it is used.

Oliva (1988: 8–9) makes a very meaningful contribution by giving a classification of definitions. Theoreticians often define 'curriculum' as one of the following:

- As 'objectives' or what is intended or what it should do (i.e. purpose), for example to contribute to the development of thinking skills

- As 'context', i.e. the particular context or perspective within which it develops, for example a specific word or philosophy of life which may serve as a starting point and which eventually determines the nature of the curriculum
- As 'strategies' utilised during the process – the particular instructional–learning strategy, for example a problem-solving strategy, that is followed throughout as the crucial strategy

Walters (1985: 1–3) alleges that the word 'curriculum' in education and in practical teaching has undergone a change of meaning, so that it has become necessary to differentiate at least amongst the following:

- **Institutional curriculum** (e.g. school curriculum), i.e. the courses and their compositional subjects offered by the institution
- **Course curriculum** (e.g. the economic or scientific streams of study for the senior secondary phase), i.e. the subjects and subject compositions offered for a particular course
- **Subject curriculum** (e.g. the curriculum for history), which is a description and systematic ordering of the objectives, goals, objects, content, methods, instructional–learning activities, curriculum material and evaluation procedures for a subject

Rowntree (1978: 1–2) sees the curriculum as part of the so-called educational technology, i.e. the design and evaluation of curricula and learning experiences which lead to implementation and evaluation. According to him, this is a rational problem-solving approach during which learning and instruction can be systematically thought through. These are not teaching media. Rowntree's (1978: 6) 'curriculum' therefore consists of identifying goals, and designing learning experience, and evaluating and improving education following on evaluation.

This change of meaning of the word 'curriculum' is closely united with the historical development of curriculum studies as a field of study in education, an aspect which has already been described and which offers necessary perspectives for anyone who wishes to become deeply involved in the curriculum as a field of study.

In spite of all these nuances of meaning which have arisen over time, the present-day word 'curriculum' still has much in common with its original Latin forebear: there is a starting place, a course which must be followed and a finishing point which must be reached, be it aim or purpose. There is even a similarity with the two-horse chariot race of old in the sense that the 'horses' quite often pull in different directions, to the great confusion of both the curriculum student and the teacher! Theoreticians even differ as to the starting point – is it the 'situation analysis', as Nicholls and Nicholls (1972) and Krüger (1980) allege; is it the 'objectives or goals', as Tyler (1949), Taba (1962) and others would have it; is it the 'needs assessment' championed by Pratt (1980); or is it perhaps 'evaluation', as propagated by Walters (1985: 2)?

It is important to take note of these various opinions so that the educational leader and teacher may have a broad frame of reference and do not waste the wide spectrum of curriculum influences by, for example, focusing only on syllabi (Becher & Maclure, 1978: 13).

A curriculum is, however, not only dealt with in the school and this has the implication that there are various curriculum development levels. These are defined more fully later on, but in brief they embrace the following (Carl, 1986: 17):

- The broader community's philosophy of life, which serves as a premise for educational considerations (and therefore also curricula)
- Government legislation to make provision for the implementation of educational considerations
- School-phase and school-type planning
- Subject syllabus development
- School curriculum
- Complete subject curriculum development, instructional–learning (classroom) or micro-curriculum development.

Within the school curriculum, both the course curriculum and co-curricular directions are encountered. The ideal is that the school principal and his or her staff, in consultation with the relevant provincial education official and the school committee or governing body, should, after an in-depth situation analysis of the needs of the relevant community, take a decision with regard to course directions which should be offered in the relevant school with a view to ensuring that the predetermined objectives are optimally achieved. Depending on, *inter alia*, the type of school and local needs, a school curriculum can be developed from a selection of various course curricula, i.e. language courses, social sciences, physical sciences, commercial courses, art-orientated courses, or courses with a stronger practical flavour.

Barrow (1984: 11) provides a clear definition in describing the curriculum as a programme of activities (by teachers and learners) so designed that learners will, as far as possible, achieve specific educational and other school objectives.

The concept 'curriculum' can be regarded as a school curriculum when a further filling in of the relevant school phases takes place. An appropriate school curriculum is designed and/or developed according to the needs of the relevant community and learners. The school curriculum must be thoroughly planned and should make provision for obligatory and optional learning activities in the form of examination and non-examination subjects, as well as for suitable after-school activities. The eventual aim in this regard would be to lead the child to adulthood. Oliva (1988: 9–10) confirms this point of view in pointing out that a curriculum 'may be a unit, a course, a sequence of courses, the school's entire programme of study – and may take place outside of class or school'.

McKernan (2008: 11–13) also debates the elusiveness of the concept. He states that curriculum is a proposal for and educational process, and that it 'is something of taste and judgment, testing the power of creativity, research and evaluation, calling upon our best powers of imagination'. He goes on to distinguish between the now well-known viewpoint that curriculum is seen by some as something narrower (i.e. what is taught and experienced in lessons) and the broader viewpoint (i.e. everything that is learned and experienced in the school).

The above descriptions serve only to place the curriculum within the education perspective and not to provide at this stage a description of curriculum development. Other educational systems would probably regard a curriculum from another point of view and, in that event, the manifestation thereof within the school would possibly be somewhat different. This is also an indication of the complexity of this concept because it has such a variety of interpretation possibilities. This must be taken into account.

Because there are other concepts which are often used synonymously with curriculum, these terms will be briefly described.

Subject syllabus

Cawood, Strydom and Van Loggerenberg (1980: 23) describe a syllabus as '*'n sistematiese keuse en ordening van kennisinhoud uit 'n bepaalde wetensgebied*' (meaning a systematic selection and organising of subject knowledge from a specific area of knowledge).

In an extension of this description by the same authors, a syllabus is regarded as

> … *'n lys, opgawe of katalogus wat die breë doelstellings en kennisinhoude vir 'n bepaalde vak op sistematiese, geordende wyse uiteensit. 'n Sillabus dui gewoonlik die doelstellings sowel as die kerninhoude wat vir eksaminering voorgeskryf word, in breë trekke aan* [meaning a list, inventory or catalogue that sets out the broad goals and knowledge content for a certain subject in a systematic, ordered way. A syllabus indicates both the goals and the core content that is prescribed for examination in broad terms] (also see HSRC, 1984: 1–2).

Tunmer (1981: 1) also sees it as 'a more detailed indication of what aspects of a subject or an area of knowledge should be presented to the learner'.

Cawood, Muller and Swartz (1982: 69–70) state that these instructional contents are usually prescribed for a fixed period by an educational authority or an examining body. This content must therefore comply with specified standards and requirements, and is chosen in accordance with the particular level of development and intellectual ability of the learners.

In reality it is not the learning content itself which is taken up in the syllabus. Learning content is found in detail in textbooks, subject literature, self-activity modules, various educational media and others. The syllabus contains the core content of what is prescribed. The classification thereof is tentative, as the class teacher may reclassify it during micro-curriculum development.

A subject syllabus is normally concerned with the particular subject's overall objectives, the core content and the possible organisation/classification thereof. Instruction and learning are then built into this organised field of objectives and content (Connell, 1955).

The curriculum model of Cawood, Carl and Blanckenberg (in Carl, 1986) (see Table 4.1 in Chapter 4) can be applied to differentiate the syllabus from the subject curriculum. All the components in this curriculum model together form a subject curriculum, while the objectives and core content together form a subject syllabus.

Subject curriculum

A subject curriculum includes more than just the objectives and selected core content as described in a syllabus. It includes all details for a specific course or school phase which the teacher may require in order to instruct effectively in the subject. It should possess enough flexibility so as not to dampen the teacher's initiative for individualisation and experimentation (Cawood *et al.*, 1982: 68–69).

It comprises a description of systematically selected and classified aims, content instruction, learning activities and experiences, teaching methods and evaluation procedures for a subject. However, it does not necessarily mean that all components must always be present (HSRC, 1984: 2).

Further to this, a subject curriculum may contain the following aspects to allow sufficient flexibility:
- The relative place of the subject with regard to the broader educational and teaching goals
- Investigations, analyses and the gauging of needs in the particular subject
- The nature of teacher training and in-service training in the relevant subject
- The particular learning needs set by the subject
- Overall aims
- Core content
- Learning content
- Instructional and learning goals
- Particular methods and techniques
- Particular media
- Particular learner activities
- Particular learner evaluation
- Particular contextual evaluation of all aspects of the subject curriculum (also called situation analysis or ongoing evaluation of the context within which development takes place)

With regard to this, subject curriculum development should take place by means of opportunities and instructional guidance possibilities, such as subject meetings, subject societies, study groups at teacher centres or subject groups in teachers' unions. Active involvement in subject curriculum affairs by the teacher can lead to a more effective instructional–learning situation, as well as to greater involvement on the part of the subject teacher.

The subject curriculum is thus an umbrella facet which consists of various components, including the syllabus.

Curriculation

Curriculation is regarded as the systematic and effective planning action during which components such as objectives; goals; situation analysis; selection and classification of content; selection and classification of teaching experiences; planning of teaching methods and teaching media; planning of the instructional–learning situation;

implementation; and learner evaluation figure strongly. Particular situations and circumstances can determine which component may serve as a point of departure. This implies that one particular component will not always necessarily serve as the point of departure. This curriculation action is thus an attempt to plan systematically and in an orderly fashion so as to bring into being an effective design.

Curriculation can take place at various curriculation levels, but not all elements will arise at all levels. Curriculation is therefore the action in terms of which each phase of curriculum development is actually brought into being and can therefore be regarded as synonymous with curriculum development.

Curriculum framework

A framework is a written document in which general policy for one or more instructional presentations in a particular subject is set out. It contains the following: the broad objectives of the instructional presentation(s), the similarly selected and classified core content in the form of subject/themes as headings, and guidelines (only in respect of frameworks which conclude with externally controlled examinations).

Frameworks are not syllabi, as these are developed from the frameworks. A framework's development also takes place in terms of curriculum development principles (namely research is done, a situation analysis is carried out, objectives are formulated, content is selected and classified, and evaluation is formatively done) (CEDH, 1991: 56–57).

Synopsis

A synopsis is a summary of the prescribed objectives, learning content and evaluation standards for an instructional presentation, the level of completeness of which is such that Umalusi (the South African Certification Council) can duly execute its certification function (CEDH, 1991: 57).

Broad curriculum

A broad curriculum is a collection of subjects/instructional presentations aimed at a specific target group and within which these subjects/presentations are structured, and connected requirements are set out. A broad curriculum is always qualified in terms of the relevant target group; for example, the broad curriculum for pre-tertiary education, the broad curriculum for the senior secondary phase, the broad curriculum for Grade 1, the broad curriculum for vocational teaching, or the broad curriculum for acquiring a specific vocational teaching certificate (CEDH, 1991: 58).

Learning programme

The learning programmes are the 'vehicles' by means of which the curriculum is implemented in the various fields, for example the school. They consist of sets of teaching and learning activities in which the learner becomes involved on the way to the realisation of one or more specific outcomes (Department of Education, 1997: 15). Learning programmes have essentially replaced syllabuses. The *National*

Curriculum Statement Grades R–9 (Schools) has been implemented in schools by means of the learning programmes. These are structured and systematic arrangements of activities that promote the attainment of learning outcomes and assessment standards for the phase. Whereas the National Curriculum Statement stipulates the concepts, skills and values on a grade-by-grade basis, learning programmes specify the scope of learning and assessment activities per phase. Learning programmes also contain work schedules that provide the pace and the sequencing of these activities each year, as well as exemplars of lesson plans to be implemented in any given period. The underlying principles and values of the National Curriculum Statement also underpin the learning programmes.

Learning programmes must ensure that all learning outcomes and assessment standards are effectively pursued and that each learning area is allocated its prescribed time and emphasis. The learning programmes are based on relationships between the learning outcomes and assessment standards across the various learning areas, without compromising the integrity of each one (Department of Education, 2002a: 15).

> In the Foundation Phase, there are three learning programmes: Literacy, Numeracy and Life Skills. In the Intermediate Phase, Languages and Mathematics remain as individual learning programmes. Other integrated learning programmes may be developed by schools, with the approval of the provincial departments of education. Provinces themselves may develop province-wide decisions on combinations in the Intermediate Phase. In the Senior Phase, there are eight learning programmes based on the learning areas. Schools may decide themselves on the eight learning programmes (Department of Education, 2002b: 3).

Learning area

(Note: As mentioned before, with the new curriculum statements to be phased in from 2012 (CAPS: Curriculum Assessment Policy Statements), the notion of learning areas will be replaced with subjects. As the concept of learning areas will still be around for a few years, the concept clarification is maintained here.)

A learning area is, in the South African context, a new grouping of content that replaces the school subjects for the General Education and Training phase (Grades 1–9). There are eight learning areas (Department of Education, 2002a: 9):

- Mathematics
- Languages
- Economic and Management Sciences
- Natural Sciences
- Social Sciences
- Arts and Culture
- Technology
- Life Orientation

Types of curricula

If one then is confronted with this wide range of possible meanings, nuances and interpretations of the concept 'curriculum' itself, one can clearly see that one's interpretation is not only influenced by the specific context, but also by how one views the curriculum (see Chapter 3 for paradigms and approaches). Figure 3.5 also provides a conceptualisation of how the different types of curricula may be transformed or changed as they are being implemented at different curriculum levels (see Chapter 3). From the literature one gets an idea of the types of curricula. The information of this section is briefly provided in table form (the mentioned sources can be consulted for further details):

Table 2.1: Types of curricula

Type	Brief description
'Hidden'/implicit/covert curriculum	Practices and goals not explicitly described in curriculum documents, but are a regular and expected part of the school experience – they are unintended and not overtly included in curriculum planning
	(Vallance, in Lewy, 1991: 40; Kelly, 2009: 10; Cortez, 1981; McKernan, 2008: 36)
Planned and received curriculum	Planned – the official curriculum of what is included in syllabuses
	Received – how learners actually experience the curriculum (Kelly, 2009: 11)
Perceived curriculum	What has officially been approved – this is not necessarily how people perceive it (Goodlad & Associates, 1979: 61–62)
Formal and informal curriculum	Formal – includes the formal activities or courses accommodated by the school timetable and institution
	Informal – focuses on those voluntary or extracurricular activities (e.g. after-school activities) (Kelly, 2009: 12; Goodlad & Associates, 1979: 61; McKernan, 2008: 35)
Overt or intended curriculum	The intentional instructional programme (Cortez, 1981) resulting in plans, materials and textbooks to control the focus and content of teaching (Eisner, 1990: 63)
Null curriculum	That which schools do not teach, but which is just as important as the formal curriculum (McKernan, 2008: 35)
Operational curriculum	The results of how the teachers mediate the intended curriculum (Eisner, 1990: 63) – also known as the taught curriculum (McKernan (2008: 35) refers to this as the actual curriculum)
Experiential curriculum	The curriculum experienced by the learners (Goodlad & Associates, 1979: 63)

Curriculum development

For the purpose of this publication, curriculum development is regarded as an umbrella and continuing process in which structure and systematic planning methods figure strongly from design to evaluation. It comprises a number of phases: curriculum design, curriculum dissemination, curriculum implementation and curriculum evaluation.

Another view is that curriculum development comprises phases, such as 'initiation', 'development', 'adoption' and 'evaluation'.

The final goal of curriculum development is to bring into being more effective education by means of a more effective and meaningful curriculum, and for that reason any change requires thorough consideration.

Development and change do not, however, have only a systematic aspect, i.e. development does not take place only when there has necessarily been planning. Often there is a natural development, but this does not mean that the development is not thoroughly considered.

Curriculum development is difficult to tie to a fixed position with regard to the phases mentioned above, because the progress from one phase to another in reality implies change and development. The interaction between these phases implies change and, as such, also development. Development is therefore implicitly built into these phases, as the purpose of each of them is in fact development. The process of curriculum development is described more fully in Chapter 3.

2.3   Summary

From the above, a perspective can be acquired on the wide and broad character of curriculum studies which the curriculum agent must take into account. It is a field of study which is difficult to capture in one clear definition, as there are so many orientations and approaches to and perspectives on the curriculum.

Curriculum studies is a multidisciplinary field, any study of which will have the effect of further accentuating its multilateral nature. It is a field of study with a particular theoretical substructure and which requires particular curriculum skills. These skills are not necessarily particular to curriculum studies but may also be found in other disciplines. Curriculum studies comprises a study of both theory and practice, and studies in this field often take place from the point of view of a particular philosophy of life or orientation.

Activities and questions

1. Is it important to have a definition of 'curriculum'?

2. Is curriculum studies an independent discipline or a conglomerate of various disciplines?

3. In what fields or areas is 'curriculum' as a notion encountered?

4. What would you regard as the most authoritative work on curriculum studies? Motivate your answer.

5. What is the most important aspect of curriculum studies: theory or practice?

6. Name at least five principles for curriculum development.

7. What is your understanding of the following concepts?

    - Curriculum

    - Curriculum development

    - Curriculum studies

8. Who has the most important functions in curriculum development: the theoretician or the curriculum practitioner? Motivate your answer.

9. Why is it necessary to be empowered with regard to curriculum studies?

10. How would you describe 'curriculum' within your specific context?

11. Describe what you understand under the notion of 'curriculum studies'.

12. Do you think that there is a typical or unique South African field of curriculum studies? Motivate your answer.

3 The Process of Curriculum Development

At the end of this chapter you should be able to

- describe the process of curriculum development and place it within the context of your subject field
- understand the various approaches to curriculum development
- give a short description, together with an example, of each of the various exponents' approaches to curriculum development
- describe the various manifestations of curriculum development with the aid of a subject-orientated example
- place the various principles of curriculum development within subject context
- appreciate the importance of empowering the teacher through effective curriculum development.

3.1 Introduction: Possible interpretations

The term or concept 'curriculum development' lends itself to different interpretations and is not easy to capture in one description or process. It is a complex, dynamic process which tends to lead to many interpretations and perspectives, of which only a few are given here. This divergence has given rise to different propositions and models.

Normally a curriculum is developed by designers at various levels (e.g. governmental or departmental) and implemented by practitioners at other levels (by teachers in schools). It is not necessarily characterised by orderliness (in other words, a strict and rigid process from which there may be no deviation), because practitioners use their own interpretations in the meaning-giving process, which does not necessarily guarantee orderliness. This, however, is the wonder of the process, because it is dynamic and lends itself to different interpretations.

Mostert's (1986b: 8–9) view of curriculum development mainly comprises a summary of internationally and nationally accepted opinions. She identifies six authoritative phases in order to show how curriculum development progresses. The phases with their corresponding actions may be summed up as shown in the following table:

Table 3.1: Global review of curriculum development phases

Phase	Actions
1. Initiation	• An introductory investigation is launched
2. Planning	• Situation analysis
	• Formulation of goals
	• Determination of criteria for the selection and classification of content
	• Planning of an experimental design
3. Development	• Selection and classification of learning content and refinement of goals
	• Supplying of didactic guidelines
	• Production of teaching material
	• Development of teaching material
	• Development of evaluation mechanisms
4. Testing	• Submission to experts for evaluation
	• Teacher preparation for the instructional task
	• Instruction
	• Formative evaluation
	• Review
5. Implementation	• Planning of learning contents
	• Dissemination
	• Teacher orientation
	• Instruction
6. Summative evaluation	• Final evaluation of the programme

As stated in Section 2.2, curriculum development is, for the purposes of this publication, regarded as an umbrella and ongoing process ranging from design to evaluation. This process is characterised by various possible phases, of which initiation, design, dissemination, implementation and evaluation are but a few. The conceptualisation in Figure 3.1 illustrates this.

A short description (see Carl, 1986: 21–46 and Carl *et al.*, 1988: 23–27 for a more comprehensive description) of each phase gives an indication as to what is to be understood by each of them.

Curriculum design is that phase during which a new curriculum is planned, or during which the replanning and review of an existing curriculum is done after a full re-evaluation has been carried out. Aspects such as flexible planning and decision making figure strongly. This phase usually has a number of characteristic components, which include purposefulness, content, methods, learning experiences and evaluation, and is dealt with in more detail in Chapter 4.

Curriculum dissemination (which is often equated with implementation in the curriculum literature) is that phase in curriculum development during which the consumers of the curriculum are prepared for the intended implementation, and information is disseminated. This is done through the distribution or publication of information, ideas and notions, and in-service training, etc., to prepare all those involved and to inform them of the proposed curriculum (see Chapter 5 for a more comprehensive description).

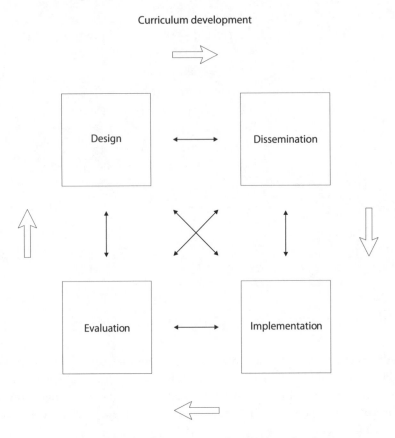

Figure 3.1: Carl's conceptualisation of the process of curriculum development

Curriculum implementation is that phase during which the relevant design is applied in practice (see Chapter 6 for a more comprehensive description).

Curriculum evaluation is that phase during which not only the success and effectiveness of the curriculum are evaluated but also the effect thereof on the learners. A distinction must therefore be drawn between curriculum-orientated and learner-orientated evaluation (see Chapter 7 for a more comprehensive description).

It appears evident that this process of curriculum development often has a specific nature and character as a result of specific orientations and approaches to curriculum development.

3.2 Approaches and paradigms to curriculum development and inquiry

Introduction

It is clear that a person's view of and how they think about curriculum and curriculum development will determine what the curriculum will look like in practice. Views and assumptions influence the construction of the curriculum and it is therefore necessary to have clarity on what these views or orientations are. Schubert (1986: 170–171) refers to ways of thinking about curriculum as paradigms of inquiry. He says that curriculum theory has given serious attention to the question of paradigms. He views paradigms with regard to the curriculum field in two ways, namely what questions are asked, and how curriculum inquiry is conducted. Frame (2003: 17, in Coleman, Graham-Jolley and Middlewood, 2003) also refers to these paradigms of curriculum inquiry as a means of exploring the variety of approaches to curriculum theorising. For the purpose of this publication, the different notions of approaches, paradigms and orientations are seen as concepts which try to portray people's views of what and how they think about curriculum. Some exponents prefer to call these views paradigms, while others refer to them as orientations or approaches.

There are various approaches to the process of curriculum development which may serve as theoretical foundations. Walters (1985: 6–17) makes a useful contribution in this connection. The approaches described by him are the academic, experience-based (experiential), technological and pragmatic approaches. The following is a synopsis of his description of these views.

The academic approach

According to this approach, curriculum development is a systematic process directed by academic rationality and theoretical logic. The approach is academic, as it is based on the application of studied logic in educational decision making, and it is a proponent of intellectual maturity and academic rationality. In this approach, the curriculum specialist or specialist team is placed in a position where curriculum decisions can be taken unilaterally (i.e. without the practitioner-teacher and others involved).

The academic approach – for which the Tyler (1949) rationale supplies the theoretical and ideological points of departure – accepts that curriculum planning is elevated above the unique nature and character of particular school situations. The process begins with the identification of objectives and goals, and then follows the further procedure of selection of content, the classification thereof, the design of methods, and the eventual evaluation of the outcomes.

Taba (1962: 197) states: 'No matter what its nature, the statement of desired outcomes sets the scope and the limits of what is to be taught and learned'.

The first principle in academic curriculum planning is therefore the identification of goals, with rational intellectual argument as a method of accomplishing this task. The sources for these goals are usually the learner, the society, subject disciplines, philosophy and learning psychology. Tyler (1949: 5, as quoted by Walters, 1985: 7) says:

> No single source of information is adequate to provide a basis for wise and comprehensive decisions about the objectives of the school ... Each source should be given some consideration in planning any comprehensive curriculum program[me].

Accordingly, no effort is spared in establishing a balanced list of goals which involve all five basic sources. Following is a short discussion of some of the sources.

In his attempt to obtain as many as possible 'reliable' inputs with regard to the kind of end behaviour which is desired (i.e. the desired change in student behaviour), the learner's characteristics and needs are analysed in terms of physical, psychosocial, intellectual and moral development. The research and theories of development psychologists and teaching theoreticians such as Piaget, Dewey, Maslow, Prescott, Kohlberg, Tanner, Having, Hurst and others are used to create compound general learner profiles (idealised learners).

The characteristics and demands of society are another important source of goals. In the US, these sources are found in publications such as the *Seven Cardinal Principles of Secondary Education* of the Committee of Ten, and reports of the Education Policies Commission. In addition, data from community records, work procurement studies, political opinions, opinion polls, and studies of marriage and family life are used. In Europe, the political climate in particular plays an important role in this connection, especially when it is catalysed by student unrest, economic crises, value conflicts, environmental pollution, racial conflict, changing moral values, and the personal alienation of the threatened individual in a technological milieu.

The great proponent of subject disciplines as a source of goals is Phenix (1964), who has argued that 'all curriculum content should be drawn from the disciplines, or, to put it another way, that only knowledge contained in the disciplines is appropriate to the curriculum'. Support for this view comes from Parker and Rubin (1966: 22, as quoted by Walters, 1985: 8).

Since the judgement of Jerome Bruner (1960) in 1958 at the now famous Woods Hole Conference, and the subsequent publication of his *Process of Education* in 1960, the academic approach has been expanded by the inclusion of the methods of directed inquiry and self-discovery, and through the development of intellectual skills or cognitive processes. Phenix (1964) amends his point of view in light of this by stating that '[i]t is more important for the student to become skilful in the ways of knowing than to learn about any product of investigation'. This 'knowledge of methods' which makes it possible for people to take their studies further and/or to carry out their own further investigation becomes more important than the content itself. Parker and Rubin (1966) support this point of view.

These skills – decision making, problem solution, reflective thought and critical thought – contain an inherent logic which lends itself to systematic academic analysis. The best known of these is probably Bloom's (1956) Taxonomy of Educational Objectives.

In conclusion, it must be mentioned that the knowledge explosion and the proliferation of school subjects necessitated other patterns, for example core programmes (also called broad fields, problems approaches, correlated curricula, combined studies, etc.); combined subjects (sociolinguistics, ethnomusicology, human ecology, etc.); interdisciplinary studies; and functional literacy skills development in the primary school (a learned name for reading instruction by means of content subject material) (Walters, 1985: 6–10).

The experiential approach

Dewey is generally regarded as the father of the experiential model. In contrast to the academic model which lays claim to objectivity and universality, and results in a subject disciplinary design, the experiential approach is subjective, personal, heuristic and transactional. It stresses the role of teachers and learners and their co-operative curriculum decisions. It makes use of self-directed, unstructured and personalised instruction programmes at 'self-paces'. Personal feelings, inclinations, values and experiences are regarded as necessary curriculum content, and the active involvement of the learner is regarded as necessary in order to obtain maximal learning outcomes. The basis is that people (children) only learn what has meaning for them personally and they create their own learning through selective perception.

The differentiating characteristics of the experiential model are probably its child-centred nature, accentuation of interpersonal relations, the syntactic suppleness of the development process and the primary role of affective content in the instruction process. It regards the psychological, social and cultural characteristics and needs of learners as the most important sources of instructional goals and at the same time regards them also as the substantive syllabus content. There is, however, a proviso, i.e. that these objectives merely give a direction to and do not necessarily specify the ultimate aims.

The function of teaching and education is pursued through curriculum content and experiences aimed at the retention of the unique human worthiness of the individual by means of sensitivity to or an appreciation of each individual's intellectual qualities, but also, and especially, his or her emotional, social, physical, aesthetic and spiritual qualities. The consideration of the learner as a being in a continuous condition of evolution towards a more mature, more complete person is therefore the directive purpose for curriculum development, while processing skills and affective experiences constitute the curriculum content. The ideal is to educate the whole person.

Walters (1985: 10) refers in his writing to the philosophy of Dewey, who stated in 1897 that the social activities of the child are the true centre of correlation on the school subjects, and not science, literature, history or geography. Dewey was of the view that education should be seen as a continuing reconstruction of experience and that the process and the goal of education were one and the same thing.

Apart from Dewey, the names of Berman and Roderick (1977), Foshay (1975), Carl Rogers (1962) and Florence Stratemeyer (Stratemeyer et al., 1957) in the US; Richmond (1971), Stenhouse (1976) and others in Britain; and the greater majority of modern Dutch curriculum workers may be mentioned in connection with this approach.

The political impact of socialist governments in Britain and the western European countries was, however, perhaps a greater driving force for the experiential approach than educationalists themselves.

In practice, this approach achieved the greatest success in curricula for primary schools, but in addition various curricula in human sciences and art subjects at high school level have been developed according to this model. Curricula in subjects less known to us, such as 'ethnic studies', 'multicultural studies', 'education for parenthood', 'death education', 'old age education', and 'female studies' are encountered in various overseas countries (Walters, 1985: 10–12).

The technological approach

As with many other aspects of education, curriculum development has also been influenced by large-scale recent technological development. The use of technological aids is more than well known. More important, however, is that the philosophies, ideologies, methods of approach and techniques generally applied in industrial planning and production are often taken over by educationists for curriculum planning, implementation and evaluation.

In essence, the technological approach is analytical, and regards instructional planning in terms of 'systems', 'management' and 'production'. It endeavours to maximise educational effectiveness by applying the same scientific management and production principles with regard to industry to the instructional situation. It is interesting to note that education was ahead of industry in this field, as the concept 'curriculum engineering' or rather 'scientific curriculum development' was already proposed according to these principles in 1918 by Franklin Bobbit (Bobbit, 1918), the first writer who identified the curriculum as a separate field of study.

The technological approach coincides with the academic model in that it also makes use of the means–end paradigm and is based on the Tyler (1949) rationale. The specification of learning outcomes or 'desired terminal behaviour' is the key in both approaches, but they differ in respect of the relationship between means and end, the methods for identification of instructional goals, the structure and formulation of the goals, and the evaluation criteria employed to measure the desired learning outcomes. The bases also differ in important aspects: while the academic model in decision making with regard to the curriculum is based on theoretical and academic logical argument, the technological model makes use of the principles of system analysis, empirical methods and management effectiveness.

The curriculum model is based on the premise that nothing is real and meaningful unless it is perceptible and subject to objective analysis (based on verifiable data). This approach declares that knowledge worth acquiring is that knowledge which prepares the learner for the functions of life; that these functions may be reduced to their distinguishable component parts; that the learning process comprises a change in behaviour; and that, as behaviour is demonstrable, learning outcomes or success is perceptibly and quantitatively measurable. Gagne (1977: 5) puts it as follows:

> A learning occurrence ... takes place when the stimulus situation together with the content of memory affect the learner in such a way that his performance changes from a time before being in that situation to a time after being in it. The change in performance is what leads to the conclusion that learning has occurred.

To ensure that the learning process takes place effectively, the curriculum must also comply with the so-called laws of proximity (context), repetition, reinforcement and preconditioning (Gagne, 1977; Gagne & Briggs, 1974). The technological approach has as its point of departure 'system analysis' (Londoner, 1972). The components of this 'system' are in sequence:

a.   Empirical analysis of needs
b.   Determination of needs priorities
c.   Specification of objectives in the form of behaviour or performance objectives
d.   Selection of content to fit in with the specified objectives
e.   Definition, description and classification of instruction procedures and learning activities
f.   Identification of quantifiable evaluation methods

The needs assessment is the point of commencement for this approach. As soon as these needs have been determined, they are converted into observable, measurable behaviour objectives. This can also, in terms of the management model, be regarded as a 'task analysis'.

In summary, the technological curriculum approach sees learning as a 'system', which can be reduced to its component parts or steps. It takes place in a predictable, systematic and controllable manner. Its effectiveness can be increased by the application of good control according to management principles. Curriculum development takes place in specific steps:

a.   Needs assessment
b.   Task analysis
c.   Structure analysis
d.   Synthesis
e.   Operational refinement

Task analysis comprises the formulation of learning tasks and activities in the form of behavioural objectives, which comprise the following:

- The observable behaviour, which must take place so that the objective can be measurable, is formulated.
- The conditions under which the end behaviour manifests itself are determined.
- The criteria for the determination of the minimum level of achievement acquired are laid down.

Structure analysis comprises the determination of the hierarchical relationships between the objectives to determine in which sequence they must be placed.

Synthesis, a 'means-to-an-end' procedure, is applied to identify and analyse all viable instructional alternatives for every end objective, with a view to selecting the instructional procedures which will most effectively produce the required learning outcomes (end behaviour). Further decisions are taken with regard to evaluation procedures and techniques designed for each of the following:

- Individual evaluation, where learner achievement can be monitored and the progressive sequence of the objectives can be controlled
- Formative evaluation of the effectiveness of the instruction in progress, with a view to improving the objectives and material while they are still in the formative development stage
- Summative evaluation so as to obtain a total image of the effectiveness of the total instruction packet (curriculum)

Operational refinement is the execution of the instructional activities as planned and the application of the evaluation criteria with a view to systematic collection of data with regard to the effectiveness of the 'system'. After data have been collected and analysed, amendments to the system are effected based on the evaluation of the data. The process of evaluation (feedback modification) is, according to Londoner (1972), a 'continuous and repeated process of evaluating each step with all prior steps and the specified terminal outcomes to ensure systematic development of all system operations for achieving the desired behaviours'.

Curriculum designs based on this approach are, *inter alia,* computer-supported instructional programmes, programmed instructional packages, achievement contracts, certain vocational and technical teaching subjects, and competency-based teacher education programmes (Walters, 1985: 13–17).

The pragmatic approach

In contrast to the above-mentioned educational view that curriculum development is a systematic scientific procedure, there are others who aver that this process is neither systematic nor rational, but rather the outcome of a long and dynamically complex process of involvement and interaction. The proponents of the pragmatic approach contend that curriculum practice is reactive and takes place fragmentarily.

It is also a political and eclectic process in which a large collection of concepts and principles derived from various theoretical models are utilised. In other words, the same curriculum elements of the academic, the experiential and the technological approaches can be used. In addition, there is the ongoing give and take within specific interest groups and political viewpoints, the negotiation phases and the eventual curriculum consensus. Decker Walker (Walker & Schaffarzick, 1974) calls it a 'naturalistic' model, while John Verduin (1967) refers to 'co-operative curriculum change'. Overseas (particularly in the US) the funding of curriculum projects also plays an important role in development and this often forces the curriculum developer to a pragmatic approach (Walters, 1985: 17).

The following is a summary of these views:

Table 3.2: Summary of the various approaches to curriculum development

Academic approach
Curriculum development is a systematic process guided by academic rationality and theoretical logic in educational decision making.
Experiential approach
This approach is subjective, heuristic and activity orientated. It emphasises teachers and learners and their co-operative decisions on the curriculum. Personal feelings, dispositions, values and experiences are regarded as essential curriculum aspects. It is strongly child centred. Aims are merely meant to provide directions and not final objectives.
Technological approach
In essence this approach is an analytical one that regards educational planning in terms of systems, management and production. Scientific management and production principles from industry are applied to teaching and education. Nothing is meaningful if it cannot be subjected to objective analysis. Learning is thus a system that can be reduced to its component parts or steps that can occur in a systematic and predictable way.
Pragmatic approach
The curriculum development process is the outcome of a long and interactive process of involvement and interaction. This approach contains elements of all the three preceding approaches.

Frame (2003: 18–28, in Coleman *et al.*, 2003) describes three paradigms:

- **The technical paradigm**. She states that this is the dominant approach in the field of curriculum. Understandings of curriculum 'are derived from an understanding of reality as an ordered set of interacting systems operating according to discernible and universal patterns of law'. This approach also enables one to 'predict, control and manipulate the environment' (2003: 19). One can then have a strong hold on precisely what the outcomes should be.

- **The practical paradigm**. According to Frame (2003: 24), this approach or paradigm accommodates the role of human agency and that 'curricular knowledge is socially constructed rather than objectively discoverable'. Human judgement and input are present in the production of knowledge, and this paradigm 'focuses on interpreting the meanings of social situations'. There must be interaction between human beings to come to a common or consensual understanding of what is to be studied. The implication is thus that all stakeholders should be involved (teachers and students).

- **The critical paradigm**. This approach acknowledges that knowledge is socially constructed and that 'the curriculum is a political question' (Frame, 2003: 27). The curriculum must be analysed and 'understood in the broader social, political and economic context'. Curriculum researchers would focus on issues such as class, gender and race, for example, to try to identify ways in which society is often disempowered so that the interests of other sectors can be improved.

Schreuder, Blanckenberg and Reddy (2000: 11–27) distinguish between the following orientations and views on curriculum: modernist (curriculum is a linear, strongly structured and centrally controlled process); interpretivist (curriculum is constructed within actual learning situations with students themselves; it addresses needs of students and teachers); critical (identification of injustices in society and ways it can be eradicated in order to serve social justice); and post-structuralist (no entity can be isolated and studied on its own: the nature of things lies in the relationships that we construct between them).

3.3   Orientations in respect of curriculum development

Introduction

Following on the above with regard to approaches to curriculum development, this process may also be influenced by developers' particular orientation with regard to a curriculum. A particular orientation may determine the character of the final curriculum. The three orientations which will be illustrated here are those of transmission, transaction and transformation. This does not mean that curriculum is mapped into little 'packages' by focusing on these orientations, but rather that it tries to promote an understanding of these different orientations/views and of what curriculum development might possibly mean. This could help one to understand the process of curriculum development and also what the underlying values, assumptions and motivations are, as these impact on the curriculum.

Orientations

Education takes place within a broader or narrower (local) community, and the norms and values of the latter often influence the curriculum. Community and school are inseparably bound in that the relevant values may eventually determine how the curriculum appears. There are also many other influences which may determine the curriculum, for example an academic preparedness, technological development, claims for relevance, human attitudes and philosophies of life.

The question then quite rightly arises as to **what** must be instructed, **how** the curriculum must appear and what must happen after the presentation of a particular curriculum. From this, two attitudes can be deduced: a process one and a product one. This attitude can be described as a person's orientation with regard to the curriculum. Normally there is a dominant orientation, as it is seldom either one or the other. It is therefore very necessary for every curriculator to be aware of his or her relevant orientation. This is not stereotyping, as educators normally move along a continuum and do not concentrate on only one orientation.

Various curriculum works touch on this aspect of orientations, and show that there are usually three which may be regarded as representative:
*   In **transmission**, the content is the most important. There is a strong product alignment, and learner participation or involvement is of lesser importance. The curriculum is therefore 'something which is done to learners'.

- In the case of **transaction** orientation, because the teacher is adapted to both the curriculum and the learner, there is a greater interaction between the learner and the teacher.
- **Transformation** requires that the learner and the curriculum must totally integrate with a view to giving meaning to the latter, and it is characterised by strong humanistic and social adaptation, as well as a high level of involvement by both the teacher and the learner.

These three orientations can be set out schematically as shown in Figure 3.2.

Figure 3.2: Orientations

What follows is a review of curriculum works that deal with these orientations. Although differing terminology is used, it is possible eventually to classify the various works within a dominant orientation.

Exponents of the various orientations

Eisner and Vallance (1974)

Eisner and Vallance (1974, as quoted in Connelly, Dukacz & Quinlan *et al.*, 1980: 14–16) give a description of particular approaches to curriculum development, called their 'conceptual framework':

- **Development of cognitive processes** stresses **how** the learner learns, rather than **what** he or she learns. The learning process is most important and for this reason the development of thinking skills is strongly accentuated. Learners must master and apply skills such as analysis, synthesisation and classification. The accent is therefore on the development of cognitive skills.
- **Curriculum as technology** links up with Walters' (1978) approach, as the process of planning and instructional methods is important. A particular end goal is set, and detailed planning takes place to achieve it. An input is made and it is expected that the learner will deliver an output in the form of a certain achievement.
- **Self-actualisation of the learner** comprises the school offering specific positive learning experiences for the learner. Opportunities for self-discovery and development must be created. Curriculum development must be relevant and topical so that this self-actualisation can take place. It does not imply total freedom but, rather, disciplined thinking.

- **Social reconstruction** requires that learners become orientated with regard to social questions, such as multiculturalism, unemployment, adaptation to change and pollution. This approach differs from the other three in that the needs of the community are strongly accentuated and receive preference. Schools must equip learners so that they will be able to maintain themselves in changing communities and, as citizens, will be critical with regard to social changes.
- In **academic rationalism** learners must master selected content as offered in the traditional subjects. Stress is also placed on the acquisition of knowledge through research. Learning and mastering facts is characteristic of this approach. This is, however, more than mere textbook memorisation, as mastering content stresses the development and change in ideas.

McNeil (1977)

McNeil (1977: 34–46) differentiates between the technological approach, the academic approach, humanism and social reconstructivism. He refers to these approaches as 'conceptions of curriculum' (1977: 1):

- By **technology** McNeil understands a fixed rigid structure which allows little flexibility. It is decided in advance what will be instructed and there is minimal departure from this. He refers to this as 'alignment learning'.
- The **academic approach** requires a strong subject and discipline alignment, and is adapted to cognitive development. Acquiring knowledge is at the heart of the curriculum (McNeil, 1977: 47; see also Walters, 1985: 6–10).
- The **humanistic approach** focuses on the learner's development as an individual and as a person. There is a shift from subject matter to the individual. The aim is now on an increase in personal awareness and a decrease in self-estrangement. This was a reaction to behaviourism. It is expected of the teacher to listen to the learner's view of reality, to respect the child as a 'fellow traveller' in life and not to manipulate the child (McNeil, 1977: 3).
- The point of departure of **social reconstructivism** is that the school must co-operate in changing the community. The learners must therefore be confronted with problem solving with regard to problems of their time and human nature, to enable them to effect social change. The curriculum is 'a vehicle for fostering critical discontent and equipping learners with skills needed for conceiving new goals and effecting social change'. Education in values is important within this view (McNeil, 2003: 19–33).

Schiro (1978)

Schiro (1978) identifies and also describes briefly some views or ideologies which link up with what is set out above. He mentions four ideologies, namely social efficiency, a scholastic academic ideology, child studies and a social reconstructivist ideology.

- **Social effectiveness** links up with the technological approach in which stress on a fixed structure and content figures strongly. Learning experiences are determined and designed in advance and follow a predetermined pattern.

- In the **scholastic academic ideology** the learner is exposed to disciplines in order to convey the essence of the subject contents. This attitude correlates with the academic approach in terms of which stress is placed on the development of cognitive processes.
- By **child study ideology** is understood the natural growth and development of the child's potential. The development of knowledge and a positive self-image in the child is a high priority.
- A **social reconstructivist ideology** arises from the premise that society is unhealthy and is threatened, and that something must be done to prevent its destruction. The school has a role to play in this. A question which arises, however, is whose values should be adopted and be valid in the process of the protection of society.

Ornstein (1982)

Ornstein (1982) mentions only two main approaches, namely subject content and learner-centredness. The stress placed on subject content focuses, *inter alia*, on subject discipline, subject structure and the basic knowledge content of each subject. The approach which focuses on learner-centredness places the child in the middle, is strongly adapted to self-activity, accentuates relevance and also focuses on humanistic aspects.

Miller (1983)

Miller (1983) describes seven possible orientations with regard to curriculum development, namely behaviourism, subject discipline alignment, social orientation, cognitive processes, development of the child, humanism and a transpersonal approach. These approaches may also be in a continuum, as no person is either one or the other. Miller classifies these seven approaches into three main categories, namely tradition, inquiring decision making and transformation. This classification may then appear as follows:

- **Tradition**
  - Behaviourism
  - Subject discipline
  - Social orientation
- **Decision making**
  - Social orientation
  - Cognitive processes
  - Development
- **Transformation**
  - Social orientation
  - Humanism
  - Transpersonal

An extension of this presentation is shown on the following page.

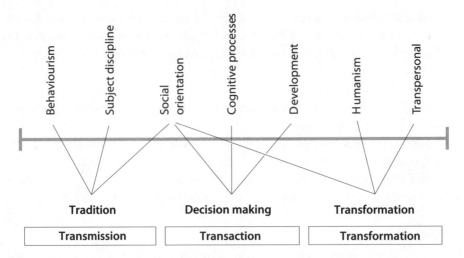

Figure 3.3: Three main categories: tradition, decision making and transformation (Eraut, 1990)

The contribution of Eraut (1990: 546–551) is based on curriculum development being determined by specific circumstances, preferences and people's consciousness of various choices. He mentions various approaches, which are briefly set out below. When these approaches are compared with those which have already been described in the previous paragraphs, the similarities and differences are clearly evident.

- The **political approach** regards the official curriculum as the product (discussion focuses on objectives, prescribed content, goals and evaluation or decision making regarding the composition of the syllabus).
- The **bureaucratic approach** places particular stress on documentation (close attention is given to regulations and administrative questions; official documents serve as guidelines for formulation). This approach can hinder creative curriculation and promote centralised rather than decentralised decision making.
- The **marketing approach** comprises the dissemination and marketing of the relevant curriculum (preparing those involved; information is distributed).
- The **scientific approach** focuses primarily on the identification and analysis of learning tasks. The outcomes arising from this approach lead to instructional design, i.e. micro-curriculum development of a lesson or lesson unit.
- The **knowledge structure** approach is primarily involved with the structure and sequence of content (Bruner, 1960, is an exponent hereof).
- The proponents of the **engineering approach** argue that a design can only be effective if the objectives are defined and a prototype is designed, applied and thereafter adapted until it is effective. Testing and adaptation are thus important characteristics of this approach.
- The criteria of the **artistic approach** are not mastering and effectiveness, but attention, participation and impact. Stress is placed on the inclusion of experiences which promote learners' interest and motivate them, because the supposition is

that learning will take place logically from involvement and reflection. It is alleged that there are too many risks attached to this.

- A **convenience or practical approach** does not regard design as a problem and regards some of the other approaches as unwieldy, unnecessary or a risk. A design is followed which is convenient and practical for specific circumstances. It may take place either dictatorially or by delegation, as long as it does not waste time and is not unwieldy. The purpose is to compile a short document with minimum planning for sufficient co-operation.
- The **problem-solving approach** puts as its point of departure firstly the condition that curriculum design requires time and effort and, secondly, that the task must be regarded as a design problem which must be solved by means of a connected, meaningful and acceptable proposal. There must be maximal utilisation of the knowledge and skills of all those involved. In addition there must be a balance between originality and creativity on the one hand and the utilisation of existing practices on the other. A logical working procedure can consist of:
  - problem formulation
  - brainstorming/think tank
  - the creation of prototype designs
  - selection of prototypes
  - the choice and refinement of a particular design.

Identifying curriculum developers' orientation

From the above it is clear that curriculum developers have differing views and approaches to curriculum development. As mentioned above, these may eventually be classified into three main categories, i.e. transmission, transaction and transformation. It is essential for curriculum developers to be conscious of their own orientations as these will determine their curriculum outcomes.

There is not always a clearly definable border between each approach, but those interested in the curriculum should determine their main orientation in respect of, or in their approach to, curriculum development. The 'curriculum orientation profile' is a useful instrument with which one may determine what this approach possibly may be. It is given here with the consent of the designer, Babin (1981). Its purpose is to help those involved to determine their approach, as it can help to prevent an over-accentuation of certain areas, to avoid certain aspects which clash with their views, or to adapt a certain part of the curriculum. The intention of this curriculum orientation profile is to help the person to:

- realise that everyone can develop a specific perspective on the curriculum
- determine specific accentuation
- obtain clarity in regard to his or her own view of purpose, methods, content and evaluation
- identify his or her role as final arbiter (together with the learner) of the curriculum potential.

Curriculum orientation profile

These statements represent a set of value signposts which may help you discover your orientation towards the content, goals and organisation of the curriculum. These statements identify a broad range of very different approaches to questions persistently asked in the curriculum field: what can and should be taught, to whom, when, and how?

a.   As you peruse the list, decide whether you agree or disagree with each statement and check the appropriate column.

b.   Once you have completed the exercise, move on to Step II, which you will find at the end of the list.

Table 3.3: Curriculum orientation profile

Value signposts	Agree	Disagree
1. The curriculum should provide students with intellectual autonomy.	1	
2. The curriculum should stress societal needs over individual needs.	4	
3. The curriculum should be primarily humanistic and existential.	3	
4. The curriculum should be preoccupied with the development of means to achieve pre-specified ends.	2	
5. The curriculum should be concerned with the technology by which knowledge is communicated and learning is facilitated.	2	
6. Not all subject matters are created equal.	5	
7. The emphasis should be on problem solving or the discovery approach to learning.	1	
8. The curriculum should feature heuristic questions – the type that stimulate curiosity and generate speculation.	1	
9. The overall goals of education should be concerned with how the curriculum relates to society, as the curriculum should be as opposed to society as it is.	4	
10. The curriculum should be deliberately value saturated.	3	
11. The curriculum reflects finding efficient means to a set of predetermined non-problematic ends.	2	
12. Objectives should be stated in specific unambiguous terms.	2	
13. The curriculum should be an active force, having direct impact on the whole fabric of its human and social context.	4	
14. Education is seen as a means of helping individuals discover things for themselves.	3	
15. The curriculum is expressed in concise, terse, skeletally logical, crystalline language.	2	➲

Value signposts	Agree	Disagree
16. The learner is seen as interactive and adaptive.	1	
17. The curriculum should focus on personal purpose – the need for personal integration.	3	
18. The curriculum should provide the learner with opportunities to acquire the most powerful products of human intelligence.	5	
19. Social reform and responsibility to the future of society are the primary goals of schooling.	4	
20. The curriculum should serve as a vehicle for fostering critical discontent in society.	4	
21. The curriculum should stress refinement of intellectual operations.	1	
22. The established disciplines of knowledge are essential.	5	
23. Education should provide content and tools for further self-discovery.	3	
24. The focus should be on the learning process *per se*.	1–2	
25. Driver training dilutes the quality of education.	5	
26. Management by objectives should be an integral part of the curriculum.	2	
27. The focus should be on the how (process) rather than the what – instructional effectiveness.	1–2	
28. The curriculum materials, when used by intended learners, should produce specified learning competencies.	2	
29. The goals of education should be formulated in dynamic, personal, process terms.	3	
30. The curriculum should be based on the structure of the academic disciplines (the primarily intellectual ones).	5	
31. The primary goal should be the development of cognitive skills that can be applied to learning virtually anything.	1	
32. The curriculum should focus on the exploitation of resources, pollution, warfare and water; the effect of population increase; the unequal use of natural resources; propaganda; and self-control in the interest of one's fellows.	4	
33. The curriculum should include action programmes designed to improve social life in the community.	4	
34. The curriculum should provide the tools for individual survival in an unstable and changing world.	4	
35. The curriculum emanates from the particular interests of particular children.	3	
36. The curriculum should include works of art that have withstood the test of time.	5	

➲

Value signposts	Agree	Disagree
37. The curriculum should provide the means to personal liberation and development.	3	
38. The curriculum should undertake community-orientated service tasks.	4	
39. The curriculum should represent cultural transmission in the most specific sense.	5	
40. The curriculum should reflect current real-life situations.	4	
41. Learning occurs in certain systematic and predictable ways.	2	
42. The curriculum should provide access to the greatest ideas and objects that human beings have created.	5	
43. The curriculum should advocate adaptation as the means of effecting smooth change.	4	
44. The concern should be very much on what is taught.	3–5	
45. Private meaning is very important.	3	
46. The curriculum should provide a satisfactory consummatory experience for each learner.	3	
47. Bloom's taxonomy with its six cognitive hierarchical levels should play an important part in the curriculum.	1	
48. The curriculum should focus on highly structured tasks, each of which builds upon what has gone before and prepares for what is to come.	2	
49. Students should play a major role in generating their own educational purposes.	3	
50. Education should stress the leading ideas that have animated humankind.	5	
51. The school should be the agent for social change.	4	
52. Education is an integrative, synthesising force – a total experience responsible to the individual's needs for growth and personal integrity.	3	
53. The real task of the educator arises in organising the material some time before the learner even enters the classroom.	2	
54. Educators should be concerned about teaching the processes by which learning occurs in the classroom.	1	
55. Problem-solving skills are more important than particular content or knowledge.	1	
56. The curriculum should emphasise not topics or subjects but forms of thought.	5	
57. Both the conceptual and the syntactical structures of the disciplines are significant factors in curriculum.	5	

Step II

Complete the first part of the exercise before you read this section. Next to each item you have checked, you will find a number or numbers which identify a specific orientation to curriculum (column 2):

1. Development of cognitive processes
2. Curriculum as technology
3. Self-actualisation, or curriculum as a consummatory experience
4. Social reconstruction
5. Academic rationalism

Check your list (the **Agree** column) and tally the total number of each of the above orientations. For example, perhaps you have a total of ten 1s (cognitive processes) and six 2s (technology). This will provide you with a 'profile' that should reflect your dominant thrust in curriculum. Plot yourself on the matrix in Figure 3.4. Virtually all curricula that have been produced reflect different degrees of each of these orientations.

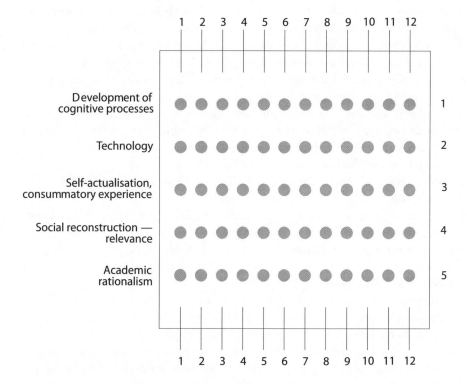

Figure 3.4: Matrix (adapted from Babin, 1981)

Summary

From the above it is clear that all persons having an interest in the curriculum must take note of the various approaches and orientations. A particular approach can be manifested in a person's practical involvement and for that reason it is essential that everyone has this self-knowledge.

It is important that those having an interest in the curriculum not only have a clear picture of their curriculum knowledge and skills, but also of their own approaches to and views on curriculum development. The latter is not always consciously present and for that reason sensitivity to curriculum approaches is most advisable.

3.4 Manifestations and functioning of curricula

We have seen that the curriculum often manifests itself in a particular manner as a result of particular orientations and approaches to curriculation. It is, however, not only differing approaches which lead to a particular manifestation as there are many other variables which also play a role. Human (1987) makes an important contribution by indicating how a curriculum is often perceived quite differently by learners from the one which was originally designed. He puts it schematically as shown in Figure 3.5.

3.5 Principles of curriculum development

As stated previously, curriculum developers may approach the process of curriculum development from a particular orientation. Their views are usually based on specific principles, as this gives direction and sense to the relevant process. It should be noted that in the curriculum literature very few descriptions are found of applicable principles for curriculum development. Principles may serve as a basic point of departure and therefore it is essential to have clarity in this regard.

It would be hazardous if curriculum development were not based on specific accountable principles. The following is a synthesis of some principles (the principles mentioned in Chapter 2 regarding the development of a new dispensation and the NQF can also be viewed as curriculum principles):

*   Purposefulness is an important aspect of effective curriculum development.
*   The rationale must be clear and communicable.
*   Curriculum development must be based on sound accountable curriculum theory.
*   Method must be an important characteristic.
*   Effective and ongoing evaluation from the design phase to the evaluation phase is essential.
*   Effective leadership is essential.
*   A particular level of curriculum ability is necessary for all those involved.
*   Effective time utilisation and orientation are determinative for effectiveness.
*   Adequate learning must be an important point of departure.
*   Relevance is an important characteristic of effective curriculum development.
*   Meaningful connection between the various elements is essential throughout the whole process.
*   Individualisation must be considered during planning.
*   The propaedeutic value of curriculum development must be considered.
*   Norm orientation is a basic principle.
*   The claims of subject content must be taken into account.
*   Applicable educational principles for learning are essential.

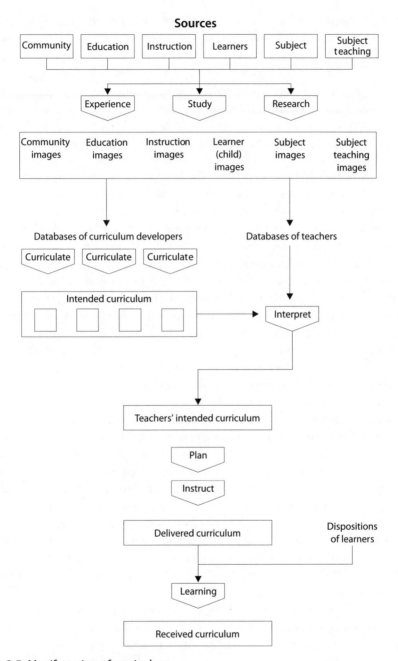

Figure 3.5: Manifestation of curriculum

With regard to the ongoing development of a curriculum, other principles also contribute to assisting the process of renewal and change. In the first instance, 'co-ordination' can contribute to curriculum development taking place on a planned basis. Skilled persons can in this manner process and utilise information countrywide to the benefit of education departments and educational institutions. Curriculum development action can also be co-ordinated on a centralised basis to bring about the closest possible co-operation with regard to dissemination, in-service training and demonstrations, etc. (Jordaan, 1989: 375–358).

A further directive principle in curriculum development is 'continuity'. According to Hill (1977: 6), this principle ensures that curriculum development is dealt with as an uninterrupted, continuous process. In this manner a continuing review rotation programme (with a view to improvement and renewal of the curriculum) prevents a curriculum from being put together on a once-off basis.

In the third place, in curriculum development there must be room for the principle of 'unity in diversity'. It must be possible for institutions to initiate their curriculum development in a distinctive manner, but it must preferably be subject to certain minimum requirements to ensure an equal standard (Jordaan, 1989: 377).

Another principle which contributes to the improvement and renewal of curriculum development is the 'directive control' exercised by skilled persons in curriculum committees. Hill (1989: 5–7, as quoted by Snyman, 1992: 82) accentuates the task of skilled persons in representative committees with regard to subject didactics, practical education, research studies and curriculum studies. The people in these committees have the necessary experience and knowledge to identify the diverse needs of communities and of learners, and through their input in curriculum development can see to it that meaningful curricula for the learning process are brought into being (Snyman, 1992: 82). This must, however, not be an autocratic process, but rather one that is characterised by active and democratic involvement.

Oliva (1988: 24–47) makes a valuable contribution in establishing accountable principles for curriculum development. There are specific forces which may give rise to these principles, for example empirical data, experimental data and society's views with regard to curriculum and reasoning. The value of the last-mentioned two sources must not be underestimated, as they may contain values, intuition, generalisations based on observation and well-thought-out decisions which may lead to effective problem solving. These sources accentuate the fact that not all solutions of educational problems are necessarily obtained from rigid empirical data, as those interested in the curriculum often have to rely on their judgement and intuition. Value judgements are therefore an important aspect in determining principles, although this may give rise to debate (Oliva, 1988: 28–29). Although Oliva (1988: 31–47) sets his principles out in detail, the following give the essence of each:

- Change is unavoidable, because life grows and develops through change.
- A curriculum does not only reflect the relevant period in which it has its origin but is also the product thereof. The curriculum planner must be aware of the powers at work and influences of the day, and decide how curriculum development will be affected by them.
- Curriculum changes which have taken place earlier may continue, together with changes brought about at a later stage. Changes may take place over a long period and even overlap newer developments. Older content may, for example, still be dealt with within History, even though more recent content has been added. The relevance and importance of older content are therefore not lost as soon

as more recent changes take place. A review of older design may even lead to new perspectives.

- Curriculum change is the result or consequence of changes that take place in people. Curriculum developers must therefore endeavour to change those people who will eventually influence curriculum change. People must be involved with curriculum development so that they may be bound to it. In this way changes and renewal may be internalised. All those involved must have the maximum opportunity to provide input to the envisaged changes, because in this way their support during the implementation phase may be obtained.

- Curriculum development is influenced by the co-operative effort of groups. Large and fundamental changes usually take place as a result of group involvement and decision making. Subject groups work together in a group identity under the leadership of instruction leaders to ensure effective curriculum development. These groups may consist of teachers, education leaders, parents, members of the community and even students. In this way school curricula may remain relevant. Curriculum development by individuals must not be dampened, because this initiative may allow for strong dynamics. Group involvement, however, has the advantage that ideas may be exchanged, and group dynamic processes definitely lead to dynamic curriculum development. Group leaders influence and help one another to change and to accept change.

- Curriculum development is basically a decision-making process. Curriculum planners must definitely make a variety of decisions in co-operation with other involved parties, decisions which may range from what objectives, content and methods must be followed to what subjects must be offered in a school. The quality of decision making will also necessarily influence the quality of curriculum development.

- Curriculum development is a never-ending process, because one must always aspire to continuous improvement. Ongoing evaluation is necessary to identify strong and weak points, and to develop or remediate them on an ongoing basis. Feedback must lead to adaptations and improvements, for example of objectives, content, media or methods. Ongoing monitoring is necessary to ensure that the design, where necessary, is successfully implemented and adapted.

- Curriculum development is more effective if it is dealt with as a comprehensive process. It cannot be dealt with on a hit-and-run basis where changes are brought about haphazardly where necessary, or where only content movements (inclusion or exclusion) take place. The overall picture must never be lost sight of, for example the broader impact on children, parents, teachers, the community and the country (i.e. the effect on those who were not involved with planning). Factors such as the utilisation of human capital, time and resources must be considered in advance. Teachers' motivation, level of energy and other commitments must be determined. Curriculum development can therefore not take place piecemeal, but must be addressed on a comprehensive basis.

- Curriculum development is more effective if it is addressed in a systematic manner. The utilisation of a curriculum model can promote systematics and organisation, and give meaningful direction to the process. It will not necessarily ensure success, as there are too many factors, such as motivation, level of curriculum ability, quality of leadership, availability of funds, quality of support and personal views, which may possibly be retarding factors and hinder success. The systematic handling of curriculum development can, however, determine success to a great extent, as structure and purpose are present.

- Curriculum development begins where the curriculum is, i.e. existing curricula are quite often the starting point. It would possibly be correct rather to speak of curriculum reorganisation than curriculum organisation. Previous attempts can therefore not be summarily dismissed, but must be taken into consideration.

Linking it to the South African context, the *Revised National Curriculum Statement Grades R–9* phased in from 2002 (Department of Education, 2002a: 10–13) and later replaced by the *National Curriculum Statement* stated that the guiding curriculum principles for the new curriculum were the following:

- Social justice, a healthy environment, human rights and inclusivity were key values.
- Outcomes-based education (OBE) was the point of departure.
- A high level of skills and knowledge for all was non-negotiable.
- Clarity and accessibility were to be key aspects in both the design and language.
- Progressive ongoing development and integrated learning were seen as integral.

Without a clear image as to what principles are valid as departure points, curriculum development may not necessarily be accountable. For that reason, those involved with the curriculum must ascertain for themselves what their fundamental principles are. This is not only valid for curriculum planners outside the school context but also for teachers within the classroom, as each one has a particular role and function which determines the success of the curriculum. A specific level of empowerment is required to be able to do this.

3.6   Summary

Curriculum development is the umbrella concept for the process which is characterised by the presence of phases such as curriculum design, dissemination, implementation and evaluation. It is an ongoing and dynamic process which involves a variety of individuals and role players. Those having an interest in the curriculum have, consciously and unconsciously, a particular approach or conceptual framework with regard to curriculum development which may also determine the nature of their involvement. Such an approach can range from an academic, experiential or technological approach to a pragmatic one.

Those having an interest in the curriculum may develop curricula from particular conceptual frameworks of curriculum development, such as development of cognitive processes, self-actualisation of the learner, social reconstruction and academic rationalisation. It would be valuable if these persons could ascertain their approach or orientation with regard to curriculum development, as it may increase the quality of their involvement and make a contribution to the process of empowerment. Empowered teachers must reflect on this aspect, as it may lead to further development.

Activities and questions

1. Are you clear as to what can be understood by 'the process of curriculum development'? Describe your understanding.

2. Within your subject group, if possible, discuss to what extent this process is founded on practice.

3. What is your particular approach to and view of curriculum development?

4. What would you say is the conceptual framework of present-day curriculum development tendencies in South Africa? A strong emphasis on development of cognitive processes? Curriculum is technology? A strong emphasis on self-actualisation by learners? Accentuation of social reconstruction? A strong emphasis on academic rationalism? A critical approach? A modernist approach? Discuss this question within your subject group and deal with it at a staff development session.

5. Complete the curriculum orientation profile (Table 3.3) individually within your subject group (if possible) and compare the profiles. Are there agreements? Are there differences? Why?

6. What would you currently regard as the five most important principles for effective curriculum development in the South African context?

7. What is the ideal profile of an empowered teacher with regard to curriculum development?

4 Effective Curriculum Design for Dynamic Curriculum Development

At the end of this chapter you should be able to

- describe the notion 'curriculum design' and its interdisciplinary nature
- understand the problems with regard to the levels at which curriculum design takes place and adopt your own point of view with regard to a particular situation
- understand curriculum design with its various components, and be able to adapt it within micro-curriculum development
- reflect on how design is manifested at different levels (national, departmental, school and classroom level).

4.1 Introduction

The dynamic of any curriculum (at whatever level) is determined to a large extent by the quality of its design. Curriculum developers must also understand precisely what curriculum design comprises, what the criteria are, how it can develop and what its nature is. The intention of this chapter is not only to show the curriculum developer **how** one may possibly go to work but also to offer a broad perspective on the nature of curriculum design. As already mentioned, this knowledge base is essential in empowering teachers.

4.2 Clarification of the concept: The interdisciplinary nature of curriculum design

Curriculum design as a phase within curriculum development relates both to the creation of a new curriculum and to the replanning of an existing one after a more complete evaluation has been made. Aspects such as method, team approach and responsible decision making should figure prominently within this phase. Barrow (1984: 7) links up with this in contending that curriculum design has largely to do with curriculum decisions. Decisions are taken, *inter alia*, with regard to the content which must be included, how it should be presented and how it should be evaluated. There are therefore various opinions and points of view as to what should be included in this design.

Various other aspects thus deserve thorough consideration during this design phase. Decision making therefore comes strongly to the fore as the following contributory factors in particular are taken into account:

- Criteria for curriculum development
- Procedure for curriculum development

- Educational and teaching objectives
- Child knowledge
- Subject knowledge
- Necessary didactic and subject didactic knowledge and skills

These aspects show clearly that curriculum design is in reality a multidisciplinary affair which should be addressed by a large team of curriculum experts, subject specialists, subject didacticians, educational psychologists and those in teaching practice who have an interest. Curriculum design is, therefore, that planning phase during which various decisions are taken which must be based on accountable criteria. It has a multidisciplinary character and may also take place at various levels. The nature and extent of decision making will also vary depending on the level at which the curriculum development is done. There are also a number of variables which the curriculum developers must take into account, once again depending on the level at which they are moving.

Barrow (1984: 40–41) offers a perspective which should be fully taken into account by every curriculum developer. He avers that there is not necessarily only one single correct method of designing with its own fixed rules which is necessarily also valid for other situations without referring to the most basic question: 'What is education and teaching about?'

Curriculum design is therefore not a fixed recipe consisting of components and set rules, but a process characterised by flexibility and pliability within which the specific variables exercise a strong influence.

4.3   Levels on which curriculum design may take place

It is clear that the nature and extent of curriculum design will differ, depending on the level on which one moves. The nature of the activities undertaken by a curriculum developer involved on national level with a curriculum committee will differ from that of the subject teacher curriculating for specific learners at a micro-level. There are differing views as to what the various levels are. The following is only one such view:

Table 4.1: One view of the various levels of curriculum design

Level	Description
MACRO	National level
MESO	Provincial or departmental level
MICRO	School level

The use of the terms 'macro', 'meso' and 'micro' is problematic in that these are relative and that all three may be just as applicable within a particular school. Preference is therefore given to the following levels, sectors or areas (Carl, 1986: 157–158):

- A community's philosophy of life and thus its views on education
- Government level and education legislation
- School-phase and school-type planning
- Syllabus/learning programme development

- School curricula
- More complete or comprehensive subject curriculum development
- Instructional–teaching/micro-curriculum development in the classroom

At each of the above-mentioned levels, aspects of curriculum design are applicable. For example, while in school-phase planning, the broad curriculum (for a total school population and country) is considered, the subject teacher in his or her classroom will be more involved with micro-curriculum development (objectives, goals, content, media, methods and evaluation for a specific learner or group of learners). This curriculum development often takes place simultaneously, although the subject teacher will be particularly involved with syllabus development, school curriculum development, more complete subject curriculum development and micro-curriculum development (see Chapter 9 for a more comprehensive description of the nature of this involvement).

Oliva (1988: 55–60) largely confirms this view in setting out a specific hierarchical presentation of the levels, pointing out that teacher involvement normally becomes less the further one moves away from the classroom. His presentation is shown below.

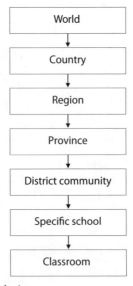

Figure 4.1: Levels of curriculum design

The fact that teachers are involved to a lesser extent on broader levels in curriculum development (e.g. syllabus design) does not at all mean that curriculum design in the classroom is of less importance or value. On the contrary, it is right there that the curriculum is implemented and its success determined.

There is in fact an interdependency and interaction between the various levels which determines the success of curriculum development. Curriculum design can therefore take place during the design of the broad curriculum, but it is filled in further during syllabus design and development by curriculum committees for a particular grade, which in turn leads to further design actions when the subject teacher designs a subject curriculum and/or a micro-curriculum. Teacher involvement is the heart of really successful curriculum development, and for this reason opportunities must be utilised to the full. It is, however, not proof of an inadequate teacher if the person is not involved at higher levels, as not everyone gets these opportunities. A teacher may be a first-class curriculum developer even though there is only a certain measure of involvement at classroom and school level. One should, however, strive to be more widely involved, for example, at least at the level of syllabus development.

An interesting contribution to the debate with regard to various levels is that of Oliva (1988: 57–58) who states that the expression 'sectors of planning' is receiving more and more approval. The problem of hierarchical classification (which sometimes wrongly characterises the involvement taking place at teaching level as of less importance) is eliminated and it is stated that curriculum design takes place in specific sectors,without giving any ranking, for example class, subject group, school, school district, province, region, country or world.

It is clear that there are different opinions as to the various levels on which curriculum design, and the phases of curriculum development following thereon, take place. Curriculum developers must rather decide what they themselves understand by this and curriculate accordingly. One must guard against curriculum agents being so caught up in a debate on semantics that curriculum development is eventually prejudiced. Curriculum design can therefore, according to Oliva (1988: 100), comprise a multilevel and/or multisector process.

4.4   The process of curriculum design

Introduction

When describing the process of curriculum design, it must be viewed against the background of Section 4.3. The extent will differ at every level or in every area or sector, but for the sake of completeness the description is given of what is normally understood by the whole process.

Curriculum design and the development level of the child

One of the most basic points of departure is that any curriculum must take account of the development level of the child. Particularly in the choice of objectives, outcomes and particular teaching content, learners' development needs must be considered, as well as the manner in which children learn. Such a curriculum design must have not only the children's intellectual development in mind but also the development of their full potential. From this it appears that the learners' needs should be a cardinal consideration. For this reason the quality of the method aspect is vital to eventual successful implementation and application.

The design must be based on a valid frame of reference, as it must help the child on the way to adulthood. The educational objectives may fulfil this cardinal function.

Carl (1986: 33) states that the following considerations may, *inter alia*, contribute to a higher quality of curriculum design:

- The design must consider not only subject content but also the methods and skills necessary for the learning process (e.g. reference skills and study methods).
- The learners should also be exercised in communication skills (reading, writing, speaking, listening and non-verbal communication).
- The design should make provision for the needs, abilities and skills of all learners, as potential differs from learner to learner.
- The design should create learning experiences which may also develop a skill in the use of free time.
- The design should correlate to a high degree with the values of the broad community and country.

Criteria for curriculum design

The phase of curriculum design is one of ongoing decision making as a result of the planning and action aspects in this process. This decision-making process is influenced by criteria which will eventually determine what the product (i.e. the design) will look like (Walters, 1978: 90).

Walters (1978: 91–92) states that there should be clarity as to the *sources* which serve as guidelines in forming criteria. He states that existing curricula, curriculum literature and interviews with curriculum developers may make a significant contribution in this regard. However, with regard to curriculum literature as a source, he sets out some problems:

- Few writers mention the sources of their criteria and there is an apparent non-critical acceptance of many criteria.
- Many criteria are founded on the personal opinion and the philosophy of life of the relevant author.
- It is apparently accepted by some that criteria which are valid for one component, for example purposefulness, are also applicable to another, such as selection of content or evaluation.

For effective curriculum design it is therefore essential to develop the design in the light of accountable criteria. Various writers have set out classifications of criteria for curriculum design (see Gorton, 1976: 236–239; Doll, 1978: 152–153; Marks *et al.*, 1978: 472; Walters, 1978: 198–199; Krüger, 1980: 105–140). When these classifications are compared, the resemblance is clear. It would appear as though there are certain basic criteria which may not and must not be disregarded. Walters' (1978) contribution is particularly valuable in that he sets out criteria for each of the separate components. He describes these as 'consensus criteria', as he has discussed this matter with curriculum specialists worldwide and has been able to arrive at a consensus opinion. (Please see Walters, 1978, for a detailed description of these criteria, as it is too extensive to include here.)

Krüger's (1980: 105–140) contribution in this connection may be summarised as follows:

- There must be a meaningful connection between the separate curriculum components.
- Curriculum contents and other components must be relevant and true to life.
- The curriculum must promote individuals' socialisation process or adaptation to their community so that learners will be able to maintain themselves later in it.
- The curriculum must provide maximally for individuals and in this way comply with the principles of individualisation.
- On an ongoing basis, one must determine whether the curriculum is still heading for its predetermined destination with regard to the learners.
- Help should be given to learners to meaningfully experience and integrate the learning content.
- The curriculum must help learners to acquire a time perspective with regard to the importance of the present as well as the future.
- The curriculum must contribute to the general education and shaping of the child.
- The curriculum's content must also be able to be used in other areas or in other situations.

The criteria of various other writers appear to be of a more general nature and to overlap those already mentioned. Gorton's (1976: 236–239) contribution in this connection is still most relevant for today and may be summarised as follows:

- Clear, well-defined educational objectives are essential. The curriculum relies on the basis or foundation of clear objectives, because without them there is no direction.
- The subject curricula and other courses must promote the realisation of the objectives. No curriculum is aimed only at itself but should bring about the objectives with regard to the broad curriculum. The instructional leader has a particular role to play here.
- The curriculum must be comprehensive and take all learners' needs into account, i.e. the weak, the average and the gifted. It must contribute to the realisation of the broader educational objective to prepare learners for a constructive and productive life. It should reflect and be relevant to the realities of life, as the following quotation clearly illustrates (Noyes & McAndrew, 1968: 65, as quoted by Gorton, 1976: 237):

  > The student is filled with facts and figures which only accidentally and infrequently have anything to do with the problems and conflicts of modern life or his own inner concern.

- The curriculum must reflect the needs of the community. The school does not exist in a vacuum and may, *inter alia,* be regarded as an agent for the community. It should therefore also be linked to the claims and expectations of the community.
- The curriculum must accentuate the cognitive, affective and psychomotor aspects. It would be a very narrow and one-sided curriculum that directed itself only to the cognitive (intellectual skills or thinking) or only to the affective (attitudes and values). The question should not be **whether** the curriculum should teach values, but rather **what** values it should develop.

- The curriculum must be relevant with regard to the development level of learners, learners' interest, degrees of difficulty and motivation aspects.
- The curriculum must ensure that correlation between subject curricula exists; in other words that the content of consecutive phases follows on. The correlation with other subjects should also be indicated.

Doll (1978: 152–153) sets out the following criteria as essential for curriculum design, namely the philosophy of life basis (of the community and the education authorities), the community within which the school is situated and its particular claims and needs, participation by all persons involved, promotion of creativity, and the needs and development level of learners.

For the purpose of this publication it is important to set criteria which may lead to more relevant and accountable curricula, and to greater teacher empowerment and involvement. To this end some general criteria for the curriculum may be set:

- The interdisciplinary nature of curriculum design must be acknowledged.
- There must be a child-directedness, which takes the child's level of development into account.
- Planning must be purposeful.
- Method must be an important characteristic of the design.
- There must be relevance with regard to practice orientation and needs.
- Comprehensiveness must be a characteristic of the design.
- Didactic demands must be taken into account.
- The demands of subject sciences must be taken into account.
- Note must be taken of educational administrative demands.
- The demands and needs of the broad community must be considered.
- Effective evaluation must be an inseparable part of curriculum design.
- There should be a balance with regard to the attention received by the cognitive, affective and psychomotor domains with a view to contributing to the development of the child's full potential.

Snyman (1992: 88) indicates by means of the following presentation what the implications of specific criteria may be.

Table 4.2: Criterion structure for an education situation

Criterion	Curriculum implication
Norm orientation	A Christian (or any other) philosophy and attitude to life is the total purpose in life in the planned and the unforeseen continuation of learning experiences.
Full human experience	Through the situation analysis, objective compilation of content and evaluation action, the full human experience (intellectual, spiritual and physical) is developed.
Viability	Learners must be exposed to viable experiences to develop them (on academic, professional and socio-cultural levels) as future-orientated adults. ➲

Criterion	Curriculum implication
Socialisation	Development and interpersonal and group interaction (with a view to community involvement) is the focus.
Individualisation	The individual's self-image is developed within the larger group (deal with situations independently).
Classification and integration	The individual classifies learning contents so that they integrate with his or her own field of experience.
Time orientation	Learning experiences are aimed at the future (relevant training).

From this table it is clear that curriculum design requires thorough and well-thought-through planning and decision making with a view to establishing a comprehensive curriculum. For effective curriculum design, it is desirable to have a thorough knowledge of relevant curriculum models, the various components, the relevant criteria, the subject, and also the child. Redesign should take place on an ongoing basis in connection with evaluation processes and for this reason it should also be flexible. Effective curriculum design may lead to effective curriculum dissemination and implementation.

Models for curriculum design

In the literature dealing with curriculum matters, a variety of models are encountered which arise from curriculum developers' methods of approach. The method of approach is, however, not the only source of variety in curriculum models, as writers' personal points of view, community needs and composition, the influence of other writers and even the nature of a particular educational system have often led to the design of a particular model.

Some models are more complex while others are simpler in nature. Some agree with others, are a refinement of already existing models or are distinctive original designs according to particular requirements. There is value in utilising a model is as it may give direction and purpose to the whole process of curriculum development. Curriculum developers can therefore take note of particular models and determine to what extent they comply with their requirements. The view of this book is that models should not be prescriptive, but rather provide a conceptual framework for planning, which should be flexible and contextualised

Marsh (2009: 24–25) also argues the issue of utilising models or conceptualisations as tools for curriculum planning. He states that this can provide useful perspectives on some curriculum issues, but not the whole context or picture. There are critics against the use of procedural and descriptive models, as it is argued they are too prescriptive.

Taba's (1962) model for curriculum design has, according to Oliva (1988: 16), an inductive approach and consists of five basic steps:
- **Step 1:** Design of experimental instructional–learning units for a particular subject/standard.
  The following eight-step sequence is part of this design:
  a. Determination of needs
  b. Formulation of objectives and goals

    c.   Selection of contents
    d.   Classification/organisation of content
    e.   Selection of learning experiences
    f.   Classification of learning experiences
    g.   Evaluation
    h.   Control for balance and sequence

- **Step 2:** Testing of experimental instructional–learning units
- **Step 3:** Review and consolidation
- **Step 4:** Development of a frame of reference (cohesion of units and rationale of design)
- **Step 5:** Establishment and dissemination of units

This approach is inductive, as the point of departure is the design of material, which then leads to generalisations.

Tyler's (1949) model has a deductive approach, as it leads from a generalisation (analysed needs) to the particular (objectives, goals). Tyler's model is introduced by Oliva (1988: 171), as shown in Figure 4.2.

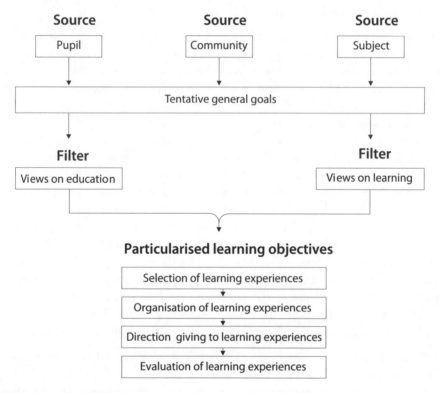

Figure 4.2: Tyler's model (1949)

Oliva (1988: 173) motivates his particular conceptualisation of a curriculum model by saying he wanted it to meet three criteria, namely it had to be simple, comprehensive and systematic. This design is shown in Figure 4.3.

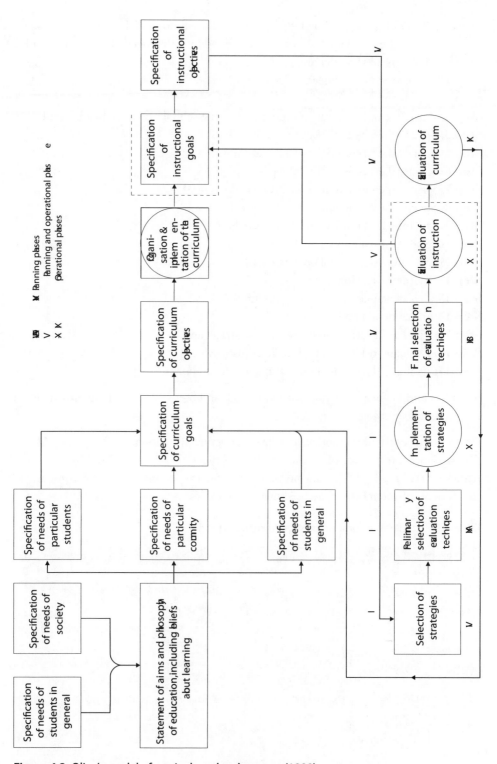

Figure 4.3: Oliva's model of curriculum development (1988)

Oliva (1988: 177) says that some might prefer a curriculum model in the form of steps, instead of a diagram and the following list might address that need. The recommended steps that flow from his model are:

Step 1: Specify the general needs of learners.

Step 2: Specify the needs of society.

Step 3: Write/formulate a mission statement of the school's philosophy and goals.

Step 4: Specify the needs of learners in the school.

Step 5: Specify the needs of the local community.

Step 6: Specify the needs of the subject.

Step 7: Specify the curriculum objectives of the school.

Step 8: Specify the curriculum goals of the school.

Step 9: Organise and implement the curriculum.

Step 10: Specify instructional goals.

Step 11: Specify instructional objectives.

Step 12: Select instructional strategies.

Step 13: Select evaluation strategies (preliminary).

Step 14: Implement strategies.

Step 15: Finalise the selection of evaluation strategies.

Step 16: Evaluate instruction and make adjustments.

Step 17: Evaluate the curriculum and make adjustments.

Steps 1–9 and 17 form a curriculum sub-model, and Steps 10–16 form an instructional (instructional–learning) sub-model.

A number of curriculum models have been designed at national level in South Africa. The design contributions of Walters (1978), Krüger (1980), and Cawood, Carl and Blanckenberg (Carl, 1986) may be mentioned in this connection. The comparable components of the models may be shown as in Table 4.3.

Table 4.3: Comparable components for curriculum models

Walters model	Krüger model	Cawood–Carl–Blanckenberg model
Initial evaluation	Situation analysis	Situation analysis (includes initial evaluation and contextual evaluation)
Selection of goals	Selection of goals	
Selection content	Planned learning experiences	Selection of goals
Classification and organisation	Selection and organisation of learning opportunities	Selection and classification of learning experiences
Outcome evaluation		Selection and classification of learning experiences
	Evaluation	Planning and application of the instructional–learning situation
		Learner evaluation

Source: Based on Walters (1978); Krüger (1980); and Carl (1986)

If these local curriculum design models are looked at more closely, it appears that the international ones have had a strong influence on most of these design forms.

The Walters (1978: 270–275) model shows a dynamic interaction between the components, as well as a close relationship and flexibility between them. In this model, evaluation especially has a testing and development function at various levels. Through initial evaluation (in which situations are analysed), progress evaluation (which is applied with regard to the formulation of objectives, selection of content, classification of content and the planning of method) and outcome evaluation (which evaluates the end result of the educational undertaking), the result of the design is continually tested and further developed.

Krüger's (1980: 333–335) model is comparable with that of Nicholls and Nicholls 1972), with an additional refinement of planned learning experiences. In respect of this model these experiences must develop into a 'vertical' and 'horizontal' educational spiral. The idea of a spiral build-up of knowledge implies, on the one hand, a vertical deepening of specialised knowledge experience in every subject terrain and, on the other hand, a horizontal integration of experiences across the different subject terrains in order to develop the learner's general education and all the values that go with it.

There are a few components or elements, such as those set out below, which seem to be in common among most of the curriculum models mentioned:
- Situation analysis/contextual evaluation/initial evaluation
- Objectives and goals
- Selection and classification of content
- Selection of methods, techniques and media
- Selection and classification of learning experiences
- Planning and implementation of the instructional–learning situation
- Evaluation of learners

A few of the problems which come to the fore when studying such curriculum models and the various components thereof are that they are either not comprehensive or not discriminatory enough, cannot be utilised on all curriculum levels, or cannot be applied in every particular educational system and community. After the application of a few models and through trial experience and intensive development work, a curriculum model has been developed in the Department of Didactics at Stellenbosch University (University of Stellenbosch, 1983), which endeavours to obviate these problems and shortcomings.

Carl (2009) has since adapted this model for the current context. It has utilisation possibilities at any curriculum level. However, it is assumed that not all components will be applicable at all levels. The dynamic interaction of the various components is also stressed and does not necessarily show a fixed progress pattern. A diagrammatic presentation of this model is given in Figure 4.4.

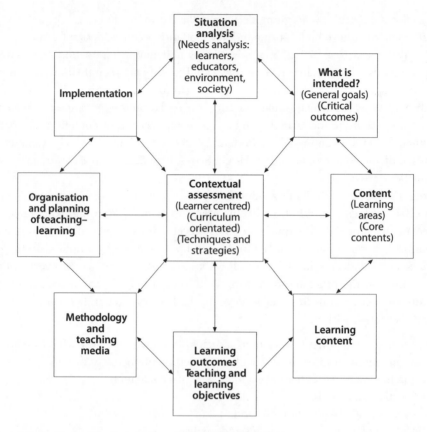

Figure 4.4: Carl's model of curriculum design (2002; 2008)

Although between 1998 and 2011 the focus on outcomes-based education was on outcomes, the place of goals and objectives in a curriculum model should not be ignored, as there is still no unanimity regarding the distinction between goals and outcomes. Some argue that outcomes should replace goals, but the difference between these two components is not clear. The model can be adapted by including the critical and specific (or learning) outcomes. The intention of this model is not to serve a specific approach (e.g. outcomes-based education), but rather to be of general use in curriculum development.

The value of Carl's model lies in the possibilities of adaptation at the various curriculum levels. Effective curriculum development is also stimulated as an ongoing evaluation takes place.

In summary it appears that there are differing rationales for the choice and design of a particular curriculum model. Whatever model is used in the planning action, it appears essential to plan any curriculum design systematically and thoroughly, as the later successful dissemination, implementation and evaluation of the curriculum depend thereon to a great degree. While the utilisation of certain models is valuable, their use must be seen against the background of the curriculum orientations described in Chapter 2 as these may influence the choice of a curriculum model and whether to make use of a model.

Oliva (1988: 177) puts it clearly that curriculum leaders must take note of the available models, must be able to test them and must decide on/develop one which is understandable and workable for their various groups. Curriculum development can then progress methodologically and purposefully. This is clearly an important aspect in the process of teacher empowerment.

4.5 Components of curriculum design for micro-curriculum development

Although the components which are normally found within curriculum design are reasonably fully described in the literature, it is nevertheless necessary for the purposes of this publication to refer to them. The components which will apply to the relevant design will also depend on the level/area/sector in which the curriculum developer is involved. A curriculum committee at national level will normally consider goals and core contents while the subject teacher will use nearly all the components (from goals, objectives, content handling and media to methods and evaluation) in a micro-curriculum development situation.

The components which will be explained are situation analysis, goals, objectives, outcomes, selection and handling of core and learning content, selection of teaching methods and evaluation.

Situation analysis

According to Oliva (1988: 223), a situation analysis is often based on the set, broad educational goals and philosophies of life. Phrases such as the following are examples of these goals: to help develop a well-rounded individual; to enrich the spirit; to develop basic skills; to help develop a well-informed citizen; and to develop certain values in the learner. They suggest the specific needs of the community and the learner.

The process of situation analysis is one of evaluation, comprising the collection and interpretation of all the information that may influence curriculum development. According to Calitz, Du Plessis and Steyn (1982: 11), all the information and variables which may play a role in goal achievement must be included. Each variable must therefore be examined and interpreted.

This process may serve as a starting point for curriculum development, but it should also take place on an ongoing basis in order to be able to make ongoing adjustments. The results of such a situation analysis should serve as a strong guideline for the design which is to follow with all its facets. Curriculum planners who look at the broad curriculum at a national level will first make a thorough analysis of the needs of the country and the broad school population, and then formulate broad objectives for the school phases accordingly. The subject teacher, however, will make an analysis of a specific class/grade/learner and use the results in micro-curriculum development for the instructional–learning situation. The process is the same but the nature and extent of the various levels/sectors lend another dimension to each respectively.

Krüger (1980: 35) avers that this situation analysis must comprise a detailed analysis of the whole terrain of curriculum studies. In this way, shortfalls, defects, needs and strong points are identified simultaneously.

It would not be wrong to refer to a situation analysis also as a needs assessment. It would in fact be an identification of needs, which include those at national and regional level to school and classroom level. A situation analysis is also a form of assessment and can be seen as a pre-assessment undertaken prior to the design and implementation of the curriculum in the teaching–learning situation.

At national level, the identification of specific needs could lead to the development of the broad curriculum, with various school types being implemented, new subjects brought in, or even obsolete subjects abolished. The broad community's needs are therefore taken into consideration. In respect of a specific school community, for example, it must be determined what the local community's needs are, such as whether the school curriculum needs to be more academic. Similarly, the needs of a school, the learners and the teacher must be determined in order to provide effectively for them.

The nature of needs may fluctuate from the more physical to the more psychological. They will also differ depending on the level at which one is moving (e.g. national or more local). At a local level, the situational analysis should be made in respect of learners, content, physical surroundings, teachers and the learning action.

a. Learners

The aspects of information regarding the learner on which one should focus include the following:

- **Learner population**, which includes the general learner population information, enrolment numbers, indications of progress and the nature of reasons for leaving school (if applicable)
- **Development and learning**, including age, physical growth and development, achievements in specific subjects, psychological needs, intellectual and creative development, personality factors, and attitudes in respect of school, home and the various subjects
- **Home, family and environmental conditions**, including home and family life/circumstances, school communities, adult population and the specific nature of the community
- **Logistic aspects**, including elements such as grade, numbers and language medium
- **More general aspects**, including attention span, motivation, leadership, skills, independence and field of interest

Mostert (1986b: 90) also mentions the following aspects in respect of the learning activity which link up with what is said above, namely what learning is, the value of motivation in learning, the nature of learning methods and the nature of learning preparedness.

b. Content

Learning content should be analysed in the light of the following: linking up with objectives, extent, relevance, degree of difficulty, available sources, demands and requirements of the syllabus, depth of study, classification, time scheduling, textbooks available, other available learning content, suitability for relevant learners, and structure of the subject content (Carl et al., 1988: 30).

Syllabus interpretation therefore makes up an important part of such a situation analysis.

c. Physical environment: school and classroom

The following may serve as a guide for what to look at in a situation analysis of the school environment: nature of the school curriculum; types and number of classrooms; number of learners in the school; language medium; number of teachers; number of males and females; community within which the school is situated; adaptation of personnel in relation to innovation leadership within the school; level of teachers' curriculum knowledge and ability; quality of subject team systems; staff development in the school; availability of resources in the library/media centre; and suitability of school climate for promoting curriculum development (Carl et al., 1988: 31).

In respect of the classroom, the following should be taken into account: physical space; lighting and ventilation; number of benches in relation to learners; subject atmosphere; change of classes; whether the teacher has a permanent subject classroom or not; and availability of reference works in class or from the class library (Carl et al., 1988: 31).

d. Teacher

During a situation analysis or a determination of teachers' requirements, the following should be considered: the relevant teachers' view on education in the broad sense; their view on learners and on the subject; the extent of the teacher's curriculum knowledge and skills; their subject knowledge; their qualifications; their teaching experience; their successes; their flexibility; their leadership style; and their teaching ability.

e. Community

It is also essential to look at the broader community and the relevant school's local community. Needs can vary from those of a more physical nature, for example food, clothing and housing, to more psychological and norm-orientated needs, such as freedom, peace, values, education, teaching, literacy, understanding of other cultures, career matters, vocational guidance, an academic or more technically orientated curriculum, and family guidance.

There are different methods that may be utilised in collecting the data, which are mentioned here without discussion. These methods include drawing up questionnaires, conducting interviews, observation, holding think tanks and drawing on available research results.

Although it has already been pointed out that the various phases of curriculum development are closely interwoven, a comprehensive or contextual evaluation or situation analysis of all variables is absolutely necessary for the effective design and later successful development and extension of the relevant curriculum. The whole spectrum must be placed under the evaluation microscope.

Aims

Introduction

It is necessary for all education to be goal orientated. Curriculum designers must have a clear understanding of the educational and teaching goals, as well as of the objectives of the particular subject. The determination of goals is an important and necessary step in order to make maximum use of instruction time. Such time is valuable, and schools should place a high premium on what is to be instructed with a view to realising the set goals (Brandt & Tyler, 1983: 40).

In this connection it is implied that having goals to guide education and focus the quality of instruction is a basic requirement for all instructional–learning situations in all subject areas and at all levels (Cawood *et al.*, 1982: 28). An educational institution may be undertaken and run more successfully if there is clarity as to what the goals are and what is intended by them. Goals may serve as a basis for the decision-making process during the drawing up of an accountable and manageable working plan.

Aims exercise a direction-giving influence on the didactic design of instructional–learning situations for learners and during its implementation in practice. The formulation of goals appears to be an important component, as the selection of learning content, the planning of learning experiences and evaluation flow directly from them. In all the models mentioned, goals and aims clearly have a special position.

Value of purposefulness

The most important values of goals, aims and objectives appear to be that they give direction and that they are determinative in the design of programmes and in the evaluation of the design. They must be in the service of the particular needs of the learner.

In this connection, Brandt and Tyler (1983: 44) state that the aims not only contain the nature of the learning contents and the nature of the claims of the community but also must take into account the precise nature of the learner. The latter moves through different development phases, of which intellectual development is one. With greater clarity as to what one seeks to achieve, the learner may develop optimally. Greater purposefulness therefore also requires a thorough knowledge of the learner. The exact formulation of aims may:
- lead to the re-evaluation and replanning of various instructional situations
- give rise to a greater variety of instructional methods and techniques
- serve as a basis for a clear communication system between teacher and learner, and among educational institutions
- define the role that teachers can play in the curriculum through their subjects
- facilitate a more precise analysis and more scientific evaluation of curricula (Kent *et al.*, 1974: 750–751, in Cawood *et al.*, 1982: 35)

- help learners to be continually self-evaluating with regard to their own progress
- help learners to have greater clarity with regard to their learning priorities and to strive for them with greater motivation (Diamond, 1975: 62–63, in Cawood *et al.*, 1982: 36; Carl *et al.*, 1988: 32–33).

The key role played by purposefulness in the didactic design of educational programmes for learners is clearly summed up by Bray (1979: 20):

> The design of a program[me] is composed of many elements, chief among which are a sense of where we are, what we have and where we hope to be …
> [T]he determination of the goal can serve as the first priority.

Hierarchy of goals and aims

Aims can, however, be seen to broaden hierarchically from the instructional aims in the classroom to the broad educational goals arising from the philosophies of life of the broader community. Although the former aims are more specific, they contribute to the realisation of the broader goals. Walters (1978: 22–23) proposes such a hierarchy, as shown in Figure 4.5.

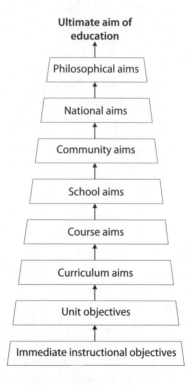

Figure 4.5: Walters' hierarchy of goals and aims (1978)

Every teacher should be thoroughly aware that goals in relation to the classroom are often in the service of a broader national and/or international philosophy of life. This often serves as a starting point for a community's view of education and, as such, also for the goals set, *inter alia,* with regard to the school, courses and classrooms. Goals and objectives may possibly be formulated at three educational levels (Carl *et al.*, 1988: 33):

- The **macro-level**, which is concerned with the identification of the final destination at national level, within a particular cultural context, within a school phase for a particular group or within the broad curriculum development for a particular subject
- The **meso-level**, which has to do with the identification of aims within a specific school curriculum or a more complete subject curriculum
- The **micro-level**, which has to do with the identification of aims within a specific subject module or even a lesson or lesson unit.

The connection between general goals, particular aims and objectives on the one hand and the three educational levels on the other is reflected in Table 4.4:

Table 4.4: Links between goals and educational levels

Educational level	Description of educational level	Types of goals
Macro-level	Goals for an educational system, instructional system within a particular culture, school phases and the broad curriculum	General goal
Meso-level	Goals for a school curriculum, a course curriculum, a subject syllabus, a more complete subject curriculum	General goals and particular aims
Micro-level	Goals for educational undertakings of limited extent (e.g. a lesson or study unit)	Particular goals and objectives

General goals, particular aims and objectives

The curriculum developer will require clarity as to the difference between a general goal, a particular aim and an objective which may be classified (and particularised):

- A general goal is, according to Cawood *et al.* (1982: 42), a general statement which describes the end condition of an undertaking (instructional activity). It is aimed at the long term, is usually broadly stated and indicates the total extent of an educational undertaking in broad terms.
- A particular aim is a broad demarcation around subjects or themes within the demarcated terrain. It is more specific and more particularised than the general goal.
- An objective is an exact, precise description of the relevant learner's required behaviour or achievement which must be realised at the end of a certain time. It is connected to the learner's final behaviour and indicates what level of achievement

must be gained and under what critical conditions this must be done. The accent therefore falls on what the learner must be able to do at the end of the instructional–learning activity or teaching undertaking (Cawood *et al.*, 1982: 39– 42). Oliva's (1988: 262–263) descriptions confirm these distinctions.

It would be incomplete merely to give definitions and not to focus on the actual practice. The broad curriculum and the various school phase curricula have as points of departure certain broad educational and teaching goals, and these are transposed to school goals. A specific education department will have specific broad goals which in turn will be particularised by a specific school. A specific school normally has general school curriculum goals, which are then further particularised by the subject teacher. The subject teacher in turn also has general subject aims which link up with this and which are eventually refined to particular aims and objectives for a particular instructional–learning situation.

Types of aims

Besides a finer differentiation being made between general and particular aims, there are also different types of aims to be found within this context.

One may distinguish between process and product aims or goals. **Product** goals or aims comprise a predominant focus on the final product, however it is achieved. For those who uplift product aims to the level of absolutes, the process, i.e. how one goes to work to achieve that product, is not of particular interest. Product aims are thus those goals or aims orientated to the introduction and control of the body of knowledge and the proficiencies and skills of a particular subject. The 'products' of a subject may be facts, concepts, principles (generalisation), algorithms, procedures, techniques, trends or theories, etc.

Process goals or aims are those goals aimed at introducing and promoting the typical working strategies of a subject and/or the thought processes which may be served through the particular subject. In this case the stress is therefore placed more on the process and not so much on the final product. The following are examples of some subjects and their relevant working strategies:

- **Mathematics**: Algorithmatising; modelling
- **Physical science**: Setting hypotheses, theorising
- **Life sciences**: Observing (orientated), classifying
- **Geography**: Collecting data; processing data
- **Languages**: Communicating effectively
- **Arithmetic**: Interpreting documents

Thought processes include using, for example, logical thought, critical thought, analytical synthetic thought, abstraction and generalisation (Carl *et al.*, 1988: 34–35).

Process goals may be broad subject goals, for example learning to study, learning to think, or learning to work together. They may, however, also be directed to the subject in a more specialised way, and in that case specific subject proficiencies and skills are envisaged.

In respect of the latter, Cawood *et al.* (1982: 31–38) indicate the following:

- Languages
  - Effective communication
  - Critical thinking
  - Logical thinking
- Mathematics
  - Ratiocination
  - Arithmetic interpretation of documents
- Geography
  - Cartography

The process goals are therefore also concerned with the development of thinking skills and require that, in dealing with the learner, very strong stress should be laid on developing these skills. Each teacher and instructional leader should take note of this and apply these goals with a view to supplying a balanced education to learners. Too much stress on product aims can result in neglecting the development of thinking skills. Conscious planning must therefore be undertaken to bring about this balance.

The empowered teacher will probably be mainly involved in classroom curriculum development, more complete subject curriculum development and syllabus development, and therefore it is essential to know about all these perspectives. Through them the quality of involvement may be increased. Not only must they know about them but they must also be well grounded in the particularisation and formulation of the various goals.

Classification systems

Various classifications of goals have been made to indicate how the thinking processes may progress during the learning process. During curriculum design the curriculum developer must have clarity as to the terrain or domain on which he or she should concentrate – whether cognitive, affective or psychomotor. In this connection knowledge of a few classification systems may contribute to maintaining a meaningful balance in respect of the various terrains.

Because the various classifications have already been described in many places in the literature, they will only be stated briefly here. The best-known system of Bloom and co-workers (1956; 1964), who drew up taxonomies on the cognitive, affective and psychomotor domains, is briefly explained (Bloom, 1956; 1964; Cawood *et al.*, 1982: 58– 61; Rowntree, 1978: 31–32; Carl *et al.*, 1988: 37–38):

a. In the **cognitive** domain, six levels have been identified, each in turn with its own further individual division. The six levels which run hierarchically are:
    Level 1: Knowledge
    Level 2: Understanding
    Level 3: Application
    Level 4: Analysis
    Level 5: Synthesis
    Level 6: Evaluation

b. In the **affective** domain there are four levels:

Level 1: Receipt
- Consciousness
- Preparedness to give attention
- Controlled or selective attention

Level 2: Response
- Consent to give attention
- Preparedness to respond
- Satisfaction

Level 3: Value determination
- Acceptance of a value
- Preferences
- Dedication

Level 4: Characterisation
- Stable value system
- Characterisation (part of behaviour)

c. In the **psychomotor** domain there are the following levels:

Level 1: Cognitive
- Knowledge acquired

Level 2: Absorption of recording

Level 3: Automation
- No effective or cognitive intervention (does it all automatically)

Other classification systems which may be consulted are the 'Structure of Intellect' by Guilford (1956; Taba, 1962: 101–103) and the systems of Bradfield and Moredock (1957); Romiszowski (1981); Rowntree (1978); and Taba (1962).

The utilisation of such classification systems can give direction to curriculum developers and help them to decide what to concentrate on.

Objectives

Carl *et al.* (1988: 41) and Oliva (1988: 282) find a strong connection between aims and objectives, stating that the objectives are the further expression and refinement of aims. This is of particular importance for the subject teacher. An objective normally describes the required behaviour and outcomes, and the level of achievement which must be obtained.

A precise and clear description of objectives gives clear direction, and cuts out vagueness regarding what learners must know or do. Well-formulated objectives also give direction to the determination of methods, media and evaluation strategies (Rowntree, 1978: 34–36). Objectives therefore offer a frame of reference against which a value determination may be made regarding the success of the curriculum development action.

For the subject teacher it is also essential during curriculum development to distinguish between instructional and learning objectives.

A **learning objective** is an objective which is formulated in such a way that it clearly spells out the expected **learning profits** on the part of the **learners**; in other words that which the learners should be able to do/know at the end of the lesson. The following serves as an example:

> After the teacher has demonstrated the following reaction for them in small groups, learners will be able to describe in less than 50 words the effect of an acid on a carbonate.

An objective may also be related to the **teacher**, and in that case it would be described as an **instructional objective**. An instructional objective is an objective formulated in such a way that it spells out the **instructional actions** of the teacher, in other words what the teacher will do at a certain time during the lesson. The following serves as an example:

> The teacher will demonstrate the effect of an acid on a carbonate to the learners in small groups.

It is essential that the subject teacher takes aspects into account with a view to extracting maximum benefit from the curriculum design.

Rowntree (1978: 17) brings forward an important perspective, namely that learner input is essential in the determination of objectives, as they are after all the learners. In this way they may utilise their own strategies to realise them. Too often learners must learn what is determined for them by others, and this can lead to a conflict between the various objectives of the system and the learner. Actually, learners must serve as a kind of filter in order that their specific needs may be served to a maximum. This then, according to Rowntree (1978: 42–52), leads to particular types of objectives, namely life skills, methodological and content objectives. These types of goals each have specific sources of origin, for example the future needs of the community (life skills objectives), analysis of subject by subject specialists (methodological objectives) and the analysis of the subject structure (content objectives) (Rowntree, 1978: 43).

A timely warning is that objectives must not be regarded as so rigid and unbending that there is no measure of flexibility and adaptability. There are so many variables which may have the effect that instructional–learning happenings do not always progress as planned. Provision must therefore be made for flexibility. Objectives should be adapted not only to product achievement; in other words only the mastery of knowledge, but also to the process. Stenhouse (1976: 84–97) is of the opinion that a process approach, during which stress is placed on the thinking skills during the instructional–learning process, is more fitting. The role of the teacher is of cardinal importance in this case, as the quality of the teacher will determine the success of the process. Professional development is necessary for the development of teachers' abilities and thinking skills, and to refine further the criteria necessary to be able to evaluate learners. The teachers' initiative and judgement ability are necessary to allow the process approach to come into its own.

The benefits of an aim-orientated approach exceed the disadvantages, as this can definitely lead to dynamic and relevant curriculum development.

Outcomes

It is necessary to reflect on the issue of outcomes-based education (OBE) and the role of outcomes, as this is the context in which teachers will still function for a number of years to come (CAPS will be phased in over a certain period).

The emphasis in OBE is on what the learner should know, understand, do and can become, rather than what the teacher envisages achieving. Most curriculum writers use the term 'outcomes-based education'. Unisa (1997), however, refers to both OBE and outcomes-based learning (OBL), while Van der Merwe (1997: 301) refers to outcomes-orientated teaching–learning (OOTL).

An outcomes-orientated curriculum may be seen as the medium which will assist in the implementation of the principles of a national curriculum framework. The key aspects of this curriculum must be examined more closely and the concept 'outcomes-orientated teaching–learning' needs to be defined.

Killen (1996: 6) recommends certain teaching procedures that can contribute towards the successful implementation of an outcomes-orientated curriculum. He states that teachers ought to prepare learners so that everyone in the class has an equal opportunity to achieve. This means that teachers must first exploit the essential prior knowledge of learners before they can grasp new content. Teachers who wish to implement outcomes-orientated teaching–learning must devote attention to several aspects, such as:

- A positive climate for learning must be created that will offer learners the assurance that they will receive assistance and support when necessary.
- Learners should be informed on what is going to be learned, why it must be mastered, and how they will know if they have mastered it.
- A variety of teaching methods must be applied so that the different learning styles of learners can be accommodated.
- Learners should be given sufficient opportunity to reinforce specialised skills, and sufficient time should be allowed for learners to be able to learn from their mistakes and for changes in their thinking to take place.
- Every lesson should be concluded with a period of retrospection, during which teachers and learners can go over learning gains. Learners should then reflect on what they have learned and on what new contents the knowledge acquired will give them access to.

Outcomes-orientated teaching–learning: a definition

Killen (1996: 10) uses Vickery's (1988, in Killen, 1996) approach to the curriculum, which is summarised below, as an example of a viable model for outcomes-orientated teaching–learning:

- Evaluation of the learners' prior knowledge
- Explaining to learners the outcomes envisaged, as well as what they will be able to do in the professional world with their acquired skills

- Use of teaching methods that will ensure the most successful learning among all learners (or the largest number of learners in the class)
- Guided reinforcement of targeted skills in terms of the outcomes
- Diagnostic evaluation of learners' progress so that meaningful proposals can be made in good time with regard to those areas that require further development
- Selecting learning activities that genuinely inculcate the necessary skills
- Formative evaluation when most learners are prepared to provide evidence of their proficiency
- Provision of more challenging outcomes (enrichment) for learners who show at a particular stage that they have mastered the stated outcomes
- Provision of additional support for learners who have not realised the module outcomes
- Eventual exposure of all learners to a summative evaluation phase. Learners who cannot demonstrate the required proficiency do not receive credits (an incomplete symbol). These learners are then responsible themselves for mastering the stated outcomes. As soon as they feel they are ready, they can be re-evaluated.

Such an approach to the curriculum links with the NQF vision of lifelong learning in that learners must accept co-responsibility for what they learn (Killen, 1996: 11):

> … [T]he teacher is responsible for creating situations in which students can learn, but the students are ultimately responsible for their own learning.

If teachers wish to implement the above key aspects of outcomes-orientated teaching–learning, then the curriculum should, according to Killen (1996: 11), include the following components:

- Clear outcomes that must be attained by everyone (the minimum requirements outcomes)
- Additional outcomes for bright learners
- An indication of the requirements that must be met by learners before they proceed to the next outcome
- Clear learning objectives in language that a learner can understand, as well as examples that can illustrate the skills required by the objectives
- Curriculum plans indicating the different teaching methods whereby learners can be guided towards realising the learning objectives
- Curriculum plans for guided support during the inculcation of subject skills, in terms of which learners can thus measure their progress according to specified criteria
- A variety of evaluation tasks whereby learners can be formatively evaluated on a continual basis
- A variety of summative evaluation tasks whereby a degree of mastery can be determined
- Sources and other teaching techniques by means of which learners can be supported if they do not achieve the required outcomes.

Content of the curriculum

Dimensions of content

When one is considering the curriculum, the content dimension is a core aspect which normally determines the nature and extent of the relevant curriculum. One cannot consider the curriculum without involving the content dimension. A traditional attitude is that content is that component which is included in a school subject; in other words the '**what**' which must be conveyed to learners. Content must, however, be seen much more broadly, as there are many other areas where content forms part of a child's development and education, for example life content and content which involves situations outside the school context. Although not always formally built into a school subject as part of the formal curriculum, these also contribute to a learner's education. Content within the educational and school context is, however, normally more formal by nature (within subject context or structured instructional–learning situations).

As already mentioned, it is normally the selected content which determines the nature and extent of the curriculum, as the content is used to achieve the set of goals or aims. It is thus necessary to illustrate the different dimensions given to content. Content is therefore more than just what is reflected in one subject, as a collection of subjects (e.g. a school curriculum) is also regarded as content.

When a **broad** curriculum is developed, content is therefore also considered. At this level one will not necessarily consider learning content but rather the subject or study fields which must be included for the various school phases. This broad curriculum's content is, for example, set out by CEDH (1991: 40) in the various fields of study and vocational fields. Languages as a field of study will comprise any language; natural sciences will include subjects such as Biology and Physical Science; while social sciences will include subjects such as History, Economics, Geography and Religious Studies. Vocational fields include fields (with examples of their subjects) such as the following: engineering field (Electro Technology, Civil Technology), business fields (Accounting, Typing and Office Administration), arts (Music, Art, Drama), agriculture (Agricultural Science, Plant Production), public utilities (Food Technology, Clothing Technology) and social services (Social Services).

The eight learning areas for the GET phase and the learning fields with their specific school subjects in the FET phase can also be used as examples in this regard.

A **school phase** curriculum also has a specific collection of subjects for those relevant phases and grades, which could be regarded as the content of the relevant school phase, while a **school** curriculum is that collection of examination and non-examination subjects (and also co-curricular activities) which has been chosen to supply the needs of the community and the learners. This collection of subjects could then be regarded as the content of the school curriculum.

During **syllabus** development, one would then normally consider the core content which must be covered within a specific subject. During this phase, a further expression of the school phases and subjects takes place, as they are now expressed by content of a more specialised nature. This content, the so-called core content, is usually described in a syllabus.

Again it is during the micro-curriculum development situation that the teacher expands, refines and develops core content to learning content. Learning content is encountered in textbooks and other literature, such as articles, notes and self-work modules. Learning content is therefore the extension of the core content. Also, the particular subject curriculum will have a specific content.

From the above it is clear that the 'content' dimension comprises more than what meets the eye and that it cannot be regarded narrowly as only the content dealt with by a teacher within a particular lesson. The nature, character and extent of the content fluctuate according to the particular level or area/sector in which curriculum development is done.

The HSRC (1981: 50–52) mentions some principles which should apply in the determination of curriculum content, namely a structural function (the learner helps to give structure to things), a content-giving function (the learner contributes to the increasing experience of adulthood content), a selective function (learners must be able to control selected reality areas completely) and an evaluative function (the learner must be able to act in an evaluating value-determining way). A specific structure is essential in the determination of curriculum content.

A further important perspective is that a distinction must be made between the selection of content on the one hand and the classification thereof on the other. The selection of content will, for example, once again be particular to the relevant levels or areas dealt with. In this way, the selection actions of a curriculum committee choosing core content at national level will be different from those of the teacher who has to choose the teaching content of a specific lesson in a micro-curriculum situation. These actions are in fact linked, but each has its own nature in each particular situation.

In the same way, the classification action of core content by a curriculum committee will appear different from the arrangement and classification of teaching content for a particular lesson by the subject teacher. It is necessary to have this perspective, as it can broaden one's curriculum insights in respect of content.

Selection and classification of content cannot take place in a haphazard manner. This is of fundamental importance for the curriculum developer, as irrelevant and incorrect content can, by its impact, drastically influence the path of life of the learner, according to Krüger (1980: 65). Therefore, content should never be heaped up in a reckless and unplanned manner. In letting the stress fall on the formative value of the content, while there is an enormous explosion of knowledge taking place currently, there should be a careful selection made as to what contains the highest priority value for the child's future adult life. Similarly, knowledge content must be subjected continuously to evaluation in the light of the rapid development in, particularly, the field of technology, so that the essential is retained and the less important omitted (Carl *et al.*, 1988: 43).

Walters (1978: 77) mentions that the traditional approach of selecting content merely for the sake of factual knowledge no longer enjoys great support. There is an ever-increasing tendency to select content which can be used to develop the whole terrain of knowledge, skills, concepts, attitudes and values. Most curricula are still put together on a subject basis, but there is a growing tendency to regard content merely as a means to promote the development of intellectual skills, abilities and attitudes.

Criteria for selection of content

Various curriculum writers offer criteria which may be valid for the selection of content (see Walters, 1978: 173–199; Hill, 1974: 284–290; Steyn, 1982: 70–72). These criteria will not be repeated in detail, but rather a synthesis of the ones that could be regarded as essential will be given:

- The content must serve the realisation of aims such as the following: aims of subject sciences, broad philosophical or life-orientated aims, broad educational goals, and particular didactic and subject didactic aims.
- The content must be realistic, manageable, accessible and viable.
- The content must be relevant.
- The content must be stimulating and motivating.
- The content must take learners' existing knowledge and needs into account.
- The content must offer opportunities for self-discovery.
- The content must promote the development of thinking skills (the cognitive), as well as attitudes and values (the affective) and psychomotor skills.
- The content must be practically achievable.
- The content must offer possibilities for learner input and choices.
- The content must have a balance in regard to extent and depth of study.
- The content must be topical with regard to needs (learners, school, local community, broad community, country, world).
- The content must promote integration of contents within a specific subject with a view to forming a meaningful whole.
- The content must be representative of the relevant subject.
- The content must be functional in the empowerment of learners to develop their full potential.

Classification of content

All curriculum developers, regardless of the level or terrain on which they curriculate, will have to take into account the classification and systematisation of the already selected content. Effective curriculum development often comes to grief particularly because this aspect does not always enjoy the necessary attention which it deserves. The handling of content comprises the selection and classification thereof, as well as the later implementation by means of specific strategies. Classification of content is, therefore, a contributory curriculum development action (from syllabus design at national level by a curriculum committee to lesson planning at classroom level by a subject teacher) towards achieving curriculum objectives.

Beauchamp (1983: 91–95) places a high priority on the classification of content and says:

> The basic curriculum question is … that of what shall be taught in schools …
> and … how shall what has been chosen to be taught in the school be organized
> so as to best facilitate the subsequent decisions about teaching and learning.

These two questions are the primary curriculum questions, and the organized decisions made in response to them culminate in a curriculum design.

A consequence of this view is that learning content in subjects and disciplines is demarcated and that certain cognitive, affective and psychomotor outcomes are linked to it.

Various aspects must be considered during the classification of content, for example the intended aims and goals, level of development and needs of learners, the teacher's subject perspective, preferences of both learners and teachers, the nature and extent of the content, aims of the relevant curriculum, the teacher's curriculum knowledge and skills, time constraints, available resources, familiarity and relevance, and the degree of difficulty of the content.

From the above it is clear that classification also dare not take place in a haphazard manner, but that certain classification principles should be taken thoroughly into consideration. These classification principles have already been fully described by, *inter alia*, Cawood *et al.* (1982: 74–76) and are now set out below in brief:

- Logical classification principle (from the simple to the complex; chronological; from basic to more advanced; from the known to the unknown)
- Psychological classification principle (from the known to the unknown)
- Punctual classification principle (a central theme serves as point of departure after which one moves to other terrains)
- Spiral or concentric classification principle (the same theme is repeated, but each time with greater depth or extent)
- Analytical synthetical principle (systematic analysis leading to conclusions and a synthesis in order to obtain a whole insight)
- Symbiotic classification principle (accentuate the topical joining up with the present or living world in order to obtain, in this manner, a better understanding of similar events in the past)
- Horizontal classification principle (puts events which took place more or less simultaneously against one another)

Summary

It is clear that the selection and classification of content is one of the most cardinal curriculum functions. It is not just a coincidental putting together and arrangement of content chosen haphazardly but should comprise accountable actions based on educational criteria and which correspond with the set objectives. It is, *inter alia*, through the content that the learner gets the opportunity better to understand reality and the world, to manage them and to be able to function meaningfully within them.

This ideal is only possible if the working methods and methodological aspects also enjoy attention during curriculum development.

Instructional–learning strategies and teaching methods

Introduction

Particularly during curriculum design at classroom level the question is asked, 'What is the best method of achieving aims and implementing the planned lesson?' At macro-level, a national curriculum committee would not normally prescribe teaching methods in a syllabus (sometimes, however, broad guidelines are given), as this may possibly dampen teacher initiative. It is therefore normally and eventually the subject teacher who must find an answer to this question within a micro-curriculum situation.

There is a close connection between learning experiences, learning opportunities and teaching methods. This connection may be described briefly as follows (Carl *et al.*, 1988: 48):

> ... by means of instruction and learning actions, in other words actions on the part of the teacher and the learner, a learning opportunity is created for the learner also to be personally and actively involved with a view to deriving the most meaningful experience from this involvement

It is from this didactic situation that the instructional–learning situation is created, in which Steyn (1982: 80–82) shows that the '... dynamic connection between ... aim, learning content, instructional learning opportunities (including teaching methods), learning activities and results' may be studied.

The mere provision and presence of content alone is no assurance whatsoever that learning and education will take place. The teacher must first appear on the scene and create a particular situation within which a particular active process is put in motion. After a decision has been made as to specific aims, it is absolutely vital that the teacher considers ways or means which will acquaint the learners with the content in a manner that will lead to learning. Ways, means or actions of this nature are called methods or didactic work forms. With the help of these methods, the potential of the learners is developed so that they may take their proper place in a future society.

The question arises as to what guidelines the teacher may follow in order to identify a suitable teaching method.

Criteria for the selection of a method

The teacher must not regard the relevant guidelines as prescriptive but only as broad criteria which may help to identify the most suitable teaching method for a particular instructional–learning situation. Such a method creates specific learning opportunities within which the learner may have optimal learning experiences.

Existing principles for instructional–learning may serve as guidelines. Wheeler (1976: 130–131) puts the following 12 principles as determinative for instructional–learning:

- Learning is an active process in which the learner must be involved.
- Learning takes place more effectively if the learner is involved and understands what must be learnt.

- Learning is strongly influenced by the individual's objectives, values and motives.
- Regular repetition is of cardinal importance in acquiring skills.
- Immediate reinforcement promotes learning. Cognitive feedback is more effective if time lapse is limited.
- The greater the variety of learning experiences offered to the learner, the greater the chance that the latter will be able to generalise and discriminate.
- Learning is to a large extent determined by the learner's observations and impressions.
- Similar situations may bring out different reactions from different learners.
- Agreements as well as differences between situations should be illustrated with a view to promoting comparison.
- The learning result and the measure of satisfaction drawn from it are determined by the group atmosphere.
- Individual differences influence learning.
- All learning is multipurpose by nature. Although the focus is placed on specific outcomes, other learning may take place simultaneously.

In the planning of learning opportunities where learner activity is to take place, the above principles should be borne in mind. Gow and Casey (1983: 118–120) link up with this by framing the following principles, namely that they must be feasible within the limitations of programme requirements, availability of sources and personnel supply; that the learning opportunity must correspond with the objectives, goals and content; that the learning opportunity must adapt to the relevant learners (within their abilities, development level, learning styles, interests); and that they must integrate with the subject content, sequence and continuity (make connections, know concepts, etc.).

Tyler (1977: 66, as quoted by Calitz *et al.*, 1982: 60) mentions the following principles: the learning experience which the learner acquires from it must be satisfactory; differing learning opportunities with the same goal must be achieved; creativity need not be repressed; and a learning opportunity may contribute to the realisation of more than one goal.

Steyn (1982: 95–97) also mentions some essential factors which should be considered in the choice of learning opportunities. These are validity and aim directedness (directed at goal realisation); comprehensivity (adaptation to and maintenance of balance between cognitive, affective and psychomotor objectives); variety (linking up with learners' intellectual ability, talents, interests, subject knowledge, general knowledge and language ability); continuity; life relevance (relevance of the skills mastered in the classroom to those applied in daily life); the nature of the learning content; time and circumstances (period time limits); size of class (the number of learners in class influences the creation and planning of learning opportunities); and the teacher (each one's personality, preferences, didactic skills, subject knowledge).

All relevant factors and aspects should therefore be thoroughly considered before decisions are made as to teaching methods.

Oliva (1988: 404–408) highlights five main sources which should be jointly considered in choosing a suitable teaching method. These are objectives and goals; subject content (facts, skills, degree of difficulty, etc.); the learner (learning styles, abilities, preferences, interest, input choice); the community (parents, parent aspirations, type of community); and the teacher (personal style, ability, preferences, abilities, initiative).

From the above it is clear that one must effectively curriculate also as far as the choice of a suitable teaching method is concerned.

Teaching methods: classification systems

The curriculum literature shows clearly that teaching methods have been extensively considered. The curriculum developer should thus be informed as to available methods so that the right choices may be made, based on the guidelines already mentioned (see Section 4.4).

By way of a definition, Cawood *et al.* (1980: 22) say that it is the method that facilitates interaction between the teacher and the learner in order to realise the set aims.

Various classification systems in regard to teaching methods have already seen the light and clearly show the tendency to create learning opportunities within which learner activities figure strongly and prominently. This has already been fully described elsewhere and only the broad approaches are given here.

De Corte's (De Corte *et al.*, 1981: 175–177) classification endeavours to promote the learner–teacher interaction in order to create maximal learning activities. He differentiates between three basic fundamental or didactic working forms, namely the recital, discussion and self-activity forms. In the recital form, the teacher presents the learning content; in the discussion form there is a continuing interaction between teacher and learner; and in the instructional self-activity form, the learner carries out the activity with the teacher in an accompanying function. Group work originates from these three didactic strategies.

Steyn (1982: 84–95) differentiates between three broad teaching strategies, namely indicative, self-discovering and interactive strategies. In each of these, specific methods are encountered. Cawood *et al.* (1980: 24–79; 1984: 32–33) differentiate between four fundamental forms:

- **Recital/lecture:** One-way communication in which a teacher conveys the learning content
- **Discussion:** Two-way communication between the teacher and the learner(s) in connection with the learning content
- **Group work:** Two-way communication during which learners communicate among themselves in connection with the learning content
- **Self-activity:** Self-activity by the learner

From these four fundamental forms a mixed form arises, namely the experience-orientated method or experiential learning. The four basic forms figure within this mixed form but the group and self-activity methods are the most prominent.

Teaching methods which create learning opportunities will not always necessarily be realised in these basic forms. As a result of the complex nature of the instructional–learning events, it is not always possible to differentiate between the actions of the teacher and those of learners, and to characterise them as one of the teaching methods.

Overlapping or clustering may take place between methods, and the difference will not always be clear.

The fundamental forms may be set out schematically, as shown in Figure 4.6, with the respective specific methods.

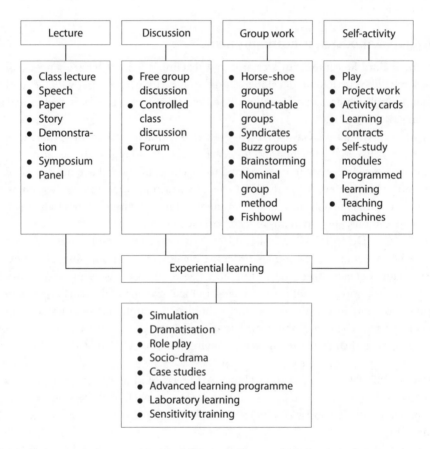

Figure 4.6: Classification of teaching methods (Cawood *et al.*, 1980: 33)

Summary

From the above it is clear that the empowered subject teacher as curriculum developer must have specific curriculum skills, of which specific abilities with regard to methodological aspects are but a few. The instructional–learning situation may lead to optimal learning if this curriculum development comes into its own. Especially within the context of an outcomes-based approach, the need to utilise learner-centred approaches becomes more important.

It is also clear that in order to ensure dynamic curriculum development, the curriculum developer must identify and utilise working methods which will ensure maximal teacher and learner participation. This is possible if basic principles and guidelines serve as a point of departure. Methods are then utilised which lead to the achievement of objectives and which promote effective learning.

Because it is necessary to determine what progress is made or success achieved, the aspect of evaluation arises.

Evaluation/assessment

For the purpose of this publication, the terms evaluation and assessment are seen as synonymous processes. The author has always been of the view that these two concepts focus on making value judgements of the success of the teaching–learning or any educational activity, which is why they are used as evaluation/assessment. They are not seen as different processes (as both make value judgements regarding success). The official view of the Department of Education, however, is that they are different processes.

Why assess?

It is often asked why we have to assess learners. Killen (2007: 321–322) states that the following reasons are normally given (see also Marsh, 2009: 75):
- To determine how well learners have achieved the learning outcomes
- To motivate learners to put even more effort into their learning
- To determine which learners are ready to progress
- For marking and/or grading purposes
- For diagnostic reasons (to determine where learning difficulties occur and what the nature of these difficulties are)
- To provide feedback
- For reporting purposes (to parents and learners)
- To determine what has to be re-taught
- To identify how teaching and learning can be improved

He proposes that these reasons can be categorised into three clusters, namely to obtain information on how to improve teaching and learning; to sensitise learners with regard to their accountability for their own learning; and to make teachers accountable as well. To achieve this, the assessment has to reliable, trustworthy and valid.

From this it is clear that assessment is not a process that 'just happens to be there' but that it plays a very important function with regard to determining the success of the teaching–learning process. Assessment is (or is supposed to be) strongly integrated/linked with all the components of the curriculum development process (goals, outcomes, methods, content) and must be seen as an integral part of the process.

Learner-orientated and curriculum-orientated evaluation/assessment

Each curriculum developer should make a value judgement of the success of the design. Evaluation, which is often regarded as synonymous with assessment, endeavours to determine to what extent learning has taken place with learners or how successful the design was. The evaluation/assessment may thus be learner or curriculum orientated.

In other words, the focus may be either on learning outcomes or on curriculum development, therefore it is essential that the initial, formative and summative evaluations are thoroughly done and that curriculum designers have clarity as to where they wish to place the emphasis.

Learner-orientated evaluation is mainly adapted to determining to what extent learners have made progress on the road to goal realisation and in regard to the lesson, series of lessons or the annual programme (Steyn, 1982: 101), while curriculum-orientated evaluation seeks to determine to what extent the objectives of the curriculum have been achieved. Learner-orientated evaluation is, in fact, only one aspect of curriculum evaluation, as the focus in regard to the latter falls on aspects other than only on the learner. The functions of evaluation/assessment are:

- to determine the success of instruction or the quality of the learning outcomes
- to determine the suitability of the curriculum
- to direct re-planning and adjustments
- to determine whether grading and advancement are possible
- to monitor progress
- to identify defects timeously and correct them.

The data which may be obtained from the evaluation are thus determinative for the further planning of the instructional–learning process and for the remainder of the successful progress of the curriculum. With a view to illustrating the above point of view and to spelling out the purpose of evaluation, Wheeler (1976: 267) says the following:

> Evaluation enables us to compare the actual outcomes with the expected outcomes, and to arrive at conclusions about this comparison with a view to future action … [W]ithout some quantitative and qualitative comparisons … it is impossible to know whether objectives have been realized, and if they have, to what extent.

It is very clear that there is a difference between learner-orientated and curriculum-orientated evaluation. The curriculum developer must be aware of this difference, as it can determine the focus of evaluation. For example, in a learner-centred approach towards curriculum development, the assessment should also be learner focused.

Curriculum-orientated evaluation as a broad phase is described more fully in Chapter 7 where the evaluation aspects which are important to the subject teacher are illustrated further.

Evaluation/assessment and measurement

There is a clear difference between evaluation/assessment and measurement, as De Corte *et al.* (1981: 356–357) clearly indicate. They regard measurement as a quantitative description of behaviour by means of a number (percentage), while evaluation is more encompassing and includes measurement. They base this point of departure, *inter alia,* on the fact that evaluation does not just include this quantitative description but also involves looking at it critically; that evaluation includes the quantitative as well as the qualitative description of achievement; and that other factors, such as the environment, intellectual development level of the learners and cultural background, are factors over and above figures which arise in value determination. Kelly (2009: 160) states that evaluation is the process by which one tries to determine the value and effectiveness of any educational activity. Marsh (2009: 71) says that evaluation is that process by which one tries to obtain information about the skills, knowledge and attitudes of students.

The clear distinction may therefore be made between evaluation and measurement. Measurement is the physical taking of tests/examinations to determine whether learners have mastered certain content and knowledge. Evaluation is a broader notion and relates to value determination which is made, *inter alia*, with the help of measurement (Carl *et al.*, 1988: 57–58).

Measurement then usually takes place by means of measuring instruments, such as written or oral tests/examinations. Calitz *et al.* (1982: 71), however, warn that the purpose and function, which is didactically based, should include the following: that learners are able to determine from them their shortcomings, learning deficiencies and inadequate knowledge, as well their strong points with regard to the learning content; that they are motivated to better achievements; that they can progress further with regard to their abilities and level of achievement; that possible shortcomings in the instructional methods of the teacher are exposed; and that they give an indication of the realisation of the didactic and educational objectives.

Tests and examinations (with question types) are not dealt with fully here. There is much criticism of the system of writing tests and examinations, but it is often the manner in which this is handled which most attracts criticism. Tests and examinations are valuable tools if they are correctly structured and are handled in an accountable fashion. Some of the advantages of tests and examinations are that they determine the level of achievement; they determine the learner's progress; they identify shortcomings and strong points; they indicate how effective the teaching methods are; they may have motivational and exhortative value; they may promote self-discipline and independence; they teach learners to work under pressure; they may teach learners to analyse and dissect information during examinations; and they supply the prognosis for future action.

The disadvantages of tests and examinations may include the following: wrong learning and study methods may develop; the fears which arise may dampen learning; and learners may become mere parrot-like repeaters if too much stress is placed on memorising. The curriculum developer will also have to obtain finality on this aspect of examination as part of curriculum development.

Methods of evaluation/assessment

The level at which curriculum development is done will determine what method of evaluation will be used. The curriculum developer at macro-level will want to determine how effective the broad curriculum or a core syllabus is and for that purpose specific methods of evaluation are used. The micro-curriculum developer (subject teacher) will on the other hand use other determined methods of evaluation to ascertain the effectiveness of the subject curriculum or lesson curriculum. The subject teachers will, however, also want to evaluate the effectiveness of their syllabi and the progress of their learners. In this connection one may therefore speak of both learner-orientated and curriculum-orientated evaluation. The respective methods of evaluation are only briefly illustrated. The core aspect is that curriculum developers must be aware of them and be able to utilise them in their specific field.

It is also important to remember that the use of a specific type of assessment, for example summative assessment, as the only form of assessment is improbable. It will most probably be used in conjunction with other ways of assessment. During formative assessment (see (*b*)), it might happen that summative assessment will be used during that process as well. In the same way, criterion assessment (see (*d*)) might be infused in the process of both summative and formative assessment. The point here is that it is very seldom that a specific way of assessment will be used in isolation as the only form of assessment, but that it will more often be used in conjunction with other forms. The following descriptions of the different forms of assessment should thus be seen in an inclusive and not in an exclusive way:

a. **Summative assessment**. During summative assessment the learning gain is determined (Calitz *et al.*, 1982: 74). It is mainly a summarising evaluation which takes place at the end of the instructional–learning process (Oliva, 1988: 446; Jacobs, Gawe & Vakalisa, 2000: 280). Killen (2007: 339) says it is a 'summation of learners' achievements' and that if it is fair and reliable, valid conclusions might be drawn from the results.

    Summative evaluation therefore takes place at the end of the instructional–learning process (or when the curriculum has been finalised). Calitz *et al.* (1982: 74) equate summative evaluation with product evaluation, as the achieved learning gain (product) is evaluated. This often takes the form of tests or examinations taken at the end of a term or year (Jacobs *et al.*, 2000: 280; Kelly, 2009: 161).

b. **Formative assessment**. Formative assessment is ongoing evaluation which may take place at one's discretion in the course of or during the instructional–learning process (Killen, 2007: 339) to determine on a continual basis whether the process is still moving towards achieving the goals or outcomes. Feedback is applied continually in this case, not only to improve the instruction of the teacher but also to indicate to the learners themselves whether and how they are progressing. Jacobs *et al.* (2000: 280), in their definition of formative assessment, focus only on the fact that it aims to assist learners to grow and develop, as it enables teachers to update their judgements about learners and it advocates a system of continuing learning with the intention of the development of the whole child. Oliva (1988: 445) is of the opinion that this may take place in a formal or informal manner. However, the view that it is there to assist the learner is only one side of the coin. Formative assessment is also there to help and support **teachers** to grow and develop. Killen (2007: 339) confirms this view when he states that it can help teachers to identify shortcomings, and correct them by making adjustments (see also Kelly, 2009: 161).

    According to De Corte *et al.* (1981: 353–354), the product should be evaluated during the development phase on an ongoing basis in order to ensure relevancy and appropriate changes. De Corte mentions further that errors may be identified and corrected at an early stage as a result of this continuing process. Ongoing evaluation also, however, offers encouragement to learners if they reflect the content correctly, and feedback to learners who do not comply with the requirements. Further guidance is then possible (Calitz, 1982: 14, in Steyn, 1982: 106). Killen (2007: 339) refers to this aspect by highlighting the diagnostic value of formative assessment in that learners can get feedback on their limitations and progress. He says that the main value is 'that it helps learners to identify gaps in their knowledge, understanding or skills and guides them towards closing those gaps'.

c. **Norm-orientated assessment**. Jacobs *et al.* (2000: 280) say that a norm is a standard that is set and that learners are assessed against it. The learner's achievement is compared with the average achievement of the group or class (Oliva, 1988: 446; Killen, 2007: 341; Warnich, 2008: 120; Marsh, 2009: 79). The teacher may, for example, accept that his or her class is a representative sample of learners and will then aim for an average of approximately 50% in order to ensure an even spread. This type of evaluation will naturally penetratively influence the teacher's choice of questions. He or she will want a normal spread with regard to the degree of difficulty.

Coetzee (1985: 7) mentions that the stress does not fall so much on full or absolute mastery but rather on personal progress. The evaluators aim for a perfect bell-shaped points spread, and if the fall-off of their group's points is too radical, they make adjustments to create an image which lies as near as possible to the median. Because norm-orientated evaluators aim for a normal points spread, they choose in their examination papers items of varying degrees of difficulty to offer to both the intelligent and the weaker learners a reasonable opportunity insofar as answering is concerned. Because in norm orientation there are usually a limited number of A and B symbols, it may encourage learners towards greater competition.

Killen (2007: 341–342) emphasises that not all learners will learn equally well, despite equal learning conditions, because they will not find assessment tasks equally easy or difficult. In norm-referenced assessment, learners are ranked according to performance, and compared to others based on this ranking. This has led, according to Killen (2007: 342), to a number of misconceptions, namely that marks are more important than how reliable or fair the assessment is; higher marks are better than lower marks; it is better to be above the average mark, no matter how it was obtained; and that it is important how learners perform compared to the rest of the group, disregarding the fairness and reliability of those marks. Killen (2007: 342) is of the view that in norm-referenced assessment, marks might not have been obtained in a fair and reliable way and that this may influence the interpretation thereof. This tends to draw attention away from what is really important, which is **what individual learners have or have not learned**.

To this can be added that one can easily tend to classify learners as to who they are and what they are based on a comparison with the group, instead of looking at the individual and the uniqueness of that learner. Learners are easily labelled as being 'slow' or as not having potential. The world is full of examples of learners who, according to a comparison with others in a group, are 'failures', but who have proved in life after their school career that they can be even more successful than those who outscored them during norm-referenced assessment. There is not always account taken of different variables, and that brings us back to the validity, fairness and reliability of norm-referenced assessment.

d. **Criterion-orientated assessment**. The learner is compared with one or other objective criterion and not with the class average. This method does not produce a good spreading of marks, but is rather striving for total mastery (Cawood *et al.*, 1982: 245–247; Oliva, 1988: 446). The focus is on total mastery and the pass level is very high. The learner him- or herself does not necessarily have a great say in the determination of the goals, as it is the evaluator who determines the relevant abilities. Should the teacher allow the learner a symbol on a criterion basis, it would be an absolute reflection of the learner's abilities with regard to the required goals and objectives (Coetzee, 1985: 6). Jacobs *et al.* (2000: 280), Killen (2007: 342) and Warnich (2008: 120) mention that these criteria are pre-determined and/or specified before the actual teaching–learning process and that learners are then assessed against them.

Killen (2007: 342–344) lists the main features of criterion-orientated assessment as the following: criteria can be defined that describe the learning that learners should achieve or demonstrate; learners can demonstrate the extent to which they have mastered the set criteria; the conditions under which the assessment is done are exactly the same for all learners; the actual marking is done in the same way and there are no exceptions; and learners 'pass' if they meet the criteria. Killen (2007: 343) says that it is very difficult to actually define the appropriate criteria and the level of performance that is required, for example setting it too low (so that everyone can pass) or too high (and everyone fails). He is of the view that this dilemma is linked with the problem of defining what is meant by competence. He calls it an 'elusive concept' as it is difficult to define. He continues to describe the dilemma of setting a benchmark and the impossibility of all learners achieving or performing equally well. Learners will not perform the same or learn equally well. There will always be differences, and Killen (2007) contends that criterion-referenced assessment is not without its problems. Teachers have to realise this and make provision for differentiation and different levels of achievement.

e. **Standards-referenced assessment**. Killen (2007: 345) is of the view that the answer to the main problems of assessment (or limitations, as he calls them) is standards-referenced assessment. This is, according to Killen (2007: 345–346), a way of assessment where learners demonstrate different levels of achievement compared to a set of standards. Learners are thus compared not with other members of the group but to the level at which they have achieved the outcome(s) (the standards). This may lead to a greater level of motivation for learners to perform better, as they now have a standard towards which they can strive. Assignments are designed so as to allow learners to demonstrate what they have achieved and are aligned with the predefined range of possible levels of achievement (standards). This can lead to a more fair and reliable assessment. The learner's work is compared with the set standards and this assists the process of judgement. Although the conditions of assessment are the same for all learners, there can be differentiation in that provision can be made for learners with special needs (Killen, 2007: 345).

f.   **Illuminative evaluation.** Illuminative evaluation is a form of process evaluation during which the change/renewal of a programme as a whole is intensively studied. This comprises a total evaluation of the rationale, development, progress, success and problems encountered. Instruments such as observation, interviews, questionnaires and analysis of documents form part of this whole process. According to Stenhouse (1976: 112–113), its purpose is to obtain an understandable version of the curriculum renewal initiatives and their outcomes, without merely falling back on measurement. Walters (1978: 266–267) mentions that this method of evaluation endeavours to describe the context within which change takes place. This method seeks to indicate not only the progress of the renewal programme but also all the influences thereon, how those involved deal with renewal, what the outstanding characteristics are, etc. The whole process makes timeous adjustments possible.

g.   **Pre-assessment.** Oliva (1988: 444) points out that most of the methods of evaluation set out above take place during or at the conclusion of the learning events. Pre-evaluation is, however, also essential in determining the knowledge and skills which the learners already possess. It may give an indication of learners' potential and interest, and the necessary planning can be made accordingly.

One can say that the situation analysis of needs assessment that one makes before the actual teaching–learning situation is actually a form of assessment and can thus be seen as pre-assessment.

h.   **Continuous assessment.** Continuous assessment is also a way of assessing learners on a continual basis by using a combination of the afore-mentioned assessment ways. Killen (2007: 339–340) refers to the gathering of reliable information about learner performances on an ongoing basis, using well-defined criteria. A variety of assessment tools and instruments (e.g. portfolios, assignments, excursions, reports) can be used during this ongoing process to determine and monitor the progress of learners. Instead of using just one final examination, reliable information is gathered and interpreted on an ongoing basis. The main emphasis on examinations is reduced in that they are seen as just one way of assessing learners. Very importantly, the idea of assessment for learning is also emphasised. Teachers are encouraged to use multiple assessment strategies. Assessment is regarded as an open and transparent process in that learners are now seen as stakeholders who have to have a clear understanding of when and why they are assessed. Recording is also an important administrative matter, and teachers must keep a detailed record.

i.   **Authentic assessment.** This is when learners have to complete an assignment which is based on real life and has to be solved within the authentic context. Skills and knowledge have to be applied in the practical, real-life (and not a simulated) situation to solve the problem. This is followed by a feedback process. This may include activities such as creating portfolios, writing journals, demonstrating, exhibiting, discussing, interviewing and role playing (Killen, 2007: 345;

Warnich, 2008: 121). Marsh (2009: 83) adds to this that authentic assessment 'encompasses far more than what students learn as measured by standardized tests or even by ordinary teacher-made tests. Authenticity arises from assessing what is most important, not from assessing what is most convenient'. The curriculum must be directed in the broadest sense at learning and how it contributes to both understanding the subject matter and to content, as well as their lives (2009: 83). Tasks and assignments might therefore be more practical and real life.

j.   **Assessment for learning**. An aspect that has been highlighted continually in the literature on assessment is the notion of **assessment for learning**. Beets (2007: 64) says that researchers still tend to make a distinction between formative assessment (assessment for learning during the teaching–learning process so as to enable learners to improve their learning) and summative assessment (assessment at the end of the teaching–learning situation to determine to what extent the learners have mastered the outcomes). Warnich (2008: 121) in his categorisation of assessment types puts assessment **of** learning equal to summative assessment, and assessment **for** learning equal to formative assessment, as if these are two different processes. Marsh (2009: 75) also sees assessment for learning as synonymous to formative assessment. It consists of a process where efforts are made to improve learning and which will satisfy the learning needs of learners. Earl (2003: 24, cited by Warnich, 2008: 121) says that performances of learners are not compared, but that there is a stronger focus on the strengths and weaknesses of learners so as to improve learning.

Beets (2007: 65) is, however, of the view that making a mere distinction on this basis is an oversimplification of a very complex issue. They should not be seen as different ways of assessment but rather as being complementary in the context of teaching and learning. They do not exclude each other during the process of assessment but should rather be seen as processes on the same continuum. Assessment for learning focuses on how learners learn; should be central to classroom practices; is sensitive and constructive in improving learning; assists learners in how to improve; and acknowledges all educational achievements. He is of the view that although a theoretical distinction can be made, they are not different types of assessment, but instead serve the same goals of a broader assessment process. The goal of making a judgement of the progress of learners during the teaching–learning process in order to support them to improve their learning is an integral component of assessment for learning (Beets, 2007: 69).

Curriculum developers need not necessarily use only one approach to undertaking an assessment. Subject teachers will make use simultaneously of a variety of methods of evaluation or assessment techniques in order either to determine learning outcomes or to evaluate the curriculum. The above-mentioned methods of evaluation may therefore be used in respect of both curriculum-orientated and learner-orientated evaluation. Specific instruments or techniques such as oral/written questioning, peer assessment, self-assessment, portfolios, journals, projects, group work, exhibitions and demonstrations, observation and interviews may be used here. From this it is clear that assessment is not a process involving only a teacher, but that it should lead to learner self-assessment as well. If we say that learners should take responsibility for their own learning and be accountable, then it is obvious that self-assessment (where they assess the outcome of their own learning) should be a core component of teaching and learning.

Recording and reporting

An important aspect of assessment is recording and reporting. Reporting is a process of sharing learners' achievements with other teachers, with students themselves, with parents, with prospective employers and with education departments. This can be communicated by means of interviews, written reports, information sessions or personal letters. These forms of communication should be based on valid and accurate recording mechanisms. Jacobs *et al.* (2000: 311–116) mention record books as a means of recording the marks of learners, and portfolios as a means of recording assessment.

Portfolios can, according to Jacobs *et al.* (2000: 316–319), assist the teacher in bridging the gap between assessing theory and assessing practice. (See also Van Wyk, 2006: 41–67 for an extensive description of the function of portfolios in the teaching–learning process, as well as Warnich, 2008: 122–123.) They continue to describe how teachers can view and use a portfolio, for example that it is a collection of the work of learners as 'it displays examples of a learner's drawings and pictures; … contains information and examples … ; … holds examples of work relating to the learner's whole curriculum'.

Van Wyk (2006: 45) and Warnich (2008: 122) both describe portfolios as the structured accumulation of evidence of learners' work, the detailed and diagnostic description of their performance, evidence of their participation in teaching–learning, and evidence of their taking ownership of their performance, possibly providing evidence of their way of thinking and of their reflection.

For the purpose of this book, however, a portfolio is seen as an instrument that can be used to demonstrate the growth and development of a learner and whether there has been progression with regard to the teaching–learning process. Within the strategy of using portfolios for this purpose, specific ways are applied to gather information on the progress that learners have made or are making.

Criteria for and principles of assessment

Evaluation or assessment, as part of design, should be based on specific criteria and principles, as these may determine the quality of evaluation to a great extent. The relevant criteria may apply to both curriculum evaluation and learner-orientated evaluation, and must thus be seen within that specific context. These criteria may include the following:

- Validity (evaluate what they are supposed to evaluate)
- Continuity, i.e. completeness/comprehensiveness (evaluate all relevant aspects)
- Correspondence (accordance between what is envisaged and what is actually evaluated)

- Objectivity
- Reliability (permanence of results)
- Comprehensiveness (utilise all relevant methods of evaluation)
- Leading to meaningful learning experiences
- Individualisation (make provision for individual differences and needs)
- Democratisation (opportunities for learner input)
- Propaedeuticality (further learning is encouraged or new learning experiences arise from the evaluation opportunity)
- Communicability (feedback of results in a complete manner which gives a true picture to the learner (see Rowntree, 1978: 157; Wheeler, 1976: 269–270; Cawood *et al.*, 1982: 240–243; Carl *et al.*, 1988: 54–56; Jacobs *et al.*, 2000: 292–295). (See Killen, 2007: 322–336, for an extensive description of reliability, validity and fairness as criteria.)

Each curriculum developer, at whatever level or in whatever field curriculum development is done, should be guided by directive criteria, of which the above are but a few.

Summary

From the above it appears that the main purpose of evaluation is to make a value determination of the success of the relevant teaching undertaking in terms of the degree to which the objectives have been realised. Evaluation is that process of value determination during which it is ascertained to what degree the curriculum is successful or to what extent the objectives have been achieved with the learners. Because it is a process, it should be an ongoing activity from the design (macro-, meso- and micro-level) to the implementation thereof (with the feedback used to make the necessary adjustments). In this connection a distinction must be drawn between curriculum-orientated and learner-orientated evaluation.

Curriculum developers who really wish to ensure dynamic curriculum development should be aware of all applicable methods of evaluation and apply them with a view to ensuring that curricula remain relevant. When looking at the broad curriculum, the utilisation of maximal methods of evaluation is essential, while the same is also valid for the subject teacher in evaluating the micro-curriculum. Accountable curriculum development is based on accountable criteria, and a thorough consideration thereof during curriculum development is necessary.

From Section 4.5 it is clear that curriculum design has a clear structure which may direct systematic planning and later implementation. To give direction to curriculum development and to ensure that curricula remain relevant and topical in order to meet all requirements, each component should receive attention. The involvement of curriculum developers and their handling of curriculum design (at their relevant level/ in their relevant field) will enhance the process of empowerment and eventually make the difference.

4.6   Summary

At the commencement of this chapter it was clearly stated that dynamic curriculum development will depend on the quality of the design. In order therefore to establish a dynamic design, whether at national level where a broad curriculum and/or core syllabi are designed, or at micro-level where the subject teacher designs a subject or lesson curriculum, thorough curriculum knowledge and skills are required. Empowered teachers will have to possess the necessary knowledge and skills to enable them to make a contribution towards relevant and dynamic curriculum development.

The value of curriculum theory must not be underestimated, as through it curriculum development and curriculum development practices are better understood. A broad perspective of the theoretical aspects of curriculum design is therefore essential if claim is to be made for a dynamic design.

Some knowledge of existing curriculum models is useful, as they may serve as guidelines in curriculum design. This knowledge may even lead to the development of an own model which is more applicable and meaningful for one's own needs. Models create a logical system or structure in terms of which planning can be carried out. Evaluation is also facilitated if the work is done according to a specific system.

Curriculum design may take place at various levels or in various fields, as set out fully in Section 4.3. Curriculum developers at the various levels/in the various fields will not necessarily utilise each component of a design but, notwithstanding this, each component may still make a contribution to a dynamic design and later to dynamic curriculum development. The quality and nature of all curriculum developers' involvement, as well as the level and quality of their curriculum development knowledge and skills, will eventually determine their level of empowerment and make the difference between either rigid or dynamic curriculum development.

Activities and questions

1. Discuss in your subject group: (a) What do you understand by curriculum design? (b) How do curriculum design and curriculum development link up? (c) What does it mean if it is said that the curriculum design is of a multidisciplinary nature?

2. Discuss the various curriculum development levels and fields in which design may take place and determine

    • where you as an individual teacher are already involved and may become involved; and

    • where you as subject group are already involved or may become involved.

3. What is more important: curriculum theory or curriculum practice?

4. After a study of the available curriculum models, design or decide upon a model for yourself/subject group which will meet your specific needs.

5. To which of the existing models would you give preference? Why?

6. Identify the five most important criteria for each of the following components:
   - Goals and objectives
   - Outcomes
   - Selection of content
   - Classification of content
   - Methods
   - Evaluation

7. Which other components would you add? Why?

8. What components of curriculum design (as set out in 6 above) will arise in each of the following levels or fields?
   - Design of a broad curriculum
   - Syllabus design through a national curriculum committee
   - School curriculum development
   - Subject curriculum development
   - Lesson curriculum development

9. How practicable is it to conduct ongoing situation analysis in your subject?

10. Is the importance of purposefulness over-emphasised?

11. Is the enumeration of behaviour goals essential for dynamic curriculum design?

12. Where would you place subject teachers in the hierarchy of objectives and goals as described in Section 4.5? How do they link up with this?

13. What is the difference between core and learning contents?

14. What could the role of the subject group be in
    - the selection and classification of core contents?
    - the selection and classification of learning contents?

15. How relevant and practically applicable are the classification principles?

16. Discuss as a subject group or reflect individually on how relevant and topical the content of your subject/learning area is today in a changing South Africa.

17. To what extent do you as an individual/subject group have freedom in the selection of (a) core content; and (b) learning content?

18. Evaluate yourself with regard to teaching methods:
    - How informed are you as to available teaching methods?
    - What is your dominant style and where do your preferences for specific teaching methods lie?
    - What variety of methods have you already utilised over the past year?
    - Are you satisfied with the results? Where would you want to improve? How will you do this?

19. Make a distinction between curriculum-orientated and learner-orientated evaluation.

20. Is too much emphasis placed on evaluation? To what extent do existing evaluation practices influence dynamic curriculum development?

21. Which of the following methods of assessment are of greater importance for you?
    - Norm-orientated assessment
    - Criterion-orientated assessment
    - Formative assessment
    - Summative assessment
    - Standard-referenced assessment
    - Assessment for learning

22. Discuss within your subject group how the ways of assessment set out in question 21 manifest themselves in practice.

23. Discuss in your subject group or reflect individually on the extent to which learner input is possible in your subject during assessment.

24. What would your response be to the statement: 'When you teach, you assess; when you assess, you teach'?

25. What do you think are the most important characteristics of an empowered teacher with regard to curriculum design?

26. How can a teacher contribute to the process of self-empowerment with regard to curriculum design?

5

Curriculum Dissemination as a Critical Phase within Dynamic Curriculum Development

At the end of this chapter you should be able to

- show an understanding of and appreciation for the necessity of effective dissemination
- describe the process of curriculum dissemination and what it comprises
- understand the necessity of the active involvement of all those interested in the curriculum and apply it in practice
- make a connection between the theory and practice of dissemination
- know the nature and essence of dissemination
- show appreciation for effective dissemination as a critical phase for the institutionalisation of a curriculum and apply it consciously in practice
- understand the role of dissemination in the process of teacher empowerment
- be more knowledgeable and empowered as to your own functions and roles in curriculum dissemination.

5.1 Introduction: Curriculum dissemination as a phase

Various curriculum development initiatives have already failed because curriculum dissemination has not come into its own. In the literature, dissemination is regarded as synonymous with implementation, while they should in fact be regarded as two separate (although linked) phases. It is during dissemination that the climate for the envisaged change is created and all users are prepared for it. The level of empowerment will probably also determine the level of dissemination.

Effective curriculum development implies change and renewal. From this, it follows that decisions that are well thought through have been taken at various levels based on available information. The information available to decision makers at these differing levels will necessarily be manifested in the decisions to be taken. It is of cardinal importance that each person in the teaching organisation be kept fully informed and involved with a view to taking the best decisions and thus to ensuring optimal development. Curriculum dissemination is the one phase in curriculum development which complies with the above requirement (Hattingh, 1989: 17).

Once the design has been finalised, the dissemination phase normally follows. Curriculum dissemination comprises the preparation of curriculum utilisers through the distribution or promulgation of information, thoughts and concepts in order to make them aware of the envisaged curriculum. According to the HSRC's 'Report of the Working Committee on Curriculum Development' (1981: 110–112), it appears that this is one of the key activities in the whole curriculum development process. As a key activity, it is an important strategy for implementing renewal and is a prerequisite for meaningful and successful implementation. Renewal has often failed as a result of defective or injudicious dissemination. Effective dissemination is a requirement not only for the effective implementation of a curriculum but also for the institutionalisation thereof – in other words, the establishment and consolidation into an accepted and inherent part of curriculation practice.

Renewal and change are often unsuccessful when sight is lost of certain critical factors and views with regard to people's readiness for change and development.

5.2 Dissemination and the involvement of those interested in the curriculum

Preparation of those involved

A critical factor in successful change and curriculum development is, according to Czajkowski and Patterson (1980: 160), the level of preparedness for such a change on the part of those involved. This process is naturally also a typical empowerment process.

Rogers' research (1962, as cited in Pratt, 1980: 427) shows that there are normally certain attitudes towards change. The manner in which information is disseminated often determines how acceptable the curriculum will eventually be. The disseminated information may be received in various divergent manners, and the designers should take this into account in planning their dissemination strategies. These divergent attitudes of future consumers are schematically depicted by Rogers (1962), as shown in Figure 5.1.

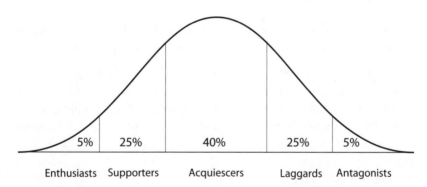

Figure 5.1: Attitudes towards change

- The **enthusiasts** are characterised by being energetic, accepting challenges and having high ambitions. They are adapted to progress and will participate in meaningful innovation. They will also enthusiastically receive and implement a newly designed curriculum.
- The **supporters** are less radical, but are also involved with professional associations and in-service training matters. They are informed as to curriculum matters and

may easily be persuaded to accept innovation if the design is thoroughly planned, well founded and tested.

- The **acquiescers** are purposeful, but although they are also adapted to development, they will not initiate it. They usually make contact only with their equals and will follow the path of least resistance.
- The **laggards** maintain a low profile and are usually sceptical about any changes. They are inclined to act dogmatically, are very rigid in their actions and will not consider any change unless the majority of their colleagues have already accepted it.
- The **antagonists** are usually loners and will resist any change, new curriculum design or revised curriculum (even if it is aimed at development).

These attitudes may vary within the same person. Any curriculum dissemination strategy should, however, take note of the above-mentioned dispositions/attitude roles, as they may eventually determine the success of the implementation phase.

Pratt (1980: 426–432) identifies some causes or factors which often lead to resistance to change and which therefore must be thoroughly taken into account during the dissemination phase. These factors, which link up with the respective roles of Rogers (1962), include the following:

- Lack of motivation
- Vulnerability as a result of uncertainty as to what the new curriculum contains
- A lack of sufficient resources, such as materials, administrative support and specialised knowledge
- Lack of clarity as to development
- Scepticism as to the credibility of the new curriculum as a result of problems in respect of the above four factors

These factors and the disposition which often exists with regard to any form of development are described as follows by Machiavelli (Pratt, 1980: 433):

> There is nothing more difficult to carry out, nor more doubtful of success, nor more dangerous to handle, than to initiate a new order of things. For the reformer has enemies in all who profit by the old order, and only lukewarm defenders in all those who would profit by the new order. This lukewarmness arises partly from fear of their adversaries, who have law in their favour, and partly from the incredulity of mankind who do not truly believe in anything new until they have had actual experience of it.

The level of preparedness of all those involved may therefore exercise a meaningful influence during the dissemination phase, and this makes the challenge of successful implementation so much more complex.

Involvement

It is clear, as already stated, that change is an inherent part of dissemination. If a curriculum stagnates, it can be detrimental to dynamic curriculum development.

Change, that is also curriculum change, endeavours to make provision for and satisfy the needs of specific groups. This may include needs of the country, community, learners and also teachers. Curriculum change therefore endeavours through dissemination to get people involved with a view to satisfying these needs. Information is distributed and there are opportunities for input by interested parties (which may later lead to a positive acceptance and support of the envisaged curriculum).

Meaningful curriculum renewal is only possible if there is active involvement and dynamic leadership. Georgiades (1980: 74) says the following in regard to the nature of involvement:

> ... [O]ur schools exist for people. Significant change in curriculum will not occur through wishful thinking but through hard work and diligent application. Meaningful change demands a deep sense of understanding and, beyond all, commitment to improve education.

Curriculum users may have differing levels of adaptation or stages of concern with regard to change. According to Hall's (1979) model, this may be determined by curriculum users. There are seven types of adaptation or involvement which potential curriculum users may have, and those leading the dissemination should take notice of and apply them.

The levels are distinguishable but not divisible. An individual may simultaneously have a certain degree of adaptation and of concern at most levels but, as renewal progresses it will become more intense at a certain level. The growth and development of individuals may be deduced according to how they move through the levels. The development character of concern and involvement can be divided into three broad dimensions – self, task and impact – with a subdivision of the seven levels under these three dimensions. Hall's (1979) model is depicted in Figure 5.2.

Hord, Rutherford, Huling-Austin and Hall (1987: 31–32) explain how curriculum users' adaptation may develop from 'no concern' to 'refocus', even to a point where own initiative begins to develop. The tempo and quality of development varies from person to person, but dissemination may result in users moving higher and more quickly through the levels to level six. This gives an indication of the measure of involvement and appropriation which has already taken place. The facilitation of change is therefore a necessary part of change.

From the above, it is clear that curriculum change can only be successful if all consumers are effectively involved. Dissemination therefore has, as one of its prime functions, the task of preparing consumers in this way so that they will be purposefully involved. In order to effect this, it is often necessary to break down resistance to change and to create a renewal climate.

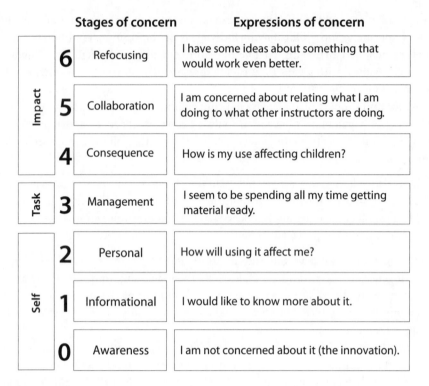

Figure 5.2: Stages of concern

Renewal climate

Park (1980: 56–57; 1981: 272) mentions that a renewal climate is necessary if one wishes to acquire enthusiasm and dedication for the implementation of the envisaged renewal. Within this climate there must also be a conscious attempt to cultivate a high group morale, as this will determine the quality of involvement and co-operation.

It is within this renewal climate that a team and individual feeling arise, as well as the appropriation of the programme as 'ours'. This climate is therefore essential not only for successful implementation but also for breaking down resistance and turning limiting powers into facilitating powers. Berman and McLaughlin (1978, in Czajkowski & Patterson, 1980: 174) even contend that the actual contribution does not lie so much in 'how to do it', but rather in giving moral support and the creation of an organisational climate which makes the envisaged changes 'lawful'. This support and assistance result in the shortcomings and resistance being timeously identified and dealt with, and the teacher having the confidence to ask for help. This personal contact may bring about greater motivation.

A great advantage of this climate is that a team approach with regard to planning and implementation is promoted. Doll (1978: 218–224) mentions that those involved may now give vent to their grievances or may put forward ideas and have the confidence to want to make a contribution. There is an openness to publicising an experimental approach and to endeavouring to realise the joint objectives. Experience in group handling is also acquired. Those involved may also experience that they are being dealt with truly as professional people.

In summary, the creation of a renewal climate appears to be of cardinal importance, not only in eliminating resistance and orientating and motivating those involved, but also possibly in determining the viability of the implementation phase. It is within this climate that planning must be done and structures created to allow implementation to progress smoothly. This climate should be maintained right through the implementation phase up to the evaluation phase.

Elimination of resistance to change

During dissemination, ways must be thought out and utilised in order to eliminate resistance to change in such a fashion that later change implementation will progress successfully. Gorton (1976: 247) warns:

> Resistance to change is a complex phenomenon, and the administrator should spend a considerable amount of time in diagnosing its source(s) before he draws any conclusions about how it might be reduced.

Boles and Davenport (1975: 330) follow this saying that 'changing people is serious business'.

There are various reasons why consumers may possibly resist change. The following are a few of them, namely fear of the unknown and the new, security of the existing, a lack of self-knowledge in regard to own abilities, a lack of motivation, fear of criticism, insufficient support by education leaders, indistinct and faulty dissemination, and ambiguity about — and lack of understanding of — the nature and extent of the envisaged change.

It is clear that the causes of resistance do not always lie with teachers as consumers, although they must often bear the blame for failures. Delahanty's remark (1978: 263, as quoted by Czajkowski & Patterson, 1980: 160) can probably not be generalised, but contains a clear warning when he states, quite correctly, that '[f]ailure is most often attributed to teachers, not innovators; success to innovators, rarely to teachers'.

Means and strategies will therefore have to be utilised during dissemination to overcome this resistance so that all consumers will be maximally involved in implementation. It is also clear that dissemination cannot be a one-way process where outsiders prescribe and pass on rules. It must be an interactive process in which outside organisations, outside persons and the eventual consumers are involved and work together on a team approach basis.

5.3 Curriculum dissemination as social structure

The social system

According to Hattingh (1989: 10), curriculum dissemination, just like the teaching organisation in which it must serve, extends over a wide variety of fields, which vary from mere organisational structures and channels, through elements such as the nature of the message and training, to social aspects such as resistance by the receiver and the characteristics of the messenger, social systems and individuals. Havelock (1973: 10) regards dissemination as a process of interaction or coupling between a potential source and a potential consumer. Different categories of the elements involved in dissemination may be distinguished in the description of the dissemination process as '**who** says **what** to **whom** by **what channel** to **what effect** for **what purpose**'. Havelock (1973: 10) sets the process out schematically as follows in Figure 5.3.

Figure 5.3: Process of social interaction in dissemination (Havelock, 1973)

Havelock (1973), however, regards the above conception as an oversimplification of a very complex system. The idea of a social system and the concept of 'flow of information' do not come to the fore in the above conception. Havelock set out the idea of a social system as follows in Figure 5.4.

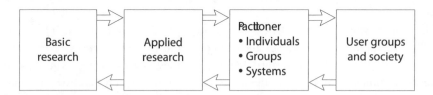

Figure 5.4: Social system and the flow of information (Havelock, 1973)

The social system to which Havelock (1973) always refers makes provision for all elements which have to do with an organisation. It therefore refers specifically to line and staff networks, the network of authority structures in the organisation, the individual's receipt and use of new knowledge, the nature of the renewal or change and the impact of it on members of the organisation, personal roles, character qualities and, therefore, actually any aspect which is connected with the people who make up the organisation (Hattingh, 1989: 20).

It seems as though dissemination in a social system is primarily related to the attitudes, tasks and responsibilities of individuals making up the organisation. Should the concept of a process be combined with that of a social system, as set out in Figure 5.5, a better picture may be developed of the many interest groups, levels and facets.

These concepts offer a simplified picture of the many different interest groups and the enormous complexity of the social system within which dissemination must take place.

Rogers (1983: 5–6) regards dissemination as a process of communication which takes place via certain channels for a period between members of the social system.

Communication in this context is seen as a two-way process in which the exchange and sharing of information takes place in order eventually to come to a clear understanding. Rogers also regards dissemination as a type of social change through which the organisation's structures and functions should be adapted to the nature of change or renewal.

Curriculum dissemination is not always strictly planned and structured. Chance dissemination or diffusion may also take place. It is, however, clear that the possibility of successful implementation decreases in the case of less-planned and chance dissemination (Ruddock & Kelly, 1976: 10). Kelly (1980: 67–69) distinguishes between these planned and unplanned activities respectively by using the terms 'dissemination' and 'diffusion'. Curriculum dissemination is regarded as part of systematic administration with meetings, plans of action, timetables, distribution of information circulars and organised in-service training programmes, and is thus a structured and planned process.

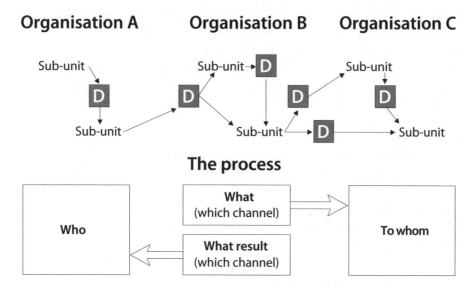

Figure 5.5: Interest groups, levels and facets in dissemination as a social process

It is clear that curriculum dissemination as a social structure must be based on good, effective and purposeful decision making, as these happenings must progress in a methodical and structured way. Within this structure, communication once again figures strongly. A lack of space does not allow a broad discussion of method as a phenomenon. However, without good planning, purposeful and meaningful dissemination cannot take place. Initial planning must have flexibility built in as ongoing adjustments must be made. Effective decision-making and problem-solving skills are also essential.

Inter- and intrapersonal aspects

As these aspects are fully described elsewhere (see Hattingh, 1989: 86–106), they are only briefly illustrated here. Curriculum consumers, as people, are influenced by inter-

and intrapersonal aspects, whether as individuals or in a group context. According to Hattingh (1989: 87), each individual has a particular deeper psychological character which comes to the fore in differing ways in certain situations and during certain interpersonal interactions. In the process of dissemination of change and renewal, it is necessary for the curriculum leader also to take note of these intrapersonal characteristics of the members of the social structure. The negation of the individual's values, norms and feelings can quite possibly cause the whole curriculum development process to miscarry. There are therefore specific psychological factors which must be taken into account during curriculum dissemination:

- Any initiative that threatens the self-esteem and self-image of the individual will be difficult to establish and have accepted. The curriculum initiative must rather strengthen the consumer's self-esteem and self-image.
- Different personalities, for example an authoritarian personality, may lead to the rejection of initiatives from outsiders.
- Values often determine attitudes and for this reason key values must be identified and strengthened with a view to cultivating positive attitudes.
- Individuals' existing needs must be taken into account.
- The individual's world of experience may play an important role; for example the more experience a person has, the more difficult it will be to accept change.
- Feelings of being threatened (anxiety, fear, uncertainty) may lead to a rejection of change.
- Fear may lead to resistance to change.
- If expectations clash with change, it may bring resistance.
- Information must be disseminated correctly and accurately, otherwise it can be distorted.
- Social influences need to be taken into account.
- Relative advantage may be obtained from participation.
- The degree of difficulty may lead to resistance.

Facilitating and inhibiting factors

It is also clear that there are specific inhibiting and reinforcing factors within the social structure which may either promote or impede curriculum dissemination.

A few **facilitating** factors are a pleasant and positive climate of renewal; thorough planning; good communication; a high level of curriculum expertise in facilitators and consumers; involvement of all interested parties; and effective leadership.

Inhibiting factors may lie within the educational system, for example a lack of financial support; political pressure from the authorities; vulnerability in terms of community needs; excessive centralisation in respect of educational control; traditions; and poor salaries.

Other inhibiting factors may lie within the organisational and social structures, for example a lack of long-term planning and objectives; excessive accentuation of bureaucracy; weakly developed channels of communication; an absence of co-ordinated action on the part of participating organisations; an absence of dissemination liaison persons from the top structure; an over-accentuation of a 'top-down' approach; inadequate availability of sources; complicated decision-making processes; exchange of personnel and curriculum leaders; the multifaceted teacher's task; expiry of periods of office; an absence of adaptability in curriculum designs; defective planning in respect of the dissemination process; professional invisibility; absence of alternative possibilities; the fact that some must design and others implement; the absence of evaluation based on feedback; the absence of specifically trained disseminators; and the tendency of educational renewal and change to be invisible and theoretical.

Human factors which may be inhibiting are poor leadership; incapability; poor training and defective skills; lack of time; other interests and divided attention as a result of private economic activities; personal and psychological qualities; other administrative duties; individual and mutual differences in preparedness; variety of educational philosophies; defective understanding by users; negative attitudes and emotions; passivity; defective self-confidence; periods of confusion; and absence of encouragement and motivation (Prescott, 1976: 11; Knoetze, 1978: 151–152; Wiles & Bondi, 1984: 351; Saylor, Alexander & Lewis, 1981: 38; Hattingh, 1989: 97–98).

From this comprehensive list of potentially inhibiting factors, the complexity and multilevel nature of the disseminator's problem becomes clear. It is, for example, theoretically possible for the dissemination team to neglect to bear in mind only one of the many possible factors in planning their dissemination effort and for that factor to cause the total planned initiative to miscarry. According to Hattingh (1989: 99), it is clearly a difficult task to give attention to all these factors during dissemination. The complexity and the extent of the initiative will influence the extent and intensity of dissemination strategy.

It is of cardinal importance for every curriculum leader and every interested party to take note of these inhibiting and facilitating factors. There must, however, be more than just taking note: one must go on to active accommodation thereof in practice.

It is clear that the social aspect gives a particular dimension to curriculum dissemination. The involvement of the variety of interested parties also determines the degree of success to a great extent. Effective strategies to utilise this degree and quality of participation must thus be applied.

5.4 Aims

Hattingh (1989: 24–26) mentions that, with a view to achieving institutionalisation in a methodical and purposeful way, the following aims, *inter alia*, are of importance:

- The **acceptance** of the initiative and application thereof
- The **adaptation** by teachers of some aspects of the initiative to their specific circumstances. This adaptation is regarded as a compromise between the ideals of the initiators and practice or the reality within which teachers find themselves.
- The experience of **renewal** – that is to say that the indirect effort or the original initiative will lead to further development and renewal in the teacher
- The **initiation** of indirect acceptance, adaptation and renewal, for example by adapting the form of examination so that it may result in a change in the subject

curriculum offered (Centre for Science Education, 1975: 7, as quoted by Hattingh, 1989: 25)

These aims imply knowledge and application of change or renewal. They imply a consciousness and understanding of the initiative behind all its consequences.

5.5   Strategies for curriculum dissemination

It has already been mentioned that the dissemination strategies must be utilised which will ensure that implementation progresses successfully at a later stage. Czajkowski and Patterson (1980: 166–168) show how education leaders may prepare their teachers for the change. It must be a conscious effort on their part. The majority of curriculum leaders have a certain adaptability with regard to curriculum change, which may be described as **individual** or as **group centred**. An individual-centred strategy would take into account personalities, homeostasis, security and variables. A group-centred strategy would concentrate mainly on social and psychological factors. The culture of the group, taking into account, *inter alia*, its norms and values, plays an important role.

Curriculum dissemination strategies may take different forms, for example power strategies and/or influencing strategies. A **power** strategy often comes from the macro-level, and the school and teachers have little control over the decision-making process. As a result of their non-involvement, teachers' response may be characterised by passivity. An **influencing** strategy seeks to make the curriculum more acceptable to all those involved, with the help of subtle persuasion on the one hand and by manipulation on the other. The key thought is that development may take place if the conditions are acceptable. Emphasis is placed on the benefits which change contains for the teacher and not so much on change itself.

Teachers often realise the need for change and are then prepared to pursue it in a purposeful manner. Involvement in this context often comprises leadership, decision making and active participation in the process.

In the investigation by Ruddock and Kelly (1976, as referred to by Whitehead, 1980: 1) into strategies of curriculum dissemination, the conclusion is reached that in general there is little question of reinstruction and that the importance of motivation of teachers – in other words the positive promotion of projects – has only been realised relatively recently. The dissemination of material, ideas and information must make informed decision making in schools possible. Until this investigation took place, the mere distribution of the resources (material, ideas and information) was regarded as dissemination, and further decision making at local level was regarded as unnecessary. The strategy which is described by these writers briefly amounts to the following:

- Phase one
  - A target group must be identified.
  - The response of the target group must be anticipated.
  - The needs of the target group must be determined and satisfied.

- Phase two
    - A general awareness and even interest must be cultivated.
    - Potential users must take note of
        - the aims;
        - the general methodology;
        - supplementary sources of information; and
        - the implications in respect of cost and time.
- Phase three
    - The application and evaluation of the initiative takes place.
    - The relevant users must have all the material and objectives of the initiative at their disposal.
    - A clear two-way network must come into being and be available.
- Phase four
    - The acceptance or rejection of the initiative takes place.
    - A structure which will keep the initiative going must be maintained, for example
        - ongoing in-service training; and
        - inclusion in formal curriculum.
    - The opportunity must be created for the teacher to adapt the material or initiative to local circumstances (see Hattingh, 1989: 27–28).

Schwartz (1980: 134–136) also identifies phases in which dissemination plays a role to a greater or lesser extent. The phases may be described as follows:

- Initiation
    - A need is determined.
    - Information is sought from outside and inside the organisation.
- Implementation
    - Planned action is determined.
    - Attitude with regard to the programme is determined.
- Evaluation
    - Mechanisms and structures are created for the determination of acceptance and implementation.
    - Corrective steps may be taken.
- Dissemination
    - An ongoing process of distribution takes place.
- Internalisation
    - Integration of the aims, values and behaviour of the original initiative takes place.

On close examination, this classification is to some extent confusing, as dissemination, internalisation and even evaluation cannot take place as separate phases in the process. These take place on a continuing basis (Hattingh, 1989: 28–29).

It is clear that the original or pilot component is essential for the later change that will take place. The question of method and structure is pivotal here. Definitive strategies are necessary to determine the success of dissemination.

5.6 Procedures for curriculum dissemination

Irrespective of the strategy applied to disseminate curriculum information, the procedures for dissemination are also essential for later successful implementation. Traditional dissemination procedures appear to comprise, *inter alia*, the following (HSRC, 1981: 111–114):

- Distribution of syllabi
- Drawing up and publishing of manuals
- Holding of courses
- Production of textbooks
- Presentation of papers
- Visits by inspectors/superintendents

A more modern procedure is found in the role which teacher centres play in dissemination, in-service training, orientation and supplying guidance in respect of syllabus interpretation and implementation. In this way, teachers need not be passive participants, but the emphasis shifts to a more active participation by them in the dissemination process, through, *inter alia*, participation in discussions, joint participation in projects, dealing with media and the establishment of active working groups.

5.7 Models for curriculum dissemination

Introduction

In order to disseminate curriculum information effectively, it may be valuable to take note of a few dissemination models which endeavour to depict or describe the process of dissemination.

Havelock's model

Havelock (1982: 137) proposes two models for the dissemination of curricula which have been reviewed or newly developed, namely the RDD model (research, development and diffusion) and the problem-solving model.

The RDD model is, according to De Lange (1984: 4), the 'top-down' model, as in this model curriculum development is initiated from the top, from government authority, and develops on a vertical basis. It often progresses over a long period and the task is carried out by means of co-ordination and team-orientated research. It may be set out schematically as in Figure 5.6:

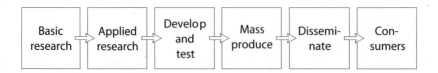

Figure 5.6: RDD Model

In the model, there are five suppositions:

- There is a rational sequence in the development and application of change and renewal. This sequence must make provision for research, development and composition of packages before dissemination can take place.
- Thorough planning, usually over a long period, must take place.
- Division and co-ordination of work forces must take place in such a manner that all phases are complemented in the process.
- A more or less passive but nevertheless clearly rational user is assumed. This user will accept change or renewal and apply it if it is conveyed to him in the right way, at the right place and time, and in the right form.
- The original high input costs with regard to the development will be accepted even before dissemination takes place. This acceptance is facilitated by the benefits which could be derived from it over the long term.

The problem-solving model apparently meets with considerable approval, as it allows for ongoing renewal to be initiated by, *inter alia*, the school or the teacher within the consumer system. In this model, therefore, the classroom serves as a starting point, and the data which is collected is distributed from the bottom upwards, which will probably encourage greater teacher participation. The problem-solving model, according to Havelock (1982: 14), is regarded as the most popular, as it makes place for the problem-solving process which takes place within the user organisation.

The process is usually seen as a succession of activities arising from the identification of a need. This need is formulated in a problem statement after which it is diagnosed. A search for ideas and information then follows, which eventually ends in the formulation of a change or renewal. This step is followed by the acceptance, testing and evaluation of the renewal (Hattingh, 1989: 54).

The focus within the organisation therefore appears to be on the user's specific needs. The task of outsiders is thus only co-operative and consultative, and is to supply information and ideas during any phase of the process. This model is depicted schematically in Figure 5.7.

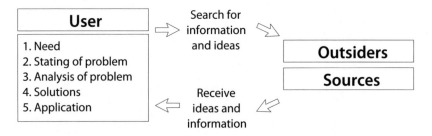

Figure 5.7: Problem-solving model

The benefits of this model are that the consumer's needs are taken as the point of departure, diagnosis of needs is continuously involved, maximal utilisation of already existing internal sources in the school takes place, and the ideas and decisions of outsiders are never forced on the consumer (Havelock, 1982: 140, as quoted by Hattingh, 1989: 55).

Havelock's social interaction model (1982: 139, as quoted by Hattingh, 1989: 52–53) accentuates the patterns in terms of which dissemination takes place in a social system. According to Havelock (1982), all research in respect of the process of dissemination points to five important generalisations:

- The individual users belong to a network of social relationships which will influence their acceptance of change and renewal.
- The individual's position in this social network (centrality, peripherality, isolation, etc.) is a good gauge of the measure in which, and the tempo at which, the new information will be accepted.
- Informal personal contact is an essential part of the influencing and acceptance process.
- Group identification and membership of a group are the principal indicators of individual acceptance.
- The tempo of dissemination by a social system follows a predictable s-curve (initially very slow, followed by a period of very quick dissemination then a long, late acceptance period). Havelock (1982) depicts the social interaction model schematically as shown in Figure 5.8.

From this figure, it appears that Havelock (1982) accentuates the communication of ideas rather than the distribution of material. It may be regarded as a reaction to the formal RDD model. Whitehead (1980: 6) regards the emphasis on communication as an attempt to convey a convincing message. It is thus not supposed to initiate criticism and modification. Through the communication, renewal and change are made known to potential appliers. The development and improvement of the individual therefore lies in the self-development of the individual after particular knowledge has been made known to him/her (Hattingh, 1989: 55).

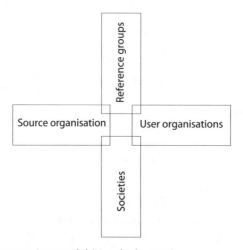

Figure 5.8: Social interaction model (Havelock, 1982)

Ruddock and Kelly's model

De Villiers (1985: 96–97) mentions that there are other dissemination models which may also be considered for effective dissemination. The dissemination model of Ruddock and Kelly (1976) distinguishes between four main components:

- **Translocation** comprises the movement of people and material with a view to implementing new aspects (who must visit the schools, whether teachers must take courses, movements of posts, and how material will be distributed).
- **Communication** describes the ways in which information of the renewal is conveyed (nature of the written pieces, channels, the nature and extent of personal interaction).
- **Animation** links up with the need to motivate teachers towards greater interest and involvement (attitudes which must be changed, ways of encouragement).
- **Retraining** is essential in order to implement renewal effectively (in-service training, experimentation by teacher).

From this model it would appear that dissemination may develop into a reasonably prescriptive process. It is, however, clear that this model is based on the author's analysis of curriculum practice. In each component, there are dominant roles or events which suggest the impression of a strongly structured succession of phases. In practice, however, it is clear that each component overlaps the others. The receptivity and acceptance on the part of the teacher play an important role, for example, in the communication and animation phases (Hattingh, 1989: 48).

Schon's model

De Villiers (1985: 97) also briefly describes Schon's (1971) three dissemination models:

- According to the **centre-periphery** model, the distribution of information is from a centre point to the consumers.
- According to the **proliferation-from-centre** model, there are secondary as well as primary centres from which information is distributed.
- According to the **periphery-centre** model, information is distributed from the consumer to the centre. The need to renew arises with the consumer and the centre proposes possible solutions.

Hattingh (1989: 49–54) expands as follows on the views of various writers regarding these models:

- In the **centre-periphery** model there is a primary source from which dissemination is done. Stenhouse (1976: 215–216) avers that Schon (1971) couches three basic conditions in this model:
  - The information exists completely before the process of dissemination begins.
  - Dissemination is the process of moving information out from a central core to the eventual users.
  - Dissemination is a planned process initiated by the source persons.

Schon expands on these general conditions and mentions four factors which he regards as critical for effective dissemination of this nature (Stenhouse, 1976: 215–216):

- The level of the source or its position of authority and the attempt at dissemination which takes place from it
- The number of points on the periphery to which distribution takes place
- The number of levels through which this dissemination must take place
- The input necessary in order to bring about a new acceptance

- Schon sees the **proliferation-from-centre** model as an extension of the first model. In this case, provision is made for primary and secondary cores from which dissemination must take place. This process is therefore based on the principle of training of trainers. The success of the primary dissemination source with regard to the total process is determined by its ability to provide suitable training to suitable persons (Schon, 1971, as quoted by Hattingh, 1989: 50).
- The process for dissemination is totally reversed in the **periphery-centre** model. Problems arising in the classroom are sent through to the central authority, from which proposals and advice may develop. The need for information therefore arises at the periphery. The necessary channels exist to satisfy this need. Information is therefore distributed from the consumers to the core (authority). The need to renew arises in the consumer, and the core proposes possible solutions (De Villiers, 1985: 97).

Functions of models

It is clear from the curriculum literature that there are different, but nevertheless linked, perspectives on the process of curriculum dissemination. The available models once again offer useful guidelines in terms of which action may be taken.

A study of these models, separately and jointly, may develop greater insight into the complexity of curriculum dissemination. Gay (1980: 143) proposes that an understanding of theoretical models may help all persons involved in the total network to improve their own planning and contribution, and to be aware of the variety of possibilities that exist, to identify weaknesses and deficiencies, to use the models as guidelines for dealing with their own circumstances, and eventually to be able to improve the quality of decision making, planning and education.

5.8   Logistical aspects

Introduction

Hattingh (1989: 56–61) makes a worthwhile contribution by giving an exposition of certain essential logistical elements of curriculum dissemination. Logistical elements are those physical aspects that arise in connection with change. They include aspects such as organisations, financial support, administrative usage and procedures, media, software and human resources. These physical aspects will eventually play a particular role in the institutionalisation of a curriculum. The value of the logistical elements must therefore not be underestimated, as they play a cardinal role. Some of these elements are briefly explained in the following paragraphs.

Administration

Effective dissemination is dependent on, *inter alia*, a good administrative structure. Good channels of communication, such as interpersonal and mass media channels, are essential within this structure to enable administration to progress smoothly.

Human aspects

The human factors can never be dissociated from effective curriculum development and dissemination. Interpersonal characteristics and determinants, such as the self-image of consumers, personalities, specific values, human needs, fears, experience, expectations and group dynamics, are all aspects which must be considered.

Physical aspects

An essential aspect of effective curriculum dissemination is the successful distribution of material to all consumers. Factors which must be considered in this regard, according to Finch and Crunkilton (1979: 211–214, as quoted by Hattingh, 1989: 58) include the following:

- The potential audience/user
- The geographic implications
- Cost factors
- Acceptance
- Nature of application
    - In-service training
    - Pre-service training
    - Redesign of existing material
- Time available for the design and composition of material
- Availability of experts
- Needs in practice
- Dissemination strategies
- Groups which must give support and guidance

Hattingh (1989: 58–60) points out that there are different types of material which are distributed during this process. These include syllabi; textbooks; teachers' handbooks; instructional packages (put together by policy-making groups); subject periodicals (published by national subject societies); reference sources; general works and subject returns (in libraries); general periodicals and pamphlets; study guides; question banks; and guides for textbook writers.

Audiovisual material, such as posters, films, video programmes, picture series, records, sets of transparencies, audiotapes, filmstrips or slide series, would also be included here.

Summary

Curriculum planners must guard against neglecting the logistical aspects during dissemination, as this can limit or hinder the institutionalisation of the curriculum. This aspect may, as a result of the implications which it contains, be pushed into the background as though it was of less importance. In context with all the other aspects of dissemination, however, it constitutes a key aspect which is essential for the marketing and institutionalisation of a curriculum.

5.9   Communication within curriculum dissemination

From the above Sections 5.1 to 5.8 it is clear that communication underlies successful curriculum dissemination. There are so many elements, materials and people involved that communication may easily miscarry. All consumers must receive, understand and accept specific information before a curriculum can be successfully applied. Within all models, strategies and procedures, it is through communication that information is distributed. As effective dissemination will depend on effective communication, it is essential that curriculum developers consider the communication aspect thoroughly.

The importance of communication becomes very clear when reviewing the large number of bodies and role players involved. On a very broad level, the following are possibly involved:

- Central government
- The Matriculation Board and Umalusi
- The national Department of Education
- Curriculum committees for the subjects

On departmental level, the following are involved:

- Curriculum committees
- Subject committees/study committees
- Departmental examination committees
- Moderators and examiners
- Instructional guidance service
- Curriculum service/bureaux

At local level/school level or in the classroom, the following are involved:

- School principals
- Departmental heads
- Teachers
- Learners

Other bodies at various levels which may be involved include the following:

- Teacher associations
- Subject study groups
- Principals' associations
- Teacher centres
- Textbook writers
- Publishers

There are different ways or techniques in which two-way communication with all these involved parties may be ensured. The HSRC Report (1981: 70) distinguishes between five categories of techniques: information techniques, techniques to involve target groups, instructional techniques, support techniques and legal techniques.

The purpose of **information** techniques is to inform, to motivate or to convince a target audience. These techniques are only applied in cases where the initiative seeks to achieve superficial change or renewal. Techniques which may be used are direct mailing, books and subject periodicals, personal contact, telephone, action research, confrontation, lectures, workshops, instructional packages and guidebooks.

A process of consultation characterises the techniques which involve the **target group**. Techniques in this connection are participation in problem identification and decision making, field testing, training of trainers and the institutionalisation of changing roles.

Training techniques are essentially suited to a climate of co-operation, where the goals have already been accepted. Such training is of two kinds, namely initial pre-service training and in-service training.

In **support** techniques, circumstances are created which facilitate the individual's participation and which may be to his or her advantage. Such techniques may include subsidisation of change, consultation, creation of temporary systems and supply of feedback systems.

The use of **legal** techniques is actually a power strategy, but laws and regulations may benefit a group's participation in the initiative.

Curriculum leaders thus have a wide variety of procedures and techniques at their disposal. The 'art' in the design of a dissemination strategy comes into play when a strategy must be designed which will make optimal implementation of the initiative possible. Pratt (1980: 438–439) links up with this thought by accentuating the curriculum leaders' ability to speak in the 'language' of the teacher. The disseminator should keep technical formulations at a level that is as understandable as possible, and must ensure that potential users understand everything connected with renewal or change (see Hattingh, 1989: 37–39).

Any factor which may limit communication must be identified and eliminated or overcome. In the same way, assisting or facilitating factors must also be considered and utilised.

5.10   Summary

It is clear that curriculum dissemination is not only a multifaceted and complex process but also a critical phase in ensuring dynamic curriculum development. There are so many aspects that must be considered and that may influence dissemination and the institutionalisation of a curriculum, such as what the nature, the essence and the objectives of dissemination are; how those involved may be prepared for change; how effective communication may be ensured; how resistance to change may be eliminated; what existing procedures may be utilised; what logistical factors must be considered; and what the facilitating powers and the inhibiting factors are.

Curriculum dissemination is therefore a highly complex and sophisticated process which must be carried out carefully and purposefully to ensure success. A haphazard way of approaching and dealing with it may seriously harm effective curriculation. South Africa as a whole is characterised by quick changes – also in the field of education. School types are amended overnight and implemented without there being effective dissemination of information and resources to schools and parent communities. This situation creates a climate for dissatisfaction and resistance, as not all the interested parties have been effectively prepared with regard to the changes envisaged. Changes in the educational system must be characterised by effective dissemination to prevent this.

South Africa has particular needs, of which the need for highly educated human capital is only one. Not only must relevant curricula be designed and relevant education be provided, but all the interested parties must be involved and effectively prepared. The development of new subjects/syllabi/learning areas must definitely take the dissemination phase into account, as the success of the later implementation and institutionalisation of curricula will be determined by it. Dissemination has a key role to play in the process of empowering teachers as curriculum agents, as the teachers will have to be able to implement and develop the curriculum.

In South Africa, with the introduction of new curricula since 1997 in the form of the *National Curriculum Statement Grades R–9* and *National Curriculum Statement Grades 10–12*, it is clear that many mistakes were made with regard to effective dissemination. New curricula were introduced and teachers were expected to implement them, initially with little in-service training and later with training during their holidays. The needs of teachers were not always considered (Carl, 2005; 2007) and this might have resulted in teachers feeling disempowered. The words '**might** have resulted' are used because, despite the dissemination strategies implemented, teachers were still motivated to make a success of the new curriculum (see Chapter 9).

It is, however, a fact that dissemination has still not come into its own in South Africa, as many aspects mentioned in this chapter are not yet considered in practice. Curriculum dissemination from national to local level is still too often defective, and curriculum initiatives suffer accordingly. The broad spectrum of dissemination will come into its own more than is the case at present but it will require dynamic leadership. It is evident that the more purposefully the teacher is empowered, the more effectively this process can progress. Only then can there be talk of dynamic and relevant curriculum development.

Activities and questions

1. Discuss in your subject group:
   - What is curriculum dissemination?
   - To what extent is this a theoretical concept for your subject group? To what extent does it have relevance in practice for you?
2. Identify at least three opportunities where
   - you were exposed to the dissemination process from the education department (syllabus-related);

- you were exposed to a dissemination action within your particular school (any teacher-related matter);
- you were exposed to a dissemination action within your subject group.

3. Study the types of attitudes of consumers to change as mentioned in Section 5.2. Evaluate where you would normally place yourself. Why? Is there room for a change in attitude?

4. Identify within your subject group or individually five aspects which are for you the core aspects of dissemination.

5. Design an action for dissemination in relation to a renewal initiative which you would like to institutionalise in your subject. You must give consideration to the following:

- Specific model (see Section 5.7)
- Objectives
- Communication (see Section 5.9)
- Logistical aspects (see Section 5.8)
- Facilitating factors
- Limiting factors
- Time scheduling
- Procedures
- Evaluation of the action

6. How can the teacher be empowered through curriculum dissemination?

6 Successful Curriculum Implementation

At the end of this chapter you should be able to

- describe the difference/connection between curriculum dissemination and implementation
- appreciate the necessity for good planning to ensure effective implementation
- identify the most important facilitating and limiting factors influencing implementation
- identify the strategies which may be followed during implementation
- design a specific implementation strategy for a particular subject curriculum which you envisage carrying through
- be more knowledgeable and empowered as a curriculum agent.

6.1 Introduction

After the relevant consumers have been prepared for the change envisaged, the implementation phase follows. The implementation is the application phase of not only core syllabi but also the school's broad curriculum, every subject curriculum and every lesson unit/lesson. The participation of the instructional leaders and teachers determines successful and effective curriculum implementation to a great extent. Schubert (1986: 42) regards curriculum implementation as follows:

> Traditionally seen as the delivery process, implementation can be considered a system of engineering that takes design specifications through various channels to the teacher and class[-]room.

Curriculum implementation depends on the level/field on which the initial design is made and for whom it is envisaged. Thus the broad curriculum will be implemented at a broad national level, while a specific subject syllabus will be implemented at school and classroom level (see Section 6.3). Schubert (1986: 42) warns that this implementation must not be a mere carrying out of instructions but should recognise that developments take place within instructional–learning situations.

It is important to note that dissemination and implementation are regarded as synonymous in most of the curriculum literature. For the purpose of this publication they are regarded as two distinguishable (but not divisible) phases, as effective dissemination must take place before there can be effective implementation. Implementation is, nonetheless, also coupled with change and therefore the aspects described in Chapter 5 with regard to change and renewal must also be taken into account here. Successful implementation, however, depends on the extent to which all consumers are informed and have been prepared for the envisaged change and whether they are also prepared to associate themselves with it.

Pratt (1980: 426) also avers that curriculum authors do not always give attention to implementation to the extent that they should, and that the condition arises where 'curriculum designers do not know how to implement what they have designed'.

The implication of this is that maximal involvement of all those having an interest in the curriculum is of cardinal importance.

Linking up with this, Moon (1990: 606) mentions that different methodologies for implementation are followed, for example the research, development and diffusion model (see Chapter 5), the problem-solving model and the social interaction strategy. The latter strives for maximal teacher involvement. He mentions that heated debate is taking place as to which should be the most suitable methodology.

Although there is merit in these three strategies, it is clear that it may impact negatively on the effectiveness of the curriculum if the teacher is involved only when the curriculum is implemented. The above strategies or methodologies must receive attention before implementation and then be continued during implementation. The importance of these strategies during implementation is not denied, but they should already have received attention during a previous phase, i.e. curriculum dissemination.

It must thus be clearly stated that aspects and processes begun in curriculum dissemination must be continued during implementation. This includes aspects such as the preparation of those involved for the envisaged change and the continuation thereof; the maintenance of a renewal climate; the continuation of attempts to eliminate resistance to change; the continuing strengthening of facilitating factors and elimination of inhibiting ones; the ongoing evaluation of the dissemination procedures which are now being applied during implementation; the ongoing evaluation of the logistic aspects in order to be able to make ongoing adjustments; and the promotion of the strengthening of good communication.

6.2 Determinative factors for successful implementation

The factors which may inhibit development must constantly be borne in mind during this phase, as resistance also manifests itself in different forms during these phases. The challenge is therefore to identify the sources of this resistance on a continuous basis and to endeavour to break them down.

The real measure of success during this application phase is determined largely by the quality of the planning, design and dissemination done beforehand. It comprises not only aspects such as involvement of all consumers, credibility, acceptable learner responses and completeness, but also the accentuation of the following four factors, as illustrated by Pratt (1980: 435–442):

- Continuous contact with consumers to give advice and help, to encourage mutual contact between consumers and to effect contact with learners and parents
- Clear communication to illustrate roles, to explain terminology, to illustrate possible means of evaluation and to supply answers to the well-known queries of 'who?', 'what?', 'when?', 'where?', 'how?' and 'why?'

- Provision of a support service through, for example, spelling out time scheduling, supplying material, setting one's own example, creating a climate within which trust and security figure, and the encouragement of teachers
- Compensation through, for example, the financial, praise, acknowledgement and also intrinsic aspects of compensation. The intrinsic aspect is realised when persons regard the successful application as sufficient compensation in itself. This attitude creates opportunities for these persons to grow professionally by way of a more extended perspective and responsibility. A further advantage of intrinsic compensation is that it is the true development which is rewarded and not its symptoms. Teachers often find their reward merely in the acceptance of the new curriculum and not so much in the implementation of it.

Jordaan (1989: 386–391) mentions, with reference to a literature study, a few further factors which are important for successful implementation. Development opportunities and the creation of a climate conducive to active involvement are key factors. He mentions that problems must be addressed continuously, that practice-orientated in-service training must be given and that support by the education department and/or school must be available continuously to offer material assistance and encouragement. Participation through active involvement in the classrooms is essential, as is a relationship of confidence between initiators and implementers. Supporting factors, such as finance, material, sources and time given for real meaningful involvement, are important and may not be ignored. Adoption, that is to say the acceptance of consumers of the new or revised curriculum, is a necessity.

To get teachers to take part in application often offers an enormous challenge in itself. The purpose of a curriculum design is still, however, to meet the needs of learners. The success of this purpose is often determined during the implementation phase. Pratt (1980: 443) stresses this purpose of meeting the needs of the learner by stating that the value of the design 'is fully discharged only when that need is satisfied'.

Czajkowski and Patterson (1980: 158) are of the opinion that, if the curriculum is to function really effectively, it must make a real contribution in the school and classroom, irrespective of at what education level it is initiated.

6.3   Levels of implementation

In Section 5.1 it is stated that implementation may take place at different levels or in different fields. Jordaan (1989: 392–400) sets out a good description of the various levels of implementation, referring to macro- and micro-implementation.

Macro-implementation

Macro-implementation is the application of policy and curriculum initiatives which have been determined at national level by curriculum authorities. This will include an interaction between this authority and the practice within which it is implemented (see also Mostert, 1986: 158, as quoted by Jordaan, 1989: 392). It is therefore the implementation of a broad curriculum or other core syllabi designed at national level, which have been distributed and applied countrywide.

Micro-implementation

Jordaan (1989: 393) and Mostert (1986b) define micro-implementation as that process during which local decisions are taken. This leads to application in practice and the eventual institutionalisation. In practice it means that core syllabi must be implemented at school and classroom level by subject teachers. Teacher participation and initiatives are normally high at this level as, through their implementation, they make their own mark on the development of a syllabus (through syllabus interpretation, subject curriculation, lesson curriculation, etc.). In this manner, the initial curriculum initiative is established in practice (institutionalised). Micro-implementation may therefore also include the implementation of a subject teacher's subject curriculum or specific lessons in a particular classroom. The micro-level is therefore that level at which the so-called curriculum consumer applies the curriculum.

Therefore, when the process of curriculum implementation is relevant, the curriculator must also consider the particular level or field, as this may determine the relevant implementation strategies which will be followed.

6.4   Implementation strategies

The success of implementation may be assured if the dissemination was effective and specific strategies are followed during implementation. Jordaan (1989: 397–398) mentions that one must distinguish between strategies which may promote or inhibit implementation and that the latter must be avoided. The strategies of Howes and Quinn (1978) and the CBAM model (concerns-based adoption model) are, to a great extent, linked with dissemination but, as already mentioned, it is clear that specific processes initiated during dissemination are, in fact, continued during implementation.

Ornstein and Hunkins (2009: 259–262) refer to three curriculum implementation models which educators may consider when they are confronted with implementation (here one can clearly see the link with dissemination). These are the following:

- Overcoming–resistance-to-change (ORC) model
- Organisational–development (OD) model
- Concerns–based adoption (CBA) model

The ORC model is normally used to motivate staff and to overcome resistance to the proposed change. Ornstein and Hunkins (2009: 257–259) state that leaders will have to address teachers' concerns and understand that people must change before the system can change. One could add that the needs of teachers and those who are stakeholders in the proposed change should be accommodated and addressed (see Ornstein & Hunkins, 2009: 259–260).

The OD model views and handles implementation as an ongoing and interactive process. It is underpinned by the need of participants to be actively involved in continually developing (designing, implementing and assessing) the system. Implementation is therefore never complete, but keeps on developing as new ideas and materials come to the fore or are created. This enables teachers to grow and develop continually due to their involvement and engagement with the curriculum (see Ornstein & Hunkins, 2009: 260–261).

The CBA model is, according to Ornstein and Hunkins (2009: 261–262), similar to the OD model. They state that 'those who use the CBA approach believe that all change originates with individuals. For individuals to favour change, they must view the change as at least partly of their own making'. It must be directly linked to their own professional and personal contexts and lives. This process may take a long time because of the many persons involved in it and because it may take a long time to develop new skills and adopt new attitudes.

The strategy of Howes and Quinn (1978: 71–83, as quoted in Jordaan, 1989: 397–398) consists of two main phases which, in turn, contain respective specific variables. Phase 1 comprises the creation of a satisfactorily orientated environment (introduction of change and preparation of consumers), and is actually a part of dissemination, but will be continued on an ongoing basis during implementation. Phase 2 comprises bringing about sufficient support networks (through instruction, communication, contact opportunities and ongoing discussion meetings) and also contains elements which should actually already have taken place during dissemination, as well as those that are initiated or continued during implementation.

The CBAM model has, as its basic point of departure, an emphasis on envisaged change and the preparation of those involved to apply it.

From the above short discussion of strategies, it is clear that the view that these strategies should actually already be being implemented during dissemination is correct. Before implementation takes place, they must already be in operation, as they will determine the success of the later implementation and eventual institutionalisation.

6.5 Summary

Many curriculum initiatives have miscarried because curriculum developers underestimated the importance of implementation. It is dangerous to take the view that the most important work has been done once the design and dissemination have been finalised. The real success is evaluated by the degree to which it is workable in practice.

It is therefore necessary for curriculum developers also to plan effectively for this phase of curriculum development, with a view to identifying facilitating and inhibiting factors, and to follow a suitable strategy which will ensure success. Dynamic curriculum development is often determined by the achievability of a curriculum in practice and in this regard the implementation phase comes strongly into the spotlight. It is also during this phase that empowered teachers have to apply the appropriate curriculum skills and knowledge that they have developed. The success may very much depend on the degree and level of their empowerment.

Activities and questions

1. What is the difference and/or similarity between curriculum dissemination and curriculum implementation?

2. Individually and/or within your subject group, identify the following:

    *   Any 10 important **facilitating** factors which may advance curriculum implementation, and arrange them in descending order from 1 to 10

    *   Any 10 important **inhibiting** factors which may limit curriculum implementation, and arrange them in descending order from 1 to 10

3. Individually and/or as a subject group, you have already designed a subject curriculum. Plan the implementation thereof, taking a specific strategy of your choice as point of departure.

4. What is the relationship between the success of implementation and the degree of teacher empowerment? Motivate your answer.

7 Comprehensive Curriculum Evaluation within Dynamic Curriculum Development

At the end of this chapter you should be able to

- give a field description of curriculum evaluation
- identify, describe and apply the various forms of curriculum evaluation
- recognise and apply the methods of evaluation
- design an own model for curriculum evaluation
- evaluate a curriculum with the help of a suitable checklist
- understand the function of the empowered teacher in curriculum development.

7.1 Introduction

An important following phase in the process of curriculum development is evaluation, although it should also take place on a continuous basis. In Section 4.5, specific aspects of evaluation were described which are also applicable to this chapter. A distinction was made between learner-orientated and curriculum evaluation. Learner-orientated evaluation is mainly adapted to determining the progress of learners on the way to goal realisation in respect of the lesson, the series of lessons, or the annual programme (Steyn, 1982: 101), while curriculum evaluation determines to what extent the objectives of the curriculum have been achieved. Learner-orientated evaluation is in reality only one aspect of curriculum evaluation, as the focus in respect of the latter also falls on other aspects. The empowerment of the teacher can also assist in bringing evaluation into its own and in its being utilised in a functional manner. Curriculum evaluation may be regarded as, *inter alia*, 'a broad and continuous effort to inquire into the effects of utilizing educational content and process according to clearly defined goals' (Doll, 1978: 433).

We are therefore concerned here with determining the value of the effectiveness of the curriculum itself, as well as the outcomes.

Rowntree (1978: 130) avers that an ongoing value determination of the standard of learning outcomes is necessary in order to determine whether aims have been achieved. The effectiveness of not only the broad curriculum but also specific instructional–learning situations should be determined.

The data thus obtained are, in turn, determinative for the further planning and successful development of the curriculum. The implications hereof are of particular interest for the schools' instruction leaders, as they must make a value determination of the curriculum's successful implementation with a view to exposing the necessary defects and the changes required to effect improvement. The learners' success will also largely be influenced by this ongoing evaluation, as they are directly involved with any development. This makes the responsibility of the instructional leaders as curriculum agents so much greater.

This chapter focuses on the broad view of curriculum evaluation. There are specific aspects of evaluation which are relevant here and which have already been mentioned in Section 4.5, namely the various methods of evaluation (see Section 4.5) and certain criteria for evaluation. These will therefore not be discussed in so much detail again.

The difference between evaluation and measuring is also relevant here, as evaluation relates to a qualitative broad value determination, while measurement is related more to the quantitative where tests and examinations are relevant. The interpretation of these tests and examination results, however, relates more to evaluation or assessment.

In some cases people prefer to use the term 'assessment' as opposed to 'evaluation', but in this publication they are used synonymously.

It is clear that ongoing evaluation of the curriculum is essential for dynamic curriculum development. McCarty and Davis (1992: 1–5) are of the opinion that assessment offers little insight into how children learn and why certain mistakes are made. According to them, a constructivist approach might be the answer, because it stresses that true education must be child-centred and have relevance to the child's experiences. This implies that alternative ways of assessment should be used to record growth over a period of time. The assessment should reflect what a learner knows and indicate how he or she learns best. This implies an exploration of the learner's mind and an increasing dialogue between teacher and learner. Evaluation should offer more valid means of assessing knowledge and growth. This would entail a focus on the whole child and individualised instruction through active interaction. Once again, the importance of teacher empowerment regarding curriculum development is stressed. McCarty and Davis (1992) also stress the need for teachers to think differently about curriculum and assessment. Theoretically, curriculum should be the driving force, but McCarty and Davis (1992: 4–5) argue that perhaps this process should be the other way around. This would ensure that assessment is more authentic and that teachers would find out more about how their learners think and learn. Authentic assessment might provide a more accurate measure of the effectiveness of the curriculum and it will also affect curriculum decision making by revising the role of the classroom teacher. McCarty and Davis (1992: 4–5) state:

> This assessment concept can be viewed as a move towards teacher empowerment[,] for much responsibility for curriculum decision-making is vested in teachers … [C]urriculum development must utilize the tremendous power and potential in the experiences and wisdom of classroom teachers. Success also depends a great deal on the personal characteristics of teachers[,] for they must be open to new ideas and willing to develop new teaching skills as they guide rather than dominate.

According to McCarty and Davis (1992: 4–5), assessment is the most powerful signal that indicates to learners what is expected of them. Authentic assessment requires more from the learners than just 'correct' answers. Their statement is extremely valid: 'It requires the use of judgment and values … The curriculum should become more meaningful for students as they see its relevance to themselves and their experiences'.

It implies learner-centredness and an approach by teachers which is based on collaboration and interaction. This once again highlights the importance of teacher empowerment with regard to curriculum development to realising this in practice.

7.2   Evaluation of the curriculum: A field description

Curriculum evaluation is the process during which a value determination of the standard and outcome of the relevant curriculum (broad, subject or lesson curriculum) is made. Evaluation should take place on an ongoing basis, as well as during and after each of the design, dissemination and implementation phases, with a view to making timeous adjustments and determining success. White (1971: 101–112, in Golby, Greenwald & West, 1982: 397) states correctly that when curriculum evaluation is placed under the spotlight, the complexity becomes clear. Specific curriculum knowledge, skills and ability are required to enable this process to be undertaken to best advantage. Curriculum evaluation does not therefore relate only to curriculum outcomes but also to curriculum development events and the thinking which precedes them. Curriculum evaluation therefore comprises the evaluation/value determination of the effectiveness/functionality of all curriculation actions and the curricula which emanate from them. The aspects of a curriculum which must be evaluated are, by their nature, very comprehensive and it may be possible that the available means are insufficient to gather all the necessary information in connection with every aspect. There are, however, two facets in respect of the curriculum which must always be evaluated, namely the effectiveness and the acceptability thereof. The effectiveness is determined by the measure in which learners have reached the envisaged objectives. As it is unrealistic to wait for all learners to reach all objectives fully, it should rather be determined whether a minimum expected number of learners have reached a specific minimum of objectives at a specific level. As far as acceptability is concerned, the curriculum must be acceptable to both learners and teachers (Mostert, 1986b: 38).

Human, Taylor, Steyn and Jansen (1986: 24–32) set out a good description of the field of curriculum evaluation. According to Human *et al.* (1986: 24), curriculum evaluation comprises the description and judgement of curriculum anticipation and realities. Stake (1967: 529–532) refers to these as 'intents' and 'observations', and Eisner (1984: 46), to the 'intended' and 'operational' curriculum. As far as the anticipations and the realities are concerned, one may distinguish between curriculum processes – being the instructional actions, contents and learning experiences to which learners are exposed, and curriculum outcomes – being the anticipated and unanticipated effects of the curriculum events on learners. These distinctions are illustrated in Table 7.1.

Table 7.1: Anticipations and realities

Curriculum	Anticipations	Realities
Processes	Curriculum plans including syllabi and curriculum material	Curriculum events including instructional acts and learning opportunities
Outcomes	Curriculum goals	Curriculum outcomes

Curriculum plans, events, goals and outcomes are not the only elements influencing the quality of a curriculum or in which this quality is manifested and which are therefore subject to evaluation. On the one hand, in addition to immediate outcomes, a curriculum may contain long-term implications for individuals and communities in the form of the dispositions of learners who have recently passed through it (compare Lawton, 1982, in McCormick & May, 1983: 170). On the other hand, curriculum anticipations, and particularly the anticipation of long-term effects, usually arise from a rationale for that particular curriculum. Stake (1967: 532) characterises a curriculum rationale as 'the philosophic background and basic purposes of the programme', and adds: 'Every programme has its rationale, though often it is only implicit'.

How Human *et al.* (1986: 25) depict the role of a rationale in this process is shown in Figure 7.1.

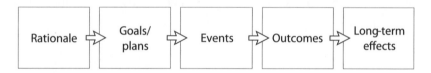

Figure 7.1: The role of a rationale

Curriculum rationale (a rationale for a particular curriculum) can be understood, on the one hand, to mean the broad objectives including the anticipated long-term effects, that, for example, knowledge of history will lead to more responsible citizenship, and knowledge of mathematics to more logical thought. On the other hand, it can also be understood to refer to the functional connections between different elements of a curriculum (Freeman & Sherwood, 1965: 13, as quoted by Human *et al.*, 1986: 26):

> ... [It is] the dynamics of how it is expected that the program[me] will have the desired effects, ... a theory which logically interrelates a set of principles and procedures with desired outcomes[,] ... a rationale that specifies the relationship between input variables and goals.

The value of a curriculum does not lie exclusively locked up in the immediate outcome thereof but is also found especially in the consequences/implications which the curriculum (including the immediate outcomes) has for individuals and the community in the long term (Human *et al.*, 1986: 26). Cooley and Lohnes (1976: 17) regard this connection as the key object of evaluation research when they say:

> What has been missing in controversies over the schools is convincing evidence which relates choices of school practices to ends which society values, ends which satisfy needs. Generating such evidence is what evaluation is all about.

What these standpoints are actually saying is that the immediate outcome of a curriculum must not be regarded as a goal in itself, but rather as a means. It means that the immediate curriculum outcome is subject to evaluation in terms of its long-term effects.

Curriculum plans and objectives are converted on the one hand from the rationale held by curriculum developers, and on the other hand from the databases available to them. The term 'databases' here refers to curriculators' knowledge, perspectives and values in regard to (Human *et al.*, 1986: 27):

- the subjects in which curriculum development is done
- the community
- the learners
- the training, instruction and learning
- education in the particular subjects.

It is not the rationale and databases of the curriculum developers only which may have an influence on curriculum anticipations and thus eventually on outcomes, but also the rationale and databases of the teachers who, in the final instance, have a determinative influence on the detailed nature and content of instructional actions and learning experiences (Human *et al.*, 1986: 28). A very simplified characterisation of the connection between evaluable curriculum elements is set out in Figure 7.2.

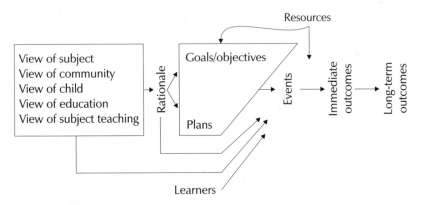

Figure 7.2: Link between evaluable curriculum elements

The term 'resources' in this scheme refers to curriculum resources, such as study material, instructional and learning aids, equipment, physical accommodation and other facilities. Such resources, by their nature, can also be evaluated. The term 'learners' refers to the dispositions (the living and meaning world, cognitive development, domestic background and circumstances, etc.) of learners, which may have an effect on curriculum events and outcomes. (Stake, 1967: 528, refers to these as 'antecedents'.) By their nature, these antecedents as premises cannot be evaluated in the same way as the other objects which have thus far been distinguished. In specific forms of curriculum evaluation, however, information with regard to antecedents is required with a view to being able to evaluate other elements in the curriculum (Human *et al.*, 1986: 30).

In the current South African educational system, the content and nature of curriculum events at school level are determined by different groups of persons who hold different positions in the dispensation. The following are examples of different curriculum agents and their roles:

- The overall planners, especially members of and those who influence the periodic interdepartmental curriculum committees, are responsible for the composition of prescribed core syllabi.
- The instructional leaders, especially school inspectors, subject advisers, superintendents, teacher trainers, subject heads and external examiners, exercise direct influence on the creators of material and on the teachers' interpretation of prescribed syllabi and choices of curriculum material.
- The detail planners, all being persons other than the teachers themselves, influence the objectives and learning experiences which are set in curriculum events. Textbook writers and other creators of curriculum material, external examiners and those who write items for item banks and standardised tests, as well as subject heads in schools, fall into this category.
- The teachers themselves are important curriculum agents.

Different people have at their disposal different databases, rationales for curricula and curriculum plans (Human *et al.*, 1986: 31). These differences may inhibit curriculum implementation. For example, it may happen that the overall planners and the teachers have totally different databases available in the case of a specific subject curriculum, and therefore they do not have the same rationale for the subject curriculum. In this case, teachers will probably have a different interpretation of the curriculum plans than the planners had themselves, eventuating in curriculum events and outcomes that do not agree with the original curriculum plans.

Even if individual teachers do not have full autonomy at their disposal in respect of curricula and the creation of curriculum material, it is possible that different databases, rationales, curriculum plans and goal packages will act on the same curriculum.

Figure 7.3 provides an overview of the possible objects of curriculum evaluation that have been distinguished thus far.

From the above descriptions taken from Human *et al.*'s (1986) work, the complexity and multifaceted nature of the field of curriculum evaluation becomes clear.

Rodgers (1983: 144–145) mentions that there are specific main categories in terms of which curriculum evaluation is addressed. These categories are the following:

- The contents of the specific curriculum programmes
- The medium of instruction (media and other material)
- The organisation and structure of the programme
- The instructional strategies
- Classroom management
- The roles of teachers

Here, too, the multifaceted nature of curriculum evaluation is apparent.

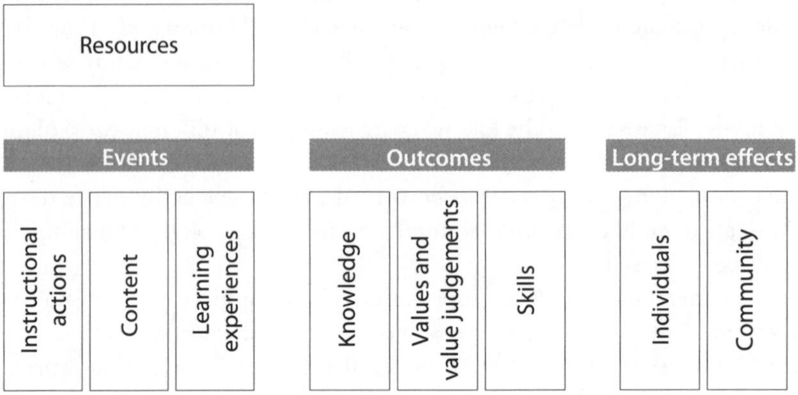

Resources

Events			Outcomes			Long-term effects	
Instructional actions	Content	Learning experiences	Knowledge	Values and value judgements	Skills	Individuals	Community

Figure 7.3: Objects of curriculum evaluation

7.3   Models for curriculum evaluation

As previously mentioned, a model may supply meaningful guidelines for the processes which are undertaken. The models of evaluation, a few of which are briefly illustrated below, differ and therefore are of value in specific circumstances. It must be noted, however, that it is vital that any model chosen to evaluate a curriculum must fit the paradigm in which it was designed. Some models might be more objective oriented and it could be problematic to use them when evaluating a process-designed curriculum.

Rodgers (1983: 145–146) sets out useful guidelines in regard to specific models which may be followed. The data which is obtained must, however, still be interpreted in relation to the specific context. The following are three points of departure which are normally valid in the determination of a model:

- Achievement of desired outcomes
- Assessment of merit
- Decision making

The 'achievement of desired outcomes' model seeks mainly to determine the level of success of learners or individuals. The curriculum developer will therefore determine to what extent the outcomes correlate with the expectations which have been set. The 'assessment of merit' model seeks to determine the merits of a specific entity according to a given standard, while the 'decision-making' model is primarily involved with future planning.

These three models are not mutually exclusive but link up with one another. Components of one model may even be encountered in another. Which model to follow is dependent on circumstances and approaches. In following on from the previous section, it will be useful to give a perspective on the evaluation of the respective levels or areas of curriculum development.

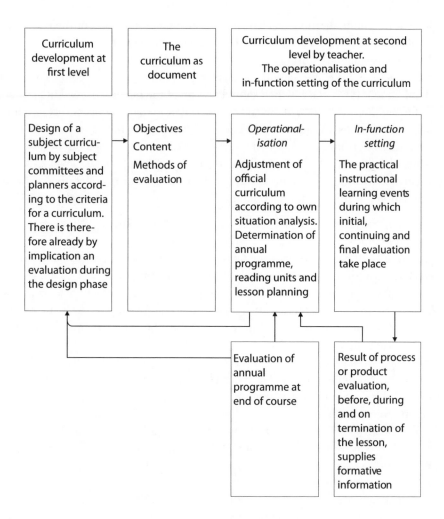

Figure 7.4: Evaluation at macro-level (Cawood *et al.*, 1982)

Blanckenberg's scheme (Cawood *et al.*, 1982: 237), shown in Figure 7.4, may serve as an illustration of possible evaluation at macro-level.

From the above model, it may be deduced that evaluation in one form or another plays a role during every phase, from the design of the curriculum up to and during the implementation thereof. Feedback to the designers is also a particular characteristic of this model. The various forms of evaluation involved are described briefly below:

- During the original design, a situation analysis or contextual evaluation which indicates the possibilities and limitations of a given curriculum is already broached. In addition, there are the criteria for a viable curriculum against which developers must test their product on an ongoing basis.
- The product of this design phase (the curriculum as official document) makes provision for the evaluation of the learner and the programme.

- During operationalisation, teachers make adjustments in respect of their contextual evaluation. Provisional curriculum development therefore takes place.
- Formative evaluation during the lesson events gives feedback to teachers for further adjustments to the instructional–learning programme, i.e. ongoing curriculum development takes place, which should also be to the benefit of current learners.
- In further final evaluation at the end of the course, in the form of final examinations and other forms of learner feedback (evaluation of the course by learners), formative information is supplied to the teacher. Further curriculum development, which should be to the benefit of the next group of learners, takes place.
- Feedback to the original designers or their successors supplies the contextual evaluation information for curriculum development at the first level.

The model of Saylor *et al.* (1981: 334) also shows how curriculum evaluation may take place at different levels.

This comprises the evaluation of the school's broad curriculum, the subject curricula, the educational authorities, as well as education at government level. Those involved at all levels should therefore be involved with this process, during which formative as well as summative evaluation is utilised. It is therefore not a question of evaluating just the learning and instructional goals within the classroom, but also the broad educational goals (Carl, 1986: 50).

Besides taking place on different levels, according to Saylor *et al.* (1981: 344–347), curriculum evaluation also comprises the evaluation of specific aspects of the relevant curriculum. This is illustrated in Figure 7.5, in which the designers' perspective of curriculum evaluation is apparent.

Oliva (1988: 481–483) gives a further model which endeavours to illustrate a logical classification and the multifaceted nature of curriculum evaluation. It is a cyclical model which accentuates interactivity. The respective steps are the following:

a. Determination of needs
b. Confirmation of validity of curriculum aims
c. Confirmation of curriculum objectives
d. Contextual evaluation (already begun with determination of needs and continued up to implementation)
e. Evaluation of input (between curriculum goals and implementation)
f. Evaluation of process during evaluation
g. Evaluation of product, summative of the whole process

The structure of the model is depicted in Figure 7.6. Oliva (1988: 482) presents an important point of view, namely that the use of any model will be more effective if a decision has been made with regard to fixed standards. He refers to one state's 'Joint Committee on Standards for Educational Evaluation' which has set out four basic characteristics for evaluation:

- Utility, under which eight utility standards are identified 'to ensure that an evaluation will serve the practical information needs of given audiences'
- Feasibility, under which, in turn, four feasibility standards have been identified to ensure that evaluation is realistic, beneficial, cautious and sensible

- Correctness and respectability, under which eight standards are set to ensure that the evaluation is justifiably ethical, taking into account the needs of interested parties
- Accuracy and reliability, under which 11 standards are set to ensure that reliable and accurate information is obtained.

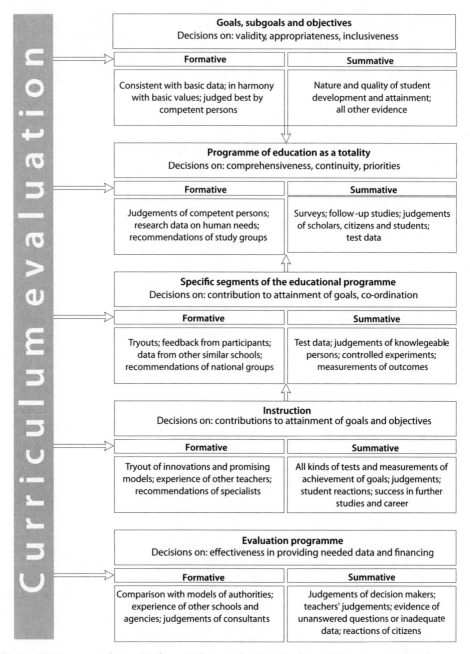

Figure 7.5: Scope and nature of curriculum evaluation (Saylor, 1981)

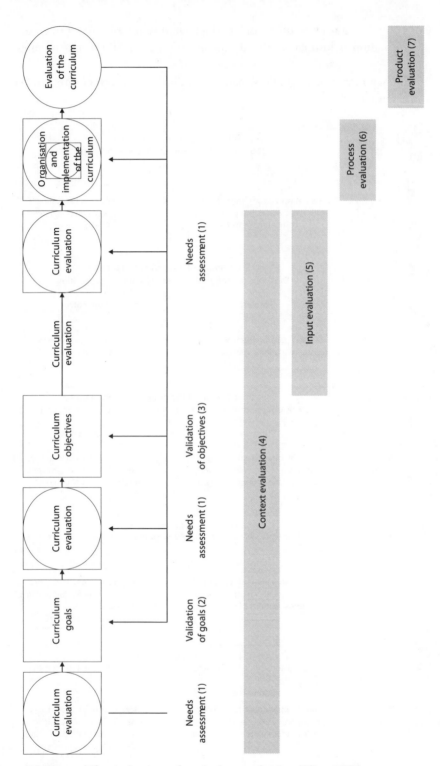

Figure 7.6: The multifaceted nature of curriculum evaluation (Oliva, 1988)

In this publication, a specific model for curriculum development is advocated (see the proposal and model (Figure 4.4) in Section 4.4). According to this proposal, evaluation is not restricted to the fourth phase in the process of curriculum development, but is continuously relevant after and during each phase. It means therefore that evaluation takes place:

a. before, during and after the design phase
b. before, during and after the dissemination phase
c. before, during and after the implementation phase; and
d. before an evaluation strategy is planned and also as it progresses.

Evaluation before, during and after the phases referred to may contribute to ensuring that dynamic curriculum development takes place. Barrow (1984: 239) warns that no instrument or model may determine the value of a curriculum empirically:

> Whether a particular curriculum is a good one has to be **thought** about … [T]he task of curriculum evaluation cannot be left in the hands of mere technicians. Adequate curriculum evaluation presupposes a sound grasp of the concepts of schooling and education.

The evaluation of a curriculum utilising a model, therefore, could degenerate into a mere technical process. It is clear from the above description that evaluation is a complex affair that must be handled with care.

7.4   Forms of curriculum evaluation

The contents of this section are, in the main, adapted from a report drawn up by Human, Taylor, Steyn and Jansen (1986: 33–57), with kind permission of the authors.

Basic differentiations

The following three essential and different basic forms of curriculum evaluation, which are expanded on below, may be distinguished, based on the activity involved:

*   The comparison of the objects which must be judged with other actual or ideal objects (comparative evaluation)
*   The linking of the different curriculum elements with one another (linking evaluation)
*   The construction of criteria or demands (fundamental evaluation)

The following forms of **comparative** evaluation may be distinguished:

a. The comparison of a curriculum or aspects of a curriculum with other curricula
b. The comparison of curriculum events, outcomes and results with curriculum anticipations
c. The comparison of the anticipations of different persons (groups of persons) of the same curriculum

The term 'comparative evaluation' is reserved for (a) above, while reference will be made to (b) as 'implementation evaluation', and to (c) as 'consensus evaluation'.

Stake's concept (1967: 536, as quoted by Human *et al.*, 1986: 33) of 'relative evaluation' is the same as comparative evaluation mentioned above. His 'absolute evaluation' refers to implementation evaluation, as well as to fundamental evaluation:

> There are two bases of judging the characteristics of a program[me], (1) with respect to absolute standards as reflected by personal judgements and (2) with respect to relative standards as reflected by characteristics of alternate program[me]s. One can evaluate mathematics with respect to opinions of what a mathematics curriculum should be or with regard to what other mathematics curricula are.

The following forms of **linking** evaluation may be distinguished:
a. Evaluation of curriculum objects by identifying the real or anticipated results or implications thereof (effect evaluation or 'pay-off' evaluation)
b. Identification of the causes of particular curriculum phenomena (diagnostic evaluation)

Effect evaluation and diagnostic evaluation comprise the identification of causal links through empirical investigation and/or logical reasoning. McCormick and May (1983: 162) refer to diagnostic evaluation as a 'diagnosis of reasons why a curriculum has succeeded or failed'. They refer to effect evaluation as a 'process product – to relate behaviour to measurable change in outcomes' (McCormick & May, 1983: 187).

Fundamental evaluating may take place with reference to:
a. theoretical criteria, such as Swartz's didactic principles; and
b. empirical data, such as the demands of parents, and social and economic circumstances (compare Scriven, 1972).

The various forms of evaluation, namely comparative, implementation, consensus, diagnostic, effect and fundamental evaluation, are further described and illustrated below.

Comparative evaluation

Comparative evaluation comprises the comparison of one or more of the databases, rationales, curriculum anticipations, resources, events, outcomes and results of two of more different curricula which broadly serve the same purpose and which are therefore comparable – for example, the History curricula in the first three school years in different regions or countries, or the existing and an alternative (renewing) curriculum in the same country or region (see also Jordaan, 1989: 408). The functions of comparative evaluation may be distinguished as follows:
• The determination of standards (achievability)
• The identification of possible shortcomings
• The maintenance of comparable norms and standards

It is often difficult to estimate with any accuracy a particular curricular outcome or result – for example, the percentage of the 18-year-old population of a country who are at least able to undertake skilled labour – or to determine on a theoretical basis what is achievable. The corresponding outcomes/results in other countries are actually the only data which may give an indication as to what may be achieved in a particular connection.

The identification of any possible shortcomings is an important function of curriculum evaluation. When other comparable countries implement a specific new curriculum component (e.g. general technology as an obligatory school subject, as is currently the case in West Germany, France and England), or abolish a traditional curriculum component (e.g. 'Euclid's Geometry'), it is obvious that the question will arise as to whether or not the same change should be made here (comparison cannot supply the answer to this question). This form of curriculum evaluation is typically the first step in curriculum renewal in one country arising from curriculum trends in other countries.

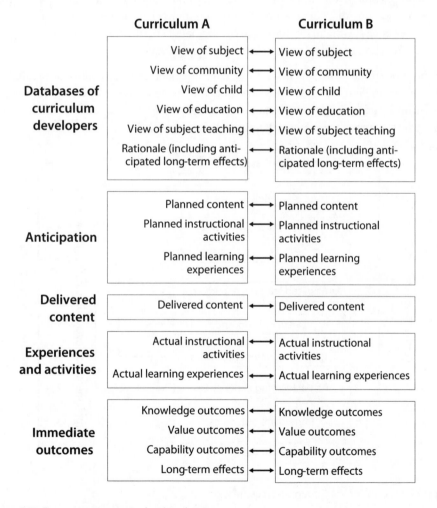

Figure 7.7: Comparative curriculum evaluation

Comparative evaluation of curricula with a view to maintaining comparable norms and standards takes place, for example, through the moderation of external examination papers. It may, however, take other forms, for example the application of the same measuring instrument to learners who have gone through the different curricula, i.e. an external examination, as used by South African education departments, with a view to, *inter alia*, maintaining comparable norms and standards between the curricula of different schools. Figure 7.7 on page 153 endeavours to set out comparable curriculum evaluation schematically (Human *et al.*, 1986: 36).

Implementation evaluation

Implementation evaluation is the evaluation of the extent to which curriculum anticipations become a reality. The following three global forms of implementation evaluation may be distinguished:
- Comparison of the (immediate) curriculum outcomes with set (anticipated) goals
- Comparison of curriculum events (content, instructional actions, learning experiences) with curriculum plans (anticipated curriculum events)
- Comparison of different elements with the rationale

Of the above three forms, the first is more correctly referred to as 'goal-based evaluation', with the term 'implementation evaluation' (in its stricter sense) being reserved for the second and third forms as rationale-based evaluation of curriculum elements. The different forms are shown schematically in Figure 7.8.

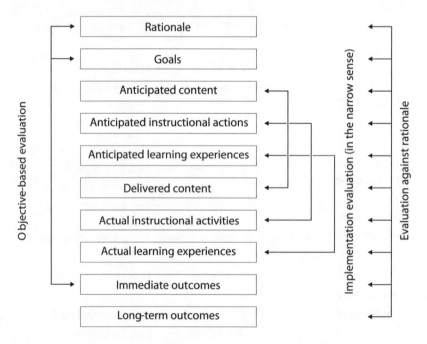

Figure 7.8: Forms of implementation evaluation

Sergiovanni (1974: 541; 550–551) uses the term 'discrepancy evaluation' for what is here referred to as implementation evaluation. Stake (1967: 532) refers to this form of evaluation as 'finding the congruencies between intents and observations'. McCormick and May (1983: 161, as quoted by Human *et al.*, 1986: 40) state:

> The major assumption underlying outcome and procedural evaluation is that it is possible to pre-specify goals, the achievement of which will be the measure of educational quality. Goals may either be framed in terms of pupil[-]learning outcomes or in terms of what 'ought to' happen if a school is functioning properly ... [B]oth these forms of evaluation require intentions to be pre-specified.

The disadvantages of the over-accentuation of objective-based evaluation have already been discussed and will not be repeated here, save to point out again that implementation evaluation in general (i.e. all three forms as shown in Figure 7.8) comprises only the comparison of curriculum realities with curriculum anticipations, or rather the evaluation of curriculum realities against curriculum anticipations as criteria. This, however, leaves unevaluated the **quality** of the anticipations (rationale aims, syllabus-anticipated instructional activities and learning experiences). Without an attendant evaluation of anticipations (fundamental evaluation) – Lawton (1982: 17) refers to this as 'justification' – implementation evaluation can quite literally be built on sand.

Implementation evaluation, in its stricter sense, has an important methodological function within the framework of other evaluation forms and is a necessary prerequisite for accountable evaluation of the effective anticipations on outcomes, as the following quotation shows (Freeman & Sherwood, 1965: 21; compare also Alkin, 1969):

> To say a program[me] fails when it is not truly implemented is indeed misguided, and the evaluation researcher's responsibility here is one of providing evidence and information that permits an accounting of what took place as well as what was the result.

Fullan and Pomfret (1977: 335–397) analyse a variety of curriculum implementation evaluations (in the stricter sense of the word) in the US and Canada, and come to the conclusion that such evaluations are aimed at the following aspects (Fullan & Pomfret, 1977: 361–364):

- The learning content and curriculum materials
- Curriculum resources and organisatorial matters
- The behaviour of teachers (instructional actions)
- The knowledge and understanding of the curriculum on the part of teachers
- The value judgements handed down by teachers with regard to the curriculum

In this sense, implementation evaluation may also refer to the interaction between curriculum functionaries at differing levels, the possibilities of which are indicated in Figure 7.9. The purpose of this bureaucratic implementation evaluation would be to determine to what extent the curriculum perspectives and anticipations of senior functionaries work through to lower order functionaries (not that this would necessarily be good).

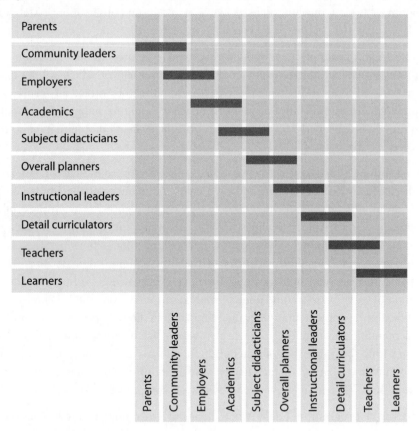

Figure 7.9: Interaction between functionaries

Bureaucratic implementation evaluation is necessarily an empirical process, in the sense that the curriculum elements must be described as consciousness contents in different persons and must then be compared for correspondences and differences. In this process, evaluators have primarily a merely descriptive role. They could, however, express themselves with regard to the merits of correspondences and differences between the curriculum elements in respect of functionaries at two levels and in different contexts. In looking at the merits they could set the bureaucratic system as a norm and therefore judge any differences as politically undesirable, whatever the effect thereof on the quality of the curriculum. Alternatively, they could have full confidence in the good curriculum judgement on the part of the relevant higher functionaries (as is often the case if the relevant higher functionary is in fact also the evaluator), and judge differences negatively on these grounds. A third possibility is that the databases, rationale and anticipations of higher order functionaries could be evaluated in another manner in order to validate them as criteria for the evaluation of the databases, rationale and anticipations of lower order functionaries and of curriculum outcomes and realities.

Consensus evaluation

Consensus evaluation is the comparison of different persons' (or groups of persons') anticipations with regard to the same curriculum and the exposure of the differences and/or correspondences. As House (1973, as quoted by Lawton, 1982: 170) points out,

> ... evaluation is the process of applying a set of standards to a programme, making judgements using the standards, and justifying the standards and their application. But there are many standards, especially in a pluralist society: which to apply? ... [I]f a school superintendent wants to defend a programme, he usually chooses the ground on which it is evaluated; if a school critic wishes to attack a programme, he chooses different standards.

Becher, Eraut and Knight (1981: 146) show that the curriculum rationales of teachers, parents and school leavers in England have, on occasion, differed drastically:

> Two opinion surveys (Schools Council, 1968, 1971) showed a marked divergence between teachers' educational priorities and those of parents and school leavers: but the findings were interpreted by the schools not as calling for any adjustment of current practice but only as a confirmation that unenlightened lay opinion must take second place to professional wisdom.

The curriculum anticipations, curriculum rationales and databases of various persons and groups of persons may differ. Consensus evaluation is the exposure of these differences by comparison. Judgement may take place within this context when a specific person's or group of persons' anticipations, rationale and/or databases are accepted as the norm. In the situation to which Becher *et al.* (1981: 146) refer, teachers accepted their own databases, rationale and anticipations as the norm. A bureaucratic educational system with central curriculum control is implicitly based on the principle that a great degree of consensus exists with regard to databases, rationales and anticipations between curriculators at various levels.

Diagnostic evaluation

Diagnostic evaluation envisages the empirical identification of the causes of specific curriculum phenomena. Suchman's description (1967, in Caro, 1977: 48) is an example of this form of evaluation:

> ... [A]n evaluation study should do more than pass or fail a program[me] ... it should attempt to find out why a program[me] was or was not effective. ... In this sense evaluation involves more than judging; it also encompasses research on conditions affecting success or failure.

Diagnostic evaluation of curricula is, according to Human *et al.* (1986: 48), important when problems in a society are identified, for example a shortage of technologically trained human capital, low productivity, an inadequate understanding and appreciation of the free-market system or a lack of acknowledgement of human worth between individuals and various culture groups. If it were considered imperative for curricula to contribute to the elimination/prevention of such problems, then their existence would indicate shortcomings in the curricula. If, for example, the above four problems are problems in present-day South African society, the question should be asked as to whether and how school curricula should make provision for:

a. creating awareness of technical/technological vocational possibilities with a degree of intensity that is comparable to that which takes place in regard to creating awareness of other vocational possibilities (e.g. through subject instruction);

b. the promotion of knowledge, values and skills which may promote productivity (do schools not often exhibit an image of low productivity in their own functioning?);

c. creating awareness and an appreciation of the free-market system as opposed to other economic systems; and

d. making acquaintance with the cultural achievements of other culture groups.

Lecturers at tertiary institutions often venture into diagnostic evaluations of school curricula, ascribing the problems experienced by tertiary students to shortcomings in those curricula.

A diagnostic evaluation need not have the identification of problems in the community as point of departure, which may be the identification of problems in any curriculum element, for example a shortage of textbooks (curriculum materials), examination question papers, the subject knowledge of teachers or the subject teaching image (subject didactic grounding) of instructional leaders. Diagnostic evaluation is therefore often a search for valid answers to the question of why a particular deficiency exists. Diagnostic evaluation must naturally be preceded by problem identification via another form of evaluation (Human *et al.*, 1986: 50).

Diagnostic evaluation may also take a more positive form. Freeman and Sherwood (1965: 13, as quoted by Human *et al.*, 1986: 50) write as follows:

> A proper evaluation ... requires not only knowing that certain effects were obtained but also knowing with some degree of probability that the effects were substantively related to a particular set of stimuli. ... The basic question is: what is it that should be repeated if the program[me] appears to work?

Pay-off evaluation

Human *et al.* (1986: 50) refer to the form of evaluation which involves assessing the value of a curriculum element (e.g. a curriculum or curriculum events) by evaluating the supposed consequences thereof (e.g. curriculum outcomes) as pay-off evaluation. Lawton (in McCormick & May, 1983: 169) refers to this form of evaluation when he states that '[e]valuation has often been seen simply as a process of measuring the success of teaching in terms of pupils' learning'.

Eisner (1985: 195–196) refers to pay-off evaluation as follows:

> ... [W]hen student performance is viewed as an index of program[me] effectiveness, the likelihood of curriculum improvement increases and a major contribution is made toward improving the quality of education.

Fundamental evaluation

Comparative evaluation refers to alternative curricula as criteria. Implementation evaluation refers to curriculum anticipations as criteria. Neither of these forms requires the making of a value judgement – the question regarding the value or quality of alternative curricula or of curriculum anticipations remains unanswered. Fundamental evaluation involves the determination of the value and/or quality of curriculum elements with reference to the primary criteria, in the form of values, points of view, needs and circumstances, which gave rise to educational programmes being instituted and maintained. Fundamental evaluation is what Lawton (in McCormick & May, 1983: 170) calls 'justification'. Eisner (1985: 236, 238) writes in this connection:

> To make such judgements requires ... the application of educational criteria. Where can such criteria be found? They can, of course, come from arbitrary, uncriticized preferences. But the truly competent educational critic is aware not only of the educational values he or she subscribes [to], but also of the values that are rejected. The educational critic will be able to provide grounds for the value choices made while recognizing that others might disagree with these choices. The grounding of such values not only requires knowledge of the history and philosophy of education, it also benefits from practical experience in the schools.

Fundamental evaluation therefore requires the identification and description of primary criteria in terms of primary values, needs and circumstances, as well as of the interpretation/operationalisation of these primary criteria into curriculum rationales and curriculum anticipations. The clarification of primary criteria is settled in curriculum databases referred to earlier, namely subject images, child images, community images, educational images and subject teaching images. These databases refer to realities, namely subject practices, children, communities, educational phenomena and subject teaching, including the particular value systems vested in these anthropological phenomena. As such, the databases themselves are subject to evaluation. The extent of congruence between the databases providing the primary criteria for a curriculum evaluation and the realities to which these databases refer is, in a fundamental sense, determinative with regard to the validity and, therefore, the value of curriculum evaluation. This means that the databases available to curriculum evaluators make up a critical component of their evaluation ability. There is also another critical component, namely their technical evaluation ability (Human et al., 1986: 55).

Fundamental curriculum evaluation therefore comprises, *inter alia*, the following processes:

a.   The establishment of databases upon which evaluation is based

b.   Determination of the logical link between these databases and the various curriculum elements, namely the databases, rationales and anticipations of curriculum developers (including teachers), the curriculum events and curriculum outcomes

Fundamental evaluation therefore refers to an evaluation of the logical consistency of curricula, that is to say whether the implications for specific items in databases are taken up in a rationale for a curriculum, or whether the objectives logically arise from the rationale or whether the content selection, anticipated instructional actions and learning experiences fit in with the objectives, etc. Each cell in the matrix given in Figure 7.10 indicates a set of links which may in a specific case be logically consistent or logically inconsistent.

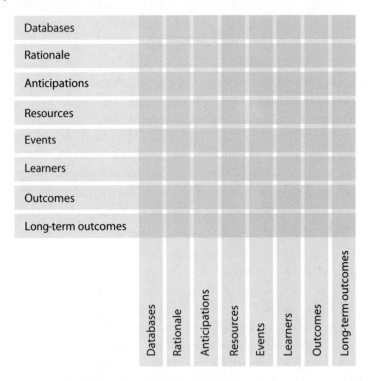

Figure 7.10: Matrix on logical consistency or inconsistency

This matrix is, however, an oversimplification, as the databases, rationale and anticipations of various kinds of functionaries may differ and influence one another. Furthermore, there are various databases and various dimensions of curriculum events and outcomes. Figure 7.11 offers a more complete review of possible connections between curriculum elements which may be the subjects of empirical or logical bonding evaluation (cause evaluation, pay-off evaluation or fundamental evaluation).

	Databases in respect of									
	Subject	Community	Learners	Subject teaching	Education and teaching	Rationale for subject curriculum	Anticipations and objectives	Content	Teaching activities	Learning experiences
Overall planners										
Instructional leaders										
Detail curriculators										
Teachers										

Figure 7.11: Connections between curriculum elements

Summary

From the above it appears that the curriculum developer must take note of these forms of evaluation and utilise them. Evaluation is therefore a broad concept and process, and can definitely lead to dynamic curriculum development if there is a thorough knowledge of, *inter alia,* the various forms of evaluation. In this way, practice may be better understood and real efforts may be made to improve evaluation practice.

7.5   Methods of evaluation

The various methods of evaluation have already been described fully in Section 4.5 and are therefore only briefly mentioned here. The methods of evaluation, such as formative, summative, criterion-oriented, norm-oriented, process and product evaluation, are also of particular importance for programme or curriculum evaluation.

7.6   The evaluation of a curriculum with the aid of a checklist

Although not valid in all circumstances, it is nevertheless useful at the conclusion of a programme to try to get an indication of the quality of the design and whether all relevant aspects have been taken into account. Such a checklist is in reality an evaluation instrument.

Once a curriculum design has been completed, the task is still far from completion. An evaluation should take place in order to determine whether it is suitable for implementation. In this connection, a few checklists which partially comply with this need have appeared.

Rowntree's checklist (1978)

Rowntree (1978: 155) poses 12 key questions in order to determine the effectiveness of a curriculum:

- Are the goals, methods and outcomes suitable for the learners?
- What is the effectiveness, and are satisfactory results achieved?
- What is the extent – in other words, what are the time, personnel and source implications; how many subjects are involved; and how many learners are involved?
- Is additional support material required?
- How difficult and complex is it for teachers and learners to work with the support material?
- Is there sufficient room for flexibility with regard to change and adaptations?
- How different is it, and how does it differ from other approaches?
- How repeatable is it, and are there any special factors which may limit repetition elsewhere?
- How compatible is it? Will it fit in with the rest of the system or will it be limiting – in other words, how unifiable is it?
- What is the status of preparedness and readiness – in other words, when may it be applied?
- Can a pre-test be carried out?
- How expensive is it? What are the initial and running costs?

The more positive the answer to each of the questions is, the greater the chance of success. The curriculum will of course also have to be subjected to evaluation on an ongoing basis, firstly to determine effectiveness and secondly to improve thereon.

Pratt's checklist (1980)

Pratt (1980: 410–413) mentions that the completion of the design phase should be followed by its submission to persons of authority who may make recommendations. As a guideline for the curriculator, he offers the following checklist in terms of which a curriculum may be evaluated:

a. Aim
   - Is the overall intended outcome clearly and concisely spelt out?
   - Does the objective include the most important aspects of the curriculum? Does it have significance?

b. Rationale
   - Is the necessity and need for the programme convincingly spelt out?
   - Are all the valid, salient and applicable motivations in favour thereof mentioned?
   - Are they valid, sound and convincing?
   - Are objections anticipated, and if so, how will they be dealt with?

- Was a needs assessment made, and how are the procedures and results described?

c. Purposefulness
- Have all major specific intended outcomes been identified?
- Is there an indication of the expected changes in learners?
- Have the type and importance of each goal been defined?
- Is each objective in agreement with or relevant to the aim?
- Is each objective precise, applicable, functional and appropriate?
- Will the aim be realised if all the objectives have been achieved?

d. Performance criteria
- Has every goal been drawn according to criteria which promote feasibility?
- Are these criteria congruent, complete, objective, reliable, efficient and discrete?

e. Grading
- Is the grading system clear and explicit?
- Does grading reflect the priorities of objectives?
- Does the grading system ensure that a goal has in fact been achieved before credit is given for it?

f. Context
- Is the social and community context described?
- Is it clear how the curriculum links with or overlaps with the programme of the learner and the school?
- Are the lines of authority clearly spelt out?
- Have other institutions been identified which may possibly make use of the curriculum?
- Has the possible impact on other courses and teachers been identified?

g. Entry requirements
- Is there a description of the learners for whom the curriculum is intended?
- Has the recruiting process been clearly spelt out?
- Are the prerequisites valid?
- Are pre-tests appropriate?
- Has provision been made for learners who do not attain admission?

h. Instruction
- Has the schedule for instruction been set out in sufficient detail?
- Is it viable?
- What is the motivational value of the content?
- Is the content relevant with regard to the goals?
- Are the educational strategies sufficiently applicable, creative and diversified?
- Does instruction contribute to the realisation of the goals?

i. Management of diversity
- Does formative evaluation take place regularly and diagnostically, and is it valid?
- Is pre-planned remediation applicable, motivational and effective?
- Is provision made for the faster learner?

j.   Logistics
  - Is there an indication of the minimum and maximum number of learners involved in the curriculum?
  - Are material and equipment specified?
  - Does this material comply with all requirements?
  - Has a realistic time allocation been made?
  - Have the capacities, responsibilities and qualities of the teachers been properly analysed?
  - Have the financial costs been analysed?

k.   Pre-testing/tryout
  - Has provision been made for sufficient pre-testing/tryout?
  - If pre-testing has been carried out, are the results available?

l.   Programme evaluation
  - Are there valid evaluation measures to determine the effectiveness and acceptability?
  - Are all aspects of the curriculum evaluated?
  - Has provision been made for the ongoing revision and monitoring of the curriculum?

m.   Implementation
  - Has a strategy and time schedule for implementation been drawn up?
  - Have roles and incentives been clearly defined?
  - Are resources available to all consumers?
  - Is it a realistic implementation strategy?

n.   Production
  - Is the curriculum guaranteed against stylistic and typographic errors, assumptions, prolixity and unnecessary word usage?
  - Has it been professionally and neatly produced?

This appears to be a very comprehensive checklist and may increase the positive value of the curriculum.

Cawood's checklist (1984)

Cawood (Cawood, Carl, Conradie, Hanekom & Blanckenberg, 1984: 44–47) has also drawn up a checklist for curriculum developers against which the extent and completeness of the curriculum design may be evaluated. He has identified six components and under each of them he poses a number of evaluation questions.

A.   General curriculum theory

  1.   Is an acknowledged curriculum model utilised?
  2.   Has each of the following cardinal components received thorough attention?
  - Contextual evaluation of the curriculum
  - Specific goal formulation in the subject
  - Specific core and learning contents in the subject

- Specific learning experiences and teaching methods for the subject
- Specific learner-orientated evaluation of learners in the subject

3. Has a strategy been planned for each of the following phases of curriculum development in the relevant subject curriculum?
   - Curriculum design
   - Curriculum dissemination
   - Curriculum implementation
   - Curriculum evaluation

B. Contextual evaluation

1. Has the subject curriculum been preceded by a thorough target audience analysis and analysis of the situation?
2. Has a strategy been planned with regard to when, how and by whom each of the following components may be evaluated on a continuing basis?
   - Goals in the subject
   - Selection of content in the subject
   - Teaching methods and media for the subject
   - The actual instructional–learning events in the subject
   - Learner-orientated evaluation in the subject

C. The formulation of goals and objectives

1. Does goal formulation in the subject curriculum join up with broader educational goals?
2. Is an acknowledged goals' taxonomy utilised in the formulation of the goals?
3. Does thinking on the higher cognitive levels figure very prominently in the goals?
4. Is there also an endeavour to formulate affective goals and to aim for them?
5. Have process goals and objectives been specifically identified in the subject and recorded?
6. Are objectives with regard to thinking skills very prominent in the goals?
7. Have goals been set aimed at:
   - leadership development in and through the subject?
   - development of creative potential?

D. Selection and classification of content

1. Does the content link up well with the set goals for the subject?
2. Does the content contain specialised knowledge and skills which are more than mere syllabus contents?
3. Does the content pre-eminently comply with the criterion of relevancy?

E. Learning activities and teaching methods

1. Has provision also been made in the subject curriculum for particular learning activities and/or teaching methods?

2. Do the following discussion teaching methods figure very prominently in the subject curriculum?
   - Controlled discussion method
   - Class discussion
   - Symposium
   - Panel

3. Do the following self-teaching methods figure very prominently in the subject curriculum?
   - Project work
   - Research
   - Learning contracts
   - Self-study modules
   - Computerised teaching
   - Investigation

4. Do the following learning activities feature very prominently in the subject curriculum?
   - Creative learning activities
   - Self-discovery
   - Problem solving
   - Joint decision making
   - Critical thinking
   - Analysis and synthesis
   - Communication
   - Concept forming

F. Learner-orientated evaluation

1. Does the learner-orientated evaluation of gifted learners in the subject curriculum differ from the evaluation of other learners in the subject?
2. Is learner-orientated evaluation an integral and natural part of the instructional–learning situation in the subject?
3. Are the following two aspects essential components in learner-orientated evaluation in your subject?
   - Self-knowledge and self-evaluation
   - Formative process evaluation

If a subject curriculum complies with these requirements, it may also be regarded as comprehensive and complete. Although it may take a long time, it is advantageous to evaluate a curriculum against the requirements.

A possible draft checklist (Carl, 1994)

An alternative checklist is proposed by Carl (1994). After the checklist has been completed, curriculum developers should have an indication of the quality of their design. The scale must be interpreted as follows:

0. Lacking
1. Very weak
2. Below average
3. Average
4. Good
5. Very good/excellent

The curriculum developer may give an indication by filling in a suitable number from the above scale against each item.

A. Curriculum development	
1. Clarity exists as to what each of the following phases comprises:	
• Curriculum design	☐
• Curriculum dissemination	☐
• Curriculum implementation	☐
• Curriculum evaluation	☐
2. Clear strategies have been set out with regard to the execution of each phase.	☐
3. Existing curricula are regularly reviewed.	☐
4. Subject groups and teachers are encouraged to deal with the syllabus critically and to identify possible amendments.	☐
5. Subject teams are regularly encouraged to channel syllabus interpretations and implementation problems.	☐
6. Opportunities have been created to channel amendments, interpretation and implementation problems.	☐
7. Teacher involvement is promoted by creating and utilising input mechanisms.	☐
8. Provision is made to counter resistance to change and to obtain co-operation.	☐
9. Teachers have the opportunity to make use of existing input mechanisms (e.g. teacher centres, departmental study committees, teachers' associations).	☐
10. There are sufficient communication channels to promote development.	☐

B. Curriculum design	
1. Pre-knowledge of curriculum design is sufficient.	☐
2. The design complies with all the required criteria in regard to the various components:	
• Contextual evaluation/assessment	☐
• Goals	☐
• Choice of core and learning content	☐
• Classification and systematisation of learning content	☐
• Selection and organisation of learning opportunities, learning experiences and teaching methods	☐
• Learner-orientated evaluation/assessment	☐
3. A thorough initial pre-evaluation/assessment has been done.	☐
4. Contextual evaluation/assessment has been thoroughly planned in respect of each component:	
• Goals	☐
• Selection of core and learning content	☐

- Classification of learning contents ☐
- Selection of learning opportunities, learning experiences and teaching methods ☐
- Practical instructional–learning process ☐
- Learner-orientated evaluation/assessment ☐

5. Goals and outcomes:
    - There is absolute clarity as to which goals and outcomes have to be pursued. ☐
    - Provision has been made for process goals. ☐
    - Provision has been made for production goals. ☐
    - Goals on the higher cognitive thought level figure in the design. ☐
    - Goals on the affective level figure in the design. ☐
    - There is clarity on the integration of the critical and learning outcomes and on how this integration will be achieved. ☐
    - There is clarity on how progress will be addressed. ☐

6. Selection and classification of core and learning contents:
    - It complies with the required criteria. ☐
    - It links up with the set objectives. ☐
    - The classification of learning content takes place according to the required classification principles. ☐
    - Learners themselves also have had input in choice and classification (where possible). ☐

7. Selection and organisation of learning opportunities, learning experiences, learning activities and teaching methods:
    - A clear distinction has been made between learning opportunities and learning experiences. ☐
    - Provision has been made for sufficient opportunities which will allow suitable learner activities. ☐
    - The most important learning principles were considered before the learning opportunities were planned. ☐
    - The basic forms of teaching methods figure in the curriculum:
        - Lecture ☐
        - Discussion ☐
        - Group work ☐
        - Group activity ☐
        - Experience-based methods ☐
    - Provision has been made for the following learning activities:
        - Creative learning ☐
        - Self-discovery ☐
        - Problem solving ☐
        - Decision making ☐
        - Analysis and synthesis ☐
        - Communication ☐

8. Evaluation/assessment:
   - Provision has been made for learner-orientated evaluation/assessment. ☐
   - Provision has been made for curriculum-orientated evaluation/assessment. ☐
   - The required criteria for evaluation/assessment have been thoroughly considered. ☐
   - Provision has been made for summative product evaluation/assessment. ☐
   - Provision has been made for formative process evaluation/assessment. ☐
   - Provision has been made for recognised measuring mechanisms. ☐
   - Provision has been made for self-evaluation/assessment. ☐
   - Provision has been made for assessment for learning. ☐
   - Provision has been made for continuous assessment. ☐
   - There is clarity on what learners have to demonstrate to indicate that they have achieved the outcomes. ☐
   - Learners will be involved in the teaching–learning situation. ☐
9. An attempt has been made to encourage colleagues to apply curriculum design within the class and lesson context. ☐
10. You have ensured that colleagues have been informed as to the purpose and process of curriculum development. ☐
11. All those involved with curriculum design have been consulted beforehand. ☐
12. Provision has been made to evaluate the design on an ongoing basis during the implementation phase. ☐

C. Curriculum dissemination

1. There is clarity as to what the concept 'dissemination' comprises. ☐
2. Knowledge as to existing dissemination procedures is evident. ☐
3. Provision has been made for a dissemination strategy. ☐
4. All those involved have been informed with regard to the curriculum. ☐
5. Sufficient channels of communication exist within the school to carry out dissemination. ☐
6. Provision has been made for a realistic implementation strategy. ☐

D. Curriculum evaluation/assessment

1. A distinction has been made between curriculum- and learner-orientated evaluation/assessment. ☐
2. There is clarity as to the functions of evaluation/assessment. ☐
3. Curriculum evaluation/assessment complies with the required criteria. ☐
4. Strategies have been planned for the ongoing and continual evaluation/assessment of the curriculum. ☐
5. All possible persons are involved. ☐

On completion of this checklist, designers may get a picture of the completeness, comprehensiveness and meaningfulness of their planning actions. A design will probably not comply with all the requirements, but the value of this checklist lies in the fact that defects can be identified and corrected. The utilisation thereof may, therefore, make a valuable contribution to curriculum development.

7.7   Summary

From the above it appears that the main purpose of evaluation/assessment is to make a value determination of the success of the relevant educational undertaking and thus to what extent the goals and outcomes have been achieved. In the process of assessment, it is necessary to distinguish between curriculum- and learner-orientated assessment. Exceptionally important aspects appear to be not just the gathering of data but also the processing thereof to determine the growth of learners, to what extent they have achieved the outcomes, their strengths and weaknesses, the support they might require and to what extent re-planning is necessary. Wheeler (1976: 267) mentions the following in order to further illustrate the above point of view, and to spell out the purpose of evaluation:

> Evaluation enables us to compare the actual outcomes with the expected outcomes, and arrive at conclusions about this comparison with a view to future action … [W]ithout some quantitative and qualitative comparisons … it is impossible to know whether objectives have been realized, and if they have, to what extent.

In order to realise this, it is necessary to take note of the broader perspectives as already described and to utilise them effectively.

It may, however, be stated that it is necessary to obtain all these perspectives so that a workable practice may be established. Curriculum developers must have knowledge of (and be competent in) the various methods of evaluation, forms of evaluation and models for evaluation, as only then can they make a meaningful contribution to an accountable evaluation practice. Each country has a particular system of practice, and in South Africa, which faces great educational challenges in meeting all the needs, it is especially necessary to establish a supple, accountable, workable and feasible practice. If there is rigidity and/or defective knowledge and skills, this can hinder effective curriculum development.

Curriculum evaluation may thus make a very substantial contribution to dynamic curriculum development and the empowerment of the teacher as curriculum agent if Barrow's (1984: 251) warning is taken to heart:

> If half the time and energy expended … were expended on *thinking* about curriculum, we might be getting somewhere.

Activities and questions

1. What do you understand by curriculum evaluation/assessment? How does it apply to your particular subject(s)?

2. (a)   Give a short description of the following forms of evaluation/assessment, and give a practice-orientated example of each (in the context of South Africa):

    •   Comparative evaluation/assessment

    •   Implementation evaluation/assessment

- Consensus evaluation/assessment
- Diagnostic evaluation/assessment
- Payoff evaluation/assessment
- Fundamental evaluation/assessment

(b) To which of the above would you give preference? Evaluate your annual programme fully in the light of your choice.

3. To which evaluation model (see Section 7.3) would you give preference in your particular situation? Why?

4. Identify and describe the five most important principles for curriculum evaluation/ assessment.

5. What is your comment on Barrow's statement that we should be thinking about curriculum?

6. Name and describe the various levels/fields in which curriculum development is done. Identify at least three ways in which you could possibly be involved in evaluation at each level.

7. What is your opinion of McCarty and Davis's viewpoint that the notion of the curriculum being the driving force for instruction and assessment should be the other way around (i.e. that one should start with assessment)? How would you apply this in practice?

8. Reflect on the role of assessment practices within the current education dispensation, and the shortcomings and strengths thereof.

8 The Operationalisation of the Curriculum

At the end of this chapter you should be able to

- make a situation analysis of your community
- make a situation analysis of your school/organisation
- formulate a mission for your school/organisation
- formulate educational, teaching and school goals for your school organisation
- do subject curriculum development in your particular subject for the year
- understand subject curriculum development more fully, and strive for the applications thereof.

8.1 Introduction

The real test for successful curriculum development is usually the operationalisation and institutionalisation; that is to say, the putting into operation and acceptance of a curriculum. Here planning must be done in order to implement and evaluate curricula at meso- and micro-level. The effectiveness thereof also determines later internalisation. The level and quality of empowerment will naturally play a determinative role in this operationalisation programme. It is through teacher participation that the success of this process is determined and for this reason the degree of empowerment is an important determinant.

This chapter will only describe possible methods, not **the** methods. Curriculum developers are free to operationalise a curriculum in their own particular manner. This description also gives only a broad framework which may and must be filled in in accordance with local, individual circumstances.

The description is given mainly at local level; that is to say, with regard to the local community and a particular school. The design of core syllabi is not described here but rather the curriculum development activities which take place in order to apply them in a particular school and class. The procedure to be followed in this method entails the following:

a. A complete situation analysis of the relevant local community
b. A complete situation analysis of the relevant school
c. Mission formulation
d. School goals formulation
e. Interpretation of the relevant subject syllabus and the formulation of subject goals
f. Identification and formulation of goals for the different grades within subject context

g. Identification of modules

h. Time scheduling of the modules for the year

The execution of this process naturally requires specific curriculum knowledge and skills by the empowered teacher. These may be obtained by various means, of which study, reading, in-service training and personnel development are but a few.

8.2 Situation analysis of the community

A situation analysis of the community within which a school is situated may produce important information that will influence planning. There are determinative aspects which may be considered. Communities may range from a high- to a low-income group and even to a squatter community. Each community will have specific needs and aspirations, and provision will have to be made for this. While one school may be situated in a very prosperous community, another may have specific handicaps precisely as a result of its particular community. An analysis of the relevant community may therefore identify specific strong and weak points, which may in turn, influence school curriculum development. A situation analysis of the relevant community may therefore take into consideration aspects such as geographical situation; income group; language preferences; occupation of parents; multiculturality; economic activities; educational organisations (e.g. number of schools, colleges, universities, technikons); community demands and expectations; parent involvement; and involvement of local authorities.

The information obtained from these aspects may give a broad image of the relevant community and how the relevant school may meet its expectations.

The information available with regard to a community may result in a school's curriculum having a specific nature and character. Thus one community will require a more academic school curriculum, while another will require a more technical one.

8.3 Situation analysis of a school

Data collection

To obtain really effective curriculum institutionalisation in the classroom, it is essential that a particular school's curriculum and its general aspects, such as organisation, climate and management, are also effective. All aspects of a school should therefore be placed in the spotlight on an ongoing basis, and a situation analysis is the first step in this process. This should actually form part of a whole strategic planning endeavour, and the results may lead to the formulation of a suitable mission and objective.

The data to be collected may include the following: the number of learners; the number of teachers; physical space (e.g. number of classrooms, the availability and absence of subject classrooms, laboratories, library, music rooms); the number of class sections and system of class exchange; the medium of instruction; structures within the school (e.g. subject teams and/or grade systems, facilitation of personnel, personal and subject development), information on the school principal (experience, leadership and management style) and the teachers (vocational aptitudes, spirit of enterprise, level of training, level and degree of empowerment in regard to curriculum studies, subject team system, personnel development, balance in regard to experience), the school curriculum (subject choices, presence of mission and objectives, reflection of expectations and needs of all interested parties), the availability of sports facilities and liaison with other schools in respect of sport and culture.

The data obtained in regard to the above-mentioned aspects may assist in maintaining a more relevant and dynamic school and subject curriculum.

8.4　Vision and mission formulation for a school

A vision is a broad idea of where the school is going, and usually contains its hopes for the future. It is not very detailed, but consists of a broad description of the dream for the school. The following is just one example: 'School X strives to achieve excellence, justice and equality, and also to make a contribution towards education of the highest quality and to optimise human potential'.

With the accumulated data, which will indicate certain needs, and clarity regarding the vision, the mission of the school may become clearer and it will become possible to formulate the ideal image that should be pursued for that particular school.

Core questions

In formulating the mission for a school, answers must be obtained to questions such as the following:

- Who are we (e.g. school type, curriculum, co-curricular activities)?
- For what basic needs (e.g. broad education, forming, results, sport activities, cultural enrichment) should we make provision?
- How do we want to acknowledge or anticipate the identified needs or problems (e.g. open communication, willingness to change and to renew, retention of high standards, retention of good staff)?
- What should our response be to key interest groups? For example:
  - Learners – quality education, good curriculum, many opportunities, good instruction, empowerment, satisfaction
  - Parents – satisfaction, safety, happy learners, empowerment
  - Personnel – good service conditions, pleasant work surroundings, professional growth, empowerment

Answers

The answers to the above questions may possibly look like this:

Who are we?

- An overwhelmingly English-speaking community
- A multicultural community
- A secondary school
- A career-orientated school
- A dual-medium school

What makes us different or unique?

- Higher standards of education
- A positive learning environment
- An infrastructure that leads to extension
- A career-orientated approach
- Service to the community
- Relevance
- Teachers' high standards for themselves
- A democratic climate to facilitate all role players

What basic needs should we provide for?

- Education for the child: spiritually, in totality, according to the values and norms of the community/to develop potential
- Educating the child to take his or her rightful place
- Career-orientated education (curriculum, teaching personnel, subject choice, physical learning facilities)
- Effectiveness and striving towards excellence (happy staff and children)
- Life skills, economic activity

How may we anticipate our needs and problems?

- Ongoing communication
  - between staff
  - between parents and staff
  - between staff and learners
  - between parents, learners and staff
  - with the private sector (community)
- Ongoing evaluation
  - of school
  - of staff
  - of learners
  - of school curriculum

Response to key interest groups

- Respect
- Mutual understanding
- Community development programme
- Creation of communication channels for learners
- Personnel development
- Vocational acknowledgement
- Empowerment

Philosophy and core values

- Preparing learners for life
- Serving the community

Core conditions: responsibility, knowledge, love, respect, empathy, sense of duty, vocational skill, perseverance, task- and people orientation, realisation of achievement, pride in self.

Mission formulation

With this information available, a school may now formulate a mission statement. It may be a shorter or longer formulation, but it must reflect the ethos of the school. The following are three examples of mission statements:

a.   High school X

The school strives to educate the total child according to the values and norms of the community so that, as a future responsible citizen, the child can develop his or her full potential and take up his or her rightful place in the community. In order to make provision for the learners' and community's needs, the school offers a balanced and relevant curriculum.

b.   High school Y

The school strives for the development of the individual to his or her full potential as a member of the broader community; and for the development of the child to a fully rounded person with high values, who has respect for work and a deep sense of responsibility, and who is adapted, with a view to building a democratic community in a progressive manner.

c.   Primary school

(With acknowledgment to Gene Louw Primary School, Durbanville, 1995)
The school is a parallel-medium school in Cape Town, which through curriculum and co-curricular activities offers its pupils optimum activities, under the leadership of a staff with particular curriculum skills and sensitive adaptation. Ours is a leading school with its unique curriculum approach which focuses on the creative control of factual knowledge through the acquisition and development of skills, attitudes and concepts. We offer pupils a pleasant and safe environment within which the educational needs of each pupil are addressed and in which the pupils are actively involved in general formative education. We endeavour to develop everyone in a balanced and integrated manner. Our school's fundamental point of departure in regard to education is Christian orientated. We pursue this by applying sound business principles and furthering partnerships between parents, school and child. We offer a balanced school curriculum to meet pupils' needs in order to maintain themselves and to develop a positive self-image. In addition, a co-curricular programme (sport and culture) is offered to guide

pupils towards balanced development in conjunction with the curriculum programme. In order to anticipate these requirements, dynamic curriculum development and curriculum management are applied. We strive to continue promoting a renewing climate and open communication within which maximal communication between all interested parties is possible, so that all relevant needs are continuously identified and addressed through dynamic curriculum development and curriculum management.

8.5   Educational, teaching and school goals

A mission statement does not normally only reflect the ethos of the school but also offers clear guidelines for the formulation of school goals. The philosophies of life of a particular school and community are also often reflected therein. Broad educational and teaching goals often figure strongly in the school goals. A few examples of these school goals are described below:

Example A

a.   To guide the child to realise his or her inherent potential to the full by:
    1.   expanding the child's unique intellectual abilities;
    2.   making the child spiritually resilient;
    3.   making the child psychosocially acceptable;
    4.   developing the child physically; and
    5.   promoting the child's aesthetic awareness.
b.   To strive for high educational standards through:
    1.   the stimulation of individuality to develop the learner's full potential according to ability, so that he or she may become a balanced member of society; and
    2.   the thorough mental, spiritual and physical development of the child
c.   To lead and support the learner to becoming an independent, balanced adult in the service of the community and a responsible, fully-fledged citizen of the country
d.   To guide the learner in the development of life skills to adapt to the changing demands and expectations of the community
e.   To instruct the learner and educate him or her in a manner which he or she may understand and comprehend and, in this way, achieve academic success
f.   To acknowledge the child as an individual, to instruct and lead him or her so that his or her talents, abilities and creative possibility may be exploited and extended so that he or she may eventually take his or her rightful place as an individual in the community
g.   To develop a pride in the school among the learners, which will serve as a basis for loyalty towards fellow learners, the staff and the school
h.   To lead the learners to self-discipline, self-motivation and human dignity through word and deed
i.   To promote good relations between teacher, learner and parent, pursuing mutual respect and regard for one another
j.   By means of ongoing evaluation of instructional methods, to improve our own instruction in the interests of the children with whom we work

Example B

a. The school's relevant, career-orientated curriculum offers the learner:
   1. training;
   2. labour skills; and ultimately
   3. economic independence.
b. Effective community involvement is promoted through ongoing liaison with:
   1. local industries;
   2. parents; and
   3. past learners.
c. Learners are equipped with the life and vocational skills necessary to become economically active and self-supporting.
d. There is a close link between school, parents and practice.
e. The teacher acts as facilitator in a democratic atmosphere.
f. There are open channels of communication.
g. A high premium is placed on teachers' professional and personal development, job security and acknowledgement of good service and achievements.
h. Learners are educated to be strong, healthy, responsible and disciplined.
i. The staff consciously pursue the broad educational objective.
j. Exceptional academic and cultural standards are maintained through the development of balanced curricular and co-curricular activities.
k. Particular attention is given to institutional curriculum and professional development.
l. Effective liaison between parent, child and school promotes maximal mutual involvement/co-operation.
m. A balanced school programme provides for the development of a healthy school pride/school ethos.
n. The school is a firm, active and viable institution characterised by a climate in which:
   1. teacher and learner may experience happiness, satisfaction and security;
   2. feelings of pride, loyalty and mutual belonging will develop spontaneously;
   3. the partnership between parent and teacher rests on mutual understanding, regard and co-operation;
   4. every teacher may live out the professionality of his or her vocation in a worthy manner in the process of empowerment; and
   5. the needs and wishes of the community are respected and receive recognition.

With these broad educational and school goals as a framework, subject teachers may progress to the process of subject curriculum development. These goals should be contextualised and further refined in the micro-curriculum situation, for example as follows:

- Overall educational goals
- Specific teaching goals
- Subject goals
- Module aims/outcomes

- Lesson aims/outcomes
- Objectives/learning outcomes

8.6   Subject curriculum development

Introduction

Subject teachers are now faced with the challenge of placing their own stamp on the development of the core syllabus of their particular subject. For a secondary school subject, for example, this includes linking the relevant subject, grade, module and lesson aims (or outcomes) with the school mission and goals. This aspect may be further amplified through the analysis of the syllabus in order to identify modules. A time schedule for the year must also be prepared. This process is known as subject curriculum development and is a critical part of the operationalisation and later institutionalisation of the curriculum.

The following are but a few examples as to how this may be done. Owing to a lack of space, examples are given of only a few subjects, followed by an explanation on developing a learning programme curriculum in an OBE context. In presenting these examples, it must once again be clearly stated that these are **only examples of ways** in which subject curriculum development can be done, as there are others. Teachers must have the freedom and initiative to follow their own strategies. Their ability to do this will depend on the nature and level of their empowerment.

Example 1: History for secondary school

Introduction

History is a systematic study of the past. History is therefore, besides its content, a means of investigating the past, which requires the acquisition and use of skills. The happenings, communities and peoples of the past are studied so that an appreciation for other times and places may be developed. History develops the imagination and understanding of peoples and communities. A study of the past is necessary for an understanding of the present, and vice versa.

Specific subject goals

a.   The goals of History at school are to bring home to learners knowledge and understanding of the past, especially with regard to:
1.   their own history and that of other peoples and cultures;
2.   the manner in which public administration has developed in their own country; and
3.   the history of important happenings and movements which influence life today.
b.   When the above goals have been realised, the study of history may be of great value for learners as:
1.   it contributes to a better understanding of present-day world trends, conditions and problems;

2.   it broadens and enriches their knowledge, so that persons, places and events referred to in books, newspapers, radio, television, films and discussions will have meaning and importance for them, and so that they may be in a position to write, think and hold discussions intelligently about them;

3.   it cultivates more appreciation and respect for basic life values, such as justice, freedom, truth and integrity;

4.   it makes them aware of their privileges and duties as citizens;

5.   it helps them to develop an understanding of time, and to appreciate the interaction between cause and result, and to evaluate humankind's achievements according to their value;

6.   it makes them aware of the changing position of historical knowledge and the contributions of applied disciplines;

7.   it contributes an understanding of history as an academic discipline, and develops the intellectual skills and perspectives which are inherent in such study;

8.   it qualifies them to apply their knowledge effectively with a view to
     - collecting and classifying information;
     - choosing from it that which is relevant to their specific needs;
     - thinking objectively, critically and empathetically; and
     - setting information out clearly both in writing and orally.

9.   it encourages working methods that will cultivate self-industry.

General aims

a.   The material is offered at the applicable level to ensure that the aims of History are achieved.

b.   The content and framework of the syllabus are such that learners will develop a broad understanding and general knowledge.

c.   Advantage is taken of the learner's natural urge to want to know what happened in the past.

d.   The syllabus will ensure that learners obtain a detailed knowledge and understanding of selected events in the history of South Africa and the rest of the world.

e.   The syllabus is designed to integrate the instruction of contents, skills and attitudes.

f.   As skills and attitudes are less-tangible objectives, they are given more conscious and systematic consideration to avoid a mere content approach.

g.   While attitudes and values are not easily tested, the goal is nevertheless to contribute to the growth and maturity of the learners.

Grade aims/outcomes

The syllabus for every year is taught in such a way that there is agreement between the learning process (the 'how') and the learning product (the 'what').

Core contents

History syllabus: Grade 12

- **Module 1:** The rise of Super Powers, 1917 to 1939
- **Module 2:** Circumstances which led to the Second World War
- **Module 3:** International relations and events 1945 to 1970
- **Module 4:** Political development and the creation of a republic:
  - The NP strengthens its position in parliament
  - The breaking of links with Britain
  - The 1960 referendum
  - Withdrawal from the Commonwealth
  - The coming of a republic
- **Module 5:** Policy with regard to race relations and the reaction following on it:
  - Apartheid, establishment laws, internal and external reaction thereto
  - Homelands policy
  - Apartheid to 1990
  - The history of anti-apartheid groups during the struggle to end apartheid
  - Moving towards a democratic South Africa (SA): 1990 to April 1994
  - The period of transformation after April 1994
- **Module 6:** Ongoing economic development and social change:
  - The development and diversification of the mining industry
  - The development of agriculture
  - Foreign trade and investment
  - Labour, urbanisation and township development
  - Economic development in rural areas
  - Economic recession and recovery
- **Module 7:** South Africa's foreign policy:
  - The World Court Judgement of 1950 – reasons, content, developments: 1950 to1970
  - Economic and social influence of SA on SWA/Namibia
  - UNO involvement by means of committees
  - World Court opinion, 1960 and the consequences
  - Efforts to isolate SA in the world
  - Efforts by SA to break the isolation

Module	1	2	3	4	5	6	7
Periods	25	30	35	25	25	30	30
Term	1	1,2	2,3	2	2	3	4

In this example, a similar breakdown of the syllabi into modules would be given for the other grades.

At this stage, this subject curriculum development is still a broad plan, which will be further divided and refined in lessons. It is especially at this micro-level of planning lessons that a subject teacher may show considerable freedom and initiative with a view to operationalising a curriculum at micro-level in the classroom.

Example 2: Accounting

The following example is given with acknowledgement to K van Staden of Swakopmund (1989).

Macro-planning schedule

Subject: Accounting Grade 11
Available instruction time: 125 hours
Lesson periods: 167 (125 × 4/3: periods are 45 min long)

Syllabus aims

1. To equip learners with accountancy concepts, principles and procedures
2. To promote learners' insight and appreciation with regard to the value and importance of accounting records and reports for personal purposes, as preparation for a career and as encouragement to further study
3. To develop the logical thinking processes of learners so that instead of relying on preconceived rules they will be able to apply the basic principles of accounting in new and strange situations
4. To encourage a systematic and discerning approach to the solution of problems and to develop the analytical abilities of learners
5. To contribute to the formative education of learners by developing characteristic accounting requirements, such as neatness, thoroughness, accuracy and healthy judgement
6. To intensify learners' insight into accountancy and management principles
7. To promote the learners' understanding of and integration with their social milieu through meaningful interpretation of accounting information which they will have to deal with in later daily life

Modules

1. Column bookkeeping, ledgers and trial balances
2. Final accounts and financial statements of the sole proprietors of commercial and service undertakings
3. Partnerships
4. Bank reconciliation
5. Departmental bookkeeping
6. Modern trends

Module numbers
Lesson periods/instruction
Most time/degree of importance

Meso-planning schedule

Subject: Accountancy Grade 11
Textbook:
Module number: 1

Column bookkeeping, ledgers and trial balances

Instructional time: 23 hours
Lesson periods: Importance value: ±17%

Module aims

To promote learners' appreciation of the practical value and importance of column bookkeeping, ledgers and trial balances for businesses and also to lead learners to an understanding with regard to the recording of transactions so that they may interpret them correctly and with insight.

Learning aims

At the end of the module the learners will be able to:
1. identify and describe basic accounting principles;
2. know and implement accounting routines on a daily and monthly basis;
3. write up transactions in the various books of account already discussed;
4. enter in ledger accounts, and balance off where necessary;
5. enter particulars of transactions from the debtors' and creditors' ledger;
6. draw up and balance off the debtors' and creditors' control account from the total of the various books of account;
7. enter transfers between the debtors' and creditors' ledger and between the debtors' and creditors' control account;
8. reconcile the balance of debtors' control account with the total of the debit and credit balances according to debtors' list, and to reconcile the balance of the creditors' control account with the totals of the debit and credit balances according to the creditors' list;
9. correct various errors which influence the debtors' and creditors' control accounts;
10. analyse transactions so as to determine what source documents and journals have been used, what ledger accounts have been affected and the effect on the accounting comparison as applicable from the accounting framework, with account identification by means of the five basic principles;
11. draw up a prepayment trial balance;
12. interpret the part played by documentation, books, ledgers and trial balances in the recording procedure.

Learning content and scheduling

Module 1	Learning content	Lesson periods	Target date	Date completed
1.1	General introduction and revision of Grade 10 work			
1.1.1	Summary of basic accounting principles			
1.1.1.1	Principles to be covered: money value, historic cost price, documentation, double entry principle, principle of debit and credit entries, classifications and summary principle and internal check principles			
1.1.2	Staff duties and staff responsibility for accounting functions			
1.1.3	The purpose of an accounting system			
1.1.4	Summary of accounting routines			
1.1.4.1	Daily routines			
1.1.4.1.1	Writing up of journals from source documents			
1.1.4.1.2	Transferring of transaction particulars from journals to ledger			
1.1.4.2	Monthly routines			
1.1.4.2.1	Casting and cross-casting of journals			
1.1.4.2.2	Entry of totals of columns in journals and diverse accounts separately to the general ledger			
1.1.4.2.3	Drawing up lists of debtor and creditor balances from ledgers			
1.1.4.2.4	Finding pencil totals of nominal accounts			
1.1.4.2.5	Balancing of bank account and other balance sheet accounts			
1.1.4.2.6	Drawing up a trial balance			
1.2	Books of original entry, general ledger, auxiliary ledgers, trial balance			
1.2.1	Auxiliary journals			
1.2.1.1	Review from preceding syllabus			
1.2.1.2	Sale of fixed assets			
1.2.1.2.1	Commencement of financial year – cash – credit			

Module 1	Learning content	Lesson periods	Target date	Date completed
1.2.1.2.2	Financial year end – cash – credit			
1.2.1.2.3	During the course of the financial year			
1.2.1.3	Bad debts collected			
1.2.2	Debtors' and creditors' ledger and control accounts			
1.2.2.1	The purpose, basic principle, necessity functions and benefits of control accounts			
1.2.2.2	Entry from auxiliary journals to debtors' and creditors' ledgers			
1.2.2.3	Entry from auxiliary journals to control accounts and the general ledger			
1.2.2.4	Reconciliation of balances of control accounts with debtors' and creditors' lists as drawn up in auxiliary ledgers			
1.2.2.5	Transfers between debtors' and creditors' ledgers and between debtors' and creditors' control accounts			
1.2.2.6	Drawing up debtors' and creditors' control accounts directly in the general ledger			
1.2.2.6.1	Debtors with credit balances and creditors with debit balances			
1.2.2.7	Comparison of debtors' and creditors' lists with the balances of control accounts			
1.2.2.7.1	Faulty casting			
1.2.2.7.2	Errors in source documents			
1.2.2.7.3	Casting errors			
1.2.2.7.4	Faulty entry from auxiliary journals			
1.2.3	Drawing up the trial balance			
1.2.4	Influence on the accounting comparison and interpretation as applicable from the accounting framework (information document 1/83), with account identification by using the following principles:			
1.2.4.1	Auxiliary journals			

Module 1	Learning content	Lesson periods	Target date	Date completed
1.2.4.2	Source documents			
1.2.4.3	Account debit account credit			
1.2.4.4	E = B = L			
1.3	Analysis and interpretation of ledger accounts			
1.3.1	Debtors' accounts			
1.3.1.1	Individual debtors' accounts			
1.3.1.2	Debtors' control account			
1.3.2	Creditors' accounts			
1.3.2.1	Individual creditors' accounts			
1.3.2.2	Creditors' control account			
1.3.3	Fixed asset accounts			
1.4	The 10-column working account Mastery testing revision: June examination and December examination			

Example 3: Life Sciences Grades 10 to 12

Subject planning

Subject aims

The teacher can include the subject aims here according to the grade level.

Modules

The subject is planned by grade and subject level, modules and time scheduling.

Grade 10

Module
1. Ecology
2. Cell anatomy
3. Plant tissue
4. Anatomy of plant roots (dicotyledon)
5. Anatomy of plant stems (mono- and dicotyledon)
6. Leaf anatomy (dorsiventral)
7. Morphology of flowers (mono- and dicotyledon)
8. Mammalian tissue (differentiation, specialisation)
   - Epithelium
   - Connective
   - Muscle
   - Nerves
9. Mammalian skeleton
   - Axial
   - Appendicular

- Joints
- Skeletal muscles
10. Transport systems (human)
    - Blood vessels
    - Lymph vessels

Module		
Lesson hours		
Term		

Grade 11

1. Cell division
   - Nucleic acids
   - Mitosis
   - Meiosis
2. Genetics
3. Viruses and bacteria
4. Mycophytes
5. Phycophytes
6. Bryophytes
7. Pteridophytes
8. Spermatophytes
   - Gymnosperms
   - Angiosperms
9. Protozoa
10. Coelenterata
11. Platyhelminthes
12. Annelida
13. Arthropoda
14. Chordata
    - Osteichthyes (bony fish)
    - Amphibia
    - Reptilia
    - Aves
    - Mammalia
15. Human reproduction

Module		
Lesson hours		
Term		

Grade 12

1. Inorganic nutrients
2. Organic nutrients
3. Enzymes and co-enzymes

4. Water relations
5. Plant growth hormones
6. Photosynthesis
7. Cell respiration
8. Nutrition (human)
9. Gas exchange
10. Excretion
11. Chemical co-ordination
12. Nerve co-ordination
13. Sensory organs
14. Homeostasis
15. Population dynamics

Module
Lesson hours
Term

Lesson units and goals/outcomes

The following serves as an example of the possible further refinement of a module.

1. Grade 11
2. Subject: Life Sciences
3. Module 4
4. Number of periods: 5
5. Time scheduling in term: week 7
6. Module aims
   - To give learners an understanding of the structural and physiological characteristics of *mucor* (bread mould)
   - To ensure an understanding and knowledge of the adaptation of *mucor* to its habitat to ensure successful existence
   - Through experience of *mucor* and other fungi, to develop an understanding of their importance and the interdependence on other organisms

7. Lesson unit	Periods	Objectives/outcomes Learners must be able to:
7.1 Habitat and growth	1	a. describe conditions necessary for growth and development; describe and illustrate by means of neat diagrams micro– and macro-structures; distinguish fungi from other plants
7.2 Nutrition	1	b. describe the heterotrophic method of nutrition
7.3 Vegetative and sexual reproduction	1	c. describe and illustrate processes of vegetative and sexual reproduction

7.4	Ecological and economic role of fungi	1	d.	appreciate: the ecological and economic role of fungi; their indispensable role in the ecosystem; the link with bacteria and their role in ecosystems
7.5	Grade test	1		

Example 4: A modular approach in the primary school

In a number of primary schools a modular approach to curriculum development is followed. This aspect is described elsewhere (see Carl *et al.*, 1988). Lack of space prevents a more comprehensive description here, but the above source may be consulted to obtain details of the following:

- A rationale for the modular approach
- Broad planning of modules and classroom management
- Micro-curriculum development
- Their application in the various subjects

8.7   More comprehensive subject curriculum development

This planning and subject curriculum development must now be followed by implementation, evaluation and development. The principle in this process is that teachers should try to **develop** the curriculum and that this development could mean much more than just planning and implementing lessons. That is why this broader view is referred to as **comprehensive** subject curriculum development.

The following, although an extensive list, gives only examples as to how this process could progress, as it may be extended and developed through local initiatives and renewal. Teachers can reflect on their own profile as curriculum agents regarding these matters.

- Purposeful dissemination, implementation and evaluation of the curriculum
- Regular evaluation of relevance
- Syllabus development
  - Regular revision
  - Reflection on the curriculum and the proposing of possible amendments (i.e. engaging with the curriculum and reflecting critically on it)
  - Critical interpretation
  - Taking note of revision procedures
  - Taking note of and participation in curriculum, syllabus and study committees
  - Linking with study groups at local level
  - Participation in subject associations
- Evaluation/assessment of the subject's position in the school curriculum
- Selection of suitable and relevant textbooks/resources
- Selection of additional textbooks
- Development from core to learning content
- Development of subject reference works in the library

- Building up an own classroom library
- The identification of community sources
- Bringing together or searching for films, posters and video material
- Drawing up supplementary notes
- Evaluation (tests, examinations, portfolios, projects, seminars)
- Drawing up a question bank
- Staying informed of departmental syllabus requirements and the execution thereof (e.g. circulars)
- Planning, completion and regular checking of work report books
- Planning for and evaluation of practical work
- Experimentation with media and renewing teaching methods continually
- Holding regular subject team meetings
- Facilitating and/or attending training opportunities (e.g. a day or weekend seminar)
- Creation of effective climate
- Consultation
- Classroom research
- Planning and implementation of instructional planning
- Experimentation
- Keeping up to date with regard to curriculum knowledge
  - Knowledge and understanding of educational views
  - Thorough child knowledge and a positive attitude towards children
  - A positive teaching attitude
  - Particular subject curricular study
  - Didactic knowledge and ability (objectives, goals, selection of contents, classification of contents, teaching methods and media, evaluation)

8.8 Summary

A few of the methods by which a curriculum may be operationalised are reflected in the ways and examples described above. These are workable because they presuppose thorough curriculum knowledge and skills, and follow a logical pattern which is strongly guided by a mission and objectives.

The *modi operandi* proposed here each represent only one particular method, as each school and subject teacher must have the freedom and initiative to follow a method which is the best for his or her particular circumstances.

May the proposition of Tanner and Tanner (1975: 589) be the incentive for every teacher: 'Teachers who participated in curriculum revision brought a new intelligence to their teaching'.

Teachers can be empowered through the process of curriculum development, which can lead to optimising teaching and learning in order to develop and guide the full potential of every learner – and also their own potential.

Activities and questions

1. Based on the information in Sections 8.2–8.4 (you may also refer to Section 4.5), do a situation analysis for your specific setting or context. The analysis must include your local community, your school and your specific teaching context (classroom).

2. Based on the data generated from the situation analysis, formulate a vision and mission for your own context (this can link up with the vision of the school).

3. Reflect on your own subject curriculum planning. To what extent have you done macro-planning? To what extent is this linked to your own and the school's vision and mission?

4. What is the extent or nature of your own subject curriculum development? (see Section 8.7)

9 The Responsibility of the Empowered Teacher with regard to Curriculum Development

At the end of this chapter you should be able to:

- formulate a rationale for teacher participation in curriculum development
- describe the curriculum functions of the teacher in the various curriculum fields
- formulate a mission of intent with regard to teacher involvement in curriculum development
- do a self-evaluation of the status and quality of your own personal involvement in curriculum development
- decide on a strategy as to how you will optimise your own involvement in curriculum development.

Why did the reforms fail? The reforms often were 'installed', that is, teachers were told to find ways of implementing change models. No wonder they couldn't – 'or wouldn't – do it: even if they understood what was wanted, chances are that they didn't agree with much of it, and therefore would never feel genuine commitment to making it work (Benham, 1977: 205).

9.1 Introductory orientation: Perspectives on teacher involvement in curriculum development

A review of the phenomenon of empowerment was given in Chapter 1. There is a direct connection between the degree and nature of empowerment on the one hand, and the degree and nature of teacher involvement in curriculum development on the other. This chapter therefore intends to illustrate further the specific curriculum functions of an empowered teacher, while also further exploring the notion of teacher involvement. The premise is that the dynamics of curriculum development are, to a great extent, determined by the teacher's role at classroom level. The extent to which the teacher accepts and carries out the role of curriculum developer determines the dynamic of the process. This also implies, naturally, an involvement in other curriculum fields. It is therefore essential for teachers not only to be sensitised to this during initial and continued teacher training but also to be empowered to do it as effectively as possible. This should also be characterised by a process of self-empowerment.

Whenever there is talk of curriculum development, the teacher's role and involvement come to the fore of necessity. At worst, in situations where the syllabus or instructions have been designed higher up in the hierarchy by other persons or organisations, the involvement of the teachers may be as mere receivers, appliers and implementers. A means of empowerment would be to bring the teacher as implementer together with the institution or person involved with the design so that greater mutual co-operation may be brought about. There must be teacher input; it should not be otherwise.

A perception often held by teachers is that the curriculum is developed 'elsewhere' and that they simply need some guidance for the 'correct application' of a curriculum which is handed down to them from the top. This might create the impression that teachers operate solely within the context of the school and the classroom, making these seem the only place where they can make a contribution to the curriculum. This view denies the broader curriculum functions which could possibly be fulfilled outside of the classroom by teachers who serve on provincial or national curriculum committees (Carl, 2005: 223). The tendency to believe that teachers have simply to implement curricula which have already been developed elsewhere probably holds true for many contexts. In South Africa, the former Curriculum 2005, for instance, was developed at national level in 1998, and teachers only became involved when they received training in its application at school and classroom level.

Curriculum development as a concept is open to many possible interpretations. For the purposes of this writing, it is regarded as the encompassing and continual process during which any form of planning, designing, dissemination, implementation and assessment of curricula may take place (see Chapters 2 and 3). This process may occur in various areas of the curriculum, ranging from national and provincial levels to schools and classrooms. It is within this process of curriculum development that the teacher can and should become involved. The scope and nature of involvement with curriculum development will understandably vary from one curriculum area to the next, as the teacher in the classroom probably focuses mainly on the micro-curriculum, while at national level the macro aspects might call for a stronger focus.

The question is, however, whether the teacher cannot also become involved in curriculum development **outside** the classroom. Obviously, change cannot be successful if the teacher focuses on the classroom only. As Hecht, Higgerson, Gmelch and Tucker (1999: 152) contend quite rightly, '[t]eaching is more than the activities defined within the classroom walls'.

It is difficult to conceptualise 'teacher participation' in one single definition. Carl (2009) rightly refers to the notion of teacher involvement in curriculum development as an 'elusive' one as it is difficult to conceptualise it and encapsulate it in one definition or description. Moreover, the nature and scope of teacher involvement is often determined by the conceptualisation. This phenomenon has already been described extensively in subject literature (compare Connelly & Clandinin, 1984; Imber & Neidt, 1990; Elbaz, 1991; Fullan & Hargreaves, 1992; Fullan, 2001; Haberman, 1992; Carl, 2005). Two main tendencies regarding teacher participation can be distinguished:

- In the one, teachers are regarded as merely the recipients of the curriculum that is developed by specialists elsewhere. Teachers' curriculum function remains limited to the correct application of what has been developed by these specialists.

This so-called top-down approach is detrimental to the process of taking ownership of the curriculum.

- In the other, teachers are regarded as partners in the process of curriculum change. There should, therefore, be an opportunity for their voices to be heard before the actual implementation; they should be given the opportunity to make an input during the initial curriculum development processes (see Carl, 2005: 223).

The context (educational system, department of education, school system) often determines which of these two interpretations or tendencies is honoured. Aspects that allow or limit input and participation, such as leadership and the centralisation or decentralisation of an educational system, may determine or influence the nature and degree of participation. For example, education authorities might, from a governmental perspective, attach a particular meaning to the specific functions or roles expected from teachers.

Kirk and Macdonald (2001: 551–567) offer a further perspective on teacher involvement and ownership, based on Bernstein's (1990) model of discourse levels. This model focuses on the relationship between meaning-making processes on various levels of the educational system. The key aspects are represented in Table 9.1.

In the model of pedagogical discourse, a distinction is made between the three levels of discourse. These three levels constitute the so-called context within which curriculum change takes place. The question arises as to which level of discourse, or within which context, the teacher can or should become involved or gain access, i.e. where the teacher should have a voice. Kirk and Macdonald (2001: 565–566) express the opinion that teachers' contributions are particularly important in respect of the local context – in other words, the classroom or school – when they mention that 'teachers' authoritative voice is rooted in the local context of implementation'.

In terms of the South African context, it would be worthwhile to try to establish on which discourse level teachers experience their own involvement, as it might bring about increased ownership and more effective curriculum development.

There are, therefore, different views on both the desirability and the nature of teacher participation in curriculum development. Connelly and Clandinin (1984: 137) ask the following questions:

> Are teachers to be seen as screens whose effect is to be minimized, as in teacher proofing? Or are they to be seen as integral parts of the curriculum situation and therefore encouraged to explore and realize the curriculum potential of curriculum material? The trick for an intelligent teacher participation is to find out what exactly is happening. Do the people running the programme want teachers to put their own stamp on the programme? Or do they simply want teachers to bring their personal traits to bear on something that the implementers have defined?

Table 9.1: Bernstein's model of discourse levels

Discourse level	Educational field (context)
Production of discourse	The intellectual field primary level of discourse where knowledge is created in the form of disciplines (e.g. in education, health sciences, sociology) at institutions such as universities and other research institutions
Recontextualisation of discourse	Meaning is given to knowledge that has been produced in the foregoing discourse level, mostly by education authorities and curriculum writers.The field is where agents have the opportunity to become involved in the process of giving meaning to the produced knowledge. Schools and teachers are not, however, normally involved in this process. If teachers are regarded as partners in curriculum change in order that they may take ownership thereof, they must also be involved within this level of discourse as active agents and role players.
Reproduction of discourse	There is real implementation and application of pre-developed ideas by teachers. Teachers experience curriculum change as a 'top-down' process (must apply that which was developed elsewhere by education authorities without having acquired any access to consultation).

(Adapted from Kirk & Macdonald, 2001: 554 and Carl, 2005; 2007)

The perception is that the curriculum has to be 'teacher proof' and this can have a negative impact on teachers' willingness to become involved. Little and McLaughlin (1993: vii) stress that teachers will not respond positively to change unless they experience that their autonomy and freedom have not been discarded. They want to maintain this right to adapt and give meaning to the curriculum. Carlgren, Handal and Vaage (1994) and Norlander-Case, Reagan and Case (1999: 11) confirm that teachers should be an integral part of change and it should not be teacher proof. Glatthorn (1987b: 4) says in this regard:

> The teacher is the curriculum. They do not neutrally implement the curriculum – they adapt, translate and modify and develop their own.

Teachers' direct involvement will determine the level of success; they must, therefore, demand that their voices be heard. Nieto (2003: 11) comments in this regard:

> I was determined to go beyond the canned curriculum. I had received a curriculum so rigid that it included not only the daily objectives and lessons that teachers had to cover, but even the words they were expected to say. ... [T]he curriculum soon tested my patience and thwarted my creativity.

Teachers want to be partners in the process of curriculum development and not mere passengers or onlookers. They are important decision makers and therefore need to be involved. Marsh (2009: 211) stresses that teachers participate in the complexities of their daily teaching and are also responsible for a vast number of classroom decisions with the view to creating order in their environment.

The nature of teacher involvement may vary in accordance with the teaching level on which one is moving, and need not necessarily require taking an active role in the design phase in order to effect change. A teacher's involvement and co-operation may take the form of consultation and feedback before and during the design phase, while there will be a greater participation during implementation. It still remains of cardinal importance that the teacher is a core person who cannot and may not be entirely ignored.

When the teacher's responsibility with regard to curriculum development is reviewed, it appears ultimately to be one of involvement. When reference is made to involvement it includes involvement in aspects such as input into the design, implementation and evaluation at the various curriculum levels.

A rationale for teacher involvement

When writers make pronouncements with regard to the principle of teacher participation, they must be interpreted against the background of their educational thinking within a particular educational system. In some educational systems, as in the US, schools will have more autonomy insofar as curriculum affairs are concerned, while in others there will be less autonomy.

It is important for success that those who are involved in the implementation of curriculum development should play an active role from the design and planning thereof to the evaluation aspect. Teachers therefore occupy – or rather should occupy – a prominent position, as they will be the implementers of the relevant curriculum. Human *et al.* (1984: 19–20) motivate this stand by regarding teachers as those who will eventually implement the curriculum and who may gather valuable insights with regard to any defects in respect of, for example, its clarity of formulation; its practical feasibility; the degree of difficulty of the content for the learners of particular age groups; and the realisation of objectives within the allowed time schedule. Kelly (2009: 137) states categorically that the 'role of the teacher is quite fundamental and crucial to the effectiveness of educational provision'. He continues to stress that the teacher 'must be the hub of all this activity'. Teachers should already be prepared for their important role in curriculum development during teacher training. Ornstein and Hunkins (2009: 266) confirm this is a central role that teachers should have with regard to any curriculum improvement.

Beauchamp (1983: 90) motivates the teacher's involvement by emphasising that the curriculum development process is an educational one. Through the teacher's active involvement in the design, the instructional–learning situation may be made more effective, and the implementation and evaluation aspect may take place more effectively.

Loucks and Lieberman (1983: 131) link up with this by ascribing lack of success to a lack of teacher participation: 'Without adequate participation, the chance of successful implementation greatly diminishes'. Saylor *et al.* (1981: 100) support this idea, and mention that lack of participation may lead to a misconception as to what is expected, and that real allocation and appropriation cannot take place.

Greater participation may lead to greater job satisfaction among teachers (Bachman & Tannenbaum, 1968: 241). If there are no opportunities for input, the morale and quality of teaching may be prejudicially influenced. The implication of this is very clear, namely that there should be opportunities for joint decision making and joint planning.

From the above it is clear that a very high priority is placed on the principle of teacher involvement. How it will appear in practice is determined, *inter alia*, by the relevant educational system. Several studies in different contexts have shown that teachers want to be involved in curriculum development (Carl, 1986, 1994, 2005; Fullan & Hargreaves, 1992; Kirk & Mcdonald, 2001). Their findings indicate that there are ways and means of involving teachers in curriculum development outside the classroom situation. According to Carl (2005: 227), mechanisms will have to be put in place to optimise this involvement, thereby ensuring that the teachers' voices are heard and that opportunities are created for participation.

Teacher involvement and professional development

Whatever the level at which the principle of teacher involvement is manifested, it is very probable that this opportunity for participation may lead to greater professionalisation. Tanner and Tanner (1975: 614) say:

> If teaching is to be a profession, the teachers must participate in curriculum development at the class[-]room, school and school system levels. Professionalism is inextricably intertwined with curriculum development.

Czajkowski and Patterson (1980: 172–173) confirm the view that it is the teacher who often has the best specialist knowledge and that the utilisation thereof may lead to greater development within the school as well as in the classroom. Professional development does not, however, take place accidentally, as it is a long process. Kelly (2009: 138) reiterates that there can be no curriculum development without teacher development, as the teacher has a vital role to ensure successful education of a high quality for learners.

Teacher involvement is therefore essential, not only for the institutional and curriculum development of a school but also for the personal professional growth and empowerment of the teacher. Teacher participation brings about positive results, which may lead to dynamic curriculum development. Unfortunately, there are certain attitudes that result in situations arising where the teacher is not granted this privilege and right, which raises the issue of a teacher's professional status.

Denial of the right to participation

According to Tanner and Tanner (1975: 580, 630), the denial of the teacher's right to participation and involvement may lead to his or her being regarded as a technician who merely needs to read the instructions to carry out the task while professional decisions are taken elsewhere by other persons. This attitude implies a lack of confidence in the teacher to initiate developments, and does not take into account that it is the teacher who, in an intellectual manner, really gives form to the content by taking into account the differences and feelings of learners. Cremin (1965: 56–57, in Tanner & Tanner, 1975: 630) says in this connection:

> Now, there is no denying that teachers must be technically competent, and the reformers have not only the right but [also] the obligation to produce careful and detailed strategies for the use of their materials. But education is too significant and dynamic an enterprise to be left to mere technicians.

If the principle of teacher participation is acknowledged, it does not necessarily mean that it will naturally come into its own in practice. It should be purposefully pursued in practice and should be effectively supported through, *inter alia,* the creation of opportunities for it and the encouragement and stimulation to utilise it. While the principle of teacher involvement may therefore be acknowledged theoretically, when it comes to the execution thereof, support is often lacking.

Elbaz (in Lewy, 1991: 366–367) mentions a few reasons which may prevent teacher participation coming into its own, namely limited training, limited time, strongly prescriptive syllabi and bureaucracy.

Tanner and Tanner (1975: 579) agree that it is unrealistic to expect this participation if teachers are left to their own devices without any positive physical and moral support. It is precisely this lack of support which leads to failure, while the blame is often placed on the teacher. This in turn leads to a crisis of confidence and a further lack of teacher participation and creativity (Tanner & Tanner, 1975: 579):

> Such class[-]rooms are desert islands with the teachers as castaways. Like Robinson Crusoe they must fall back upon their own resources. However, whereas no one ever blamed Robinson Crusoe for not being more creative, the castaway teacher is continually under fire for being 'traditional' instead of 'forward looking' and for failing to produce spectacular new curriculum designs. In truth, his (or her) main concern may be educational and/or physical survival.

Teachers and curriculum change

The perception is often that teachers are against curriculum change and that they would therefore resist it because they have not been involved. Fullan (1991; 2001) sheds light on the phenomenon of the role of teachers' subjective realities by saying that one should always bear in mind that change is much more than just implementing a new policy. It is important to change the culture of teachers' schools and classrooms if they are to take ownership of the change. Too often they do not know how to handle the change, or they are uncertain of what is expected of them. This perceived negativity does not necessarily mean that they are resistant to change but rather that they are uncertain of what is expected. Fullan (2001: xiv) states:

> It isn't that people resist change as much as they don't know how to cope with it. If we know one thing about innovation and reform, it is that it cannot be done successfully to others.

Fullan (2001) then argues that to enable teachers to take ownership of the proposed curriculum change, these subjective realities will have to be considered. By subjective realities is meant the fears and uncertainties that teachers experience in their real life and contexts. A false perception is often created that teachers have taken ownership of the change, whereas it might only be a superficial acceptance and not real ownership. Change is multidimensional, and the pedagogical assumptions and belief systems of teachers are often not considered or taken into account: their subjective realities (fears, uncertainties, anxieties) are thus ignored (see Carl, 2007: 205). Fullan is of the opinion that if the belief systems are taken into consideration, then it can be seen that the nature of change is very complex. Fullan (2001: 42) states in this regard:

> ... [T]he development of a clear belief system is essential, because it provides a set of criteria for overall planning and a screen for sifting valuable from not-so-valuable learning opportunities.

It is essential to accommodate the world and reality of teachers and to consider their subjective realities to ensure optimal teacher involvement. Teachers play a major role in effective curriculum change and development, but are very often perceived to be resisting change, when actually the 'resistance' is a result of these realities having been ignored.

Ornstein and Hunkins (2009: 267) argue that if one wants teachers to commit themselves to change and innovation, involve them. They must have opportunities to make a contribution to curriculum improvement so that they may 'develop their individual identities as curriculum innovators'. They should therefore be fully involved in curriculum improvement and not be mere receivers of the curriculum. If one wants change to be successful, the involvement of the key role players (teachers) is essential and critical.

Summary

From the above paragraphs, the following principles become clear:
- Teacher participation in and involvement with curriculum development are essential and necessary principles in the process of teacher empowerment.
- A lack of involvement may have negative implications for the school and the teacher.
- The promotion of teacher participation in curriculum development may lead to greater professionalisation and empowerment.
- Attempts to limit teacher participation are unrealistic and unproductive.
- Teacher involvement with regard to curriculum development varies at the various curriculum levels.

9.2 The teacher's curriculum functions in the respective curriculum fields/sectors

Introduction

The responsibility of the teacher with regard to greater involvement with and participation in curriculum development in the respective curriculum fields will now be described. The curriculum fields and levels which are pertinent here correspond with those mentioned in Section 7.4. The more advanced the level of empowerment is, the higher the level and standard of involvement will most probably be. The curriculum fields are the following:

- Philosophy of the broad community
- Broad education policy and legislation
- School phase planning
- Syllabus development
- School curriculum development
- Comprehensive subject/learning programme development
- Micro-curriculum development

The teacher's responsibility with regard to the broad community's philosophy of life and therefore its attitude to and view of education

The broad philosophy of life usually has a directive function with regard to the determination of goals, which may be seen in the broader community's educational goals; the goals of the local community and school; the aims of the subject, lesson unit and lesson; and the instructional and learning objectives. There is mutual interaction, as the goals and objectives at all these levels should still be linked to the broader community's educational views and philosophies of life. Subject objectives and broad school objectives should serve the realisation of the broader national objectives. They should strongly promote the educational process, as well as the goal of providing quality education for all learners.

Besides the fact that teachers should also be the co-determiners of the philosophy of life of the broad community, at this level they probably have other responsibilities as well. In the first instance, the teacher is required to have a thorough knowledge of the relevant community's view of education. Teachers should also continuously evaluate whether their instruction is still in agreement with this broad philosophy of life and the broad goals of the education system. It may also mean that they must interpret the philosophy of life of the relevant community and school, and determine whether the community and school's objectives serve the relevant philosophy of life.

If, in addition, they act as subject heads, this interpretation function will also be carried through in respect of their subject colleagues. It would then be possible from time to time, for example during a subject group meeting, to remind the subject group leaders that all instruction and instruction-related activities should actually serve the broad educational objectives. A form of evaluation could even be used to determine whether each one's educational and subject goals are still in agreement with the broader educational ones. The privilege of fulfilling this function need not necessarily be reserved for a subject head but may also be carried out by every subject group member.

To give value to this evaluation effort, however, if it should appear that there are defects in this regard, there should be a follow-up action to bring subject teaching into agreement again with the broad educational goals.

It would appear as though the teacher's responsibility in this field is to be found particularly in the ongoing review of subject education, and also other education-related matters, with a view to determining whether it is still in agreement with the broad philosophy of life and the broad goals of education.

The teacher's responsibility with regard to broad educational policy and legislation

The role the government may play in curriculum development comprises a thorough situation analysis and interpretation of the community's philosophies of life, and also its attitude to and view of education, as this analysis and interpretation function may supply guidelines for suitable legislation. Carson (1984: 19) contends that this function may be ideally fulfilled by the government, as it has access to a variety of sources that could act in a consultative capacity, for example subject specialists from universities and other government organisations.

A community's or nation's view of education is often embodied in educational goals and, to give lawful acknowledgement to it, it is often recorded in legislation. Examples in this regard are the South African Qualifications Authority Act, Act 58 of 1995, through which SAQA was instituted, and the Constitution of the Republic of South Africa. It is improbable that teachers will participate in drawing up educational legislation. Their responsibilities will probably be limited to taking note of the relevant educational legislation and carrying it out. If they are subject heads, they will then probably play a leading role in ensuring a greater awareness thereof and ensuring that it is carried out.

The teacher's responsibility with regard to school phase planning

In the pre-1994 system, provision was made for four school phases: the junior primary school phase; the senior primary school phase; the junior secondary school phase and the senior secondary school phase. In the new dispensation, as mentioned earlier, the system now consists of the following:

Table 9.2: The school phase system

Education and training phases	Subdivisions
General Education and Training Phase	Receptive Phase (preschool, Grade R or 0)
	Foundation Phase (Grades 1–3)
	Intermediate Phase (Grades 4–6)
	Senior Phase (Grades 7–9)
Further Education and Training Phase	Grades 10–12
Higher Education and Training Phase	Higher Education

Provision has also been made for differing types of schools (schools with ordinary fields of study, commercial schools, technical schools, etc.) to make provision for differing educational needs. It is highly improbable that the teacher would have any direct part in the amendment thereof. It has already been mentioned that the school principal would probably also not have a direct share in any amendment hereof, but his or her function would relate rather to the filling out of the various phases. This filling out refers to the implementation of the rules and requirements as prescribed by the education authorities: entry requirements valid for every grade; rules with regard to examination and non-examination subjects; the number of periods per subject; subject choices for matriculation exemption purposes; and the rules affecting the import of new subjects or the elimination of existing ones.

Although it is probably mainly the school principal's responsibility to ensure that the particularisation takes place according to these rules and requirements, and he or she should therefore have a thorough knowledge of all the requirements, it does not mean that the teacher need not have any knowledge of these rules. Inherent in this, however, is the implication that the teacher should also have a thorough knowledge of school phase planning, subject choice possibilities, matriculation exemption requirements and syllabus development procedures, and that he or she may make an input in curriculum development in one way or another.

The ideal is, therefore, for each teacher to be informed as to these rules and requirements. It will facilitate the school principal's task in that a whole team of teachers may, on an ongoing basis, monitor whether all the requirements have been complied with. Thus all teachers may also evaluate their subject against the requirements, for example whether their pacing is relevant with regard to time scheduling and what adjustments should be made.

With regard to school phase and school type planning, teachers' responsibility appears to be one of awareness of the rules and requirements valid in respect of each school phase. This awareness should, however, have a further outcome, namely that they will not only continuously evaluate whether the relevant requirements are still relevant and realistic but also whether their particular subject complies with them. Depending on their rank in the school, their responsibility in this regard may be broader, for example subject choice composition within the school.

The teacher's responsibility with regard to syllabus development

Syllabus development comprises the design of a new syllabus, as well as the revision or changing of existing subject syllabi. Subject syllabi for every grade indicate what must be finalised in that particular grade. Core syllabi are planned according to a determined procedure, but each education department may adapt this core syllabus to local needs.

As teachers are the implementers of the syllabus they may identify deficiencies and defects in respect of, for example, the relevance of content; the practical feasibility of the syllabus; the degree of difficulty; the realisation of the objectives or outcomes within the specific time schedule; the clarity of formulation; and the realism of the relevant syllabus content. It is therefore essential for there to be a greater teacher input so that teachers will be curriculum developers and not merely implementers of syllabi designed elsewhere (Carl, 1987b: 113).

When teachers' responsibility with regard to syllabus development is reviewed therefore, it appears that they should be more involved in the development of the syllabus by means of, *inter alia*, the following:

- Thorough awareness of the relevant subject's syllabus review procedures
- Thorough awareness of input channels by which to submit syllabus amendments and proposals
- Active utilisation of these input channels
- Lodging of proposals and suggestions for amendments
- Reaction to proposals concerning syllabus amendments
- Awareness of the functions and activities of the respective curriculum committees
- Active participation in the activities of the relevant subject committee
- Active participation in the activities of teacher centres
- Active participation in the activities of the relevant subject-related societies (if they exist) at regional, national or even international level (e.g. through the attendance of their conferences)
- The writing of school textbooks or curriculum-related material (should the opportunity arise)

There are various sources which may be utilised in order to obtain the above-mentioned knowledge, which is, after all, a prerequisite for effective involvement. This information may be obtained in various ways, *inter alia* during initial teacher training; during in-service training opportunities; during ongoing formal study; through official educational documents/circulars; through the official journals of teachers' societies; through involvement in national subject societies; through personnel development programmes; during discussions with colleagues; through instructional guidance by school principals and superintendents; and through the activities of teacher centres or the forming of subject study groups. These sources may even serve as input mechanisms and be supplemented by input channels, such as departmental subject or study committees, or any curriculum committee.

The mass utilisation of these input mechanisms, however, would be impractical and would bring about a clumsy control system. Rather, teachers acting as representatives in committees or associations are the mouthpiece of the other teachers, and may make a contribution on their behalf. This reduces the awkwardness of a system which has too many representatives. In this way, the respective education departments can create a golden opportunity for teacher participation in syllabus development, not only through the creation of department subject or study committees but also through the manner in which they are composed and through the manner in which provision is made for orderly teacher input.

Mention was made earlier of the principle of approaching teachers to submit suggestions and proposals for possible syllabus amendments and that the reaction to this is not always positive. There may be various reasons as to why the teacher would not always react to requests to submit syllabus amendments, for example:

- The existing input channels are too limited.
- The teacher is satisfied with the present syllabus in its existing form.
- There is a disinclination to become involved.
- The workload at school is too time consuming.
- The teacher is unaware and ignorant of existing channels.

It appears that there is unanimity with regard to the principle of teacher input in syllabus development. Teacher participation is apparently limited, but there should be channels or input mechanisms which at least offer teachers the opportunity to convey their needs and to submit proposals with regard to syllabus development.

Various input channels have been indicated in the preceding paragraphs, but there is uncertainty with regard to the frequency of the utilisation of such mechanisms. This uncertainty is emphasised when one looks at responses to attempts, *inter alia* by means of subject committees, to ensure greater teacher input. There are three factors in particular which may determine the extent of teacher input:

- The education system and its composition and organisational structure
- The attitude and initiative of the individual teacher
- The degree of empowerment and self-empowerment

The final responsibility, however, lies with the teacher: however many input mechanisms there may be, they will be this in name only if there is little teacher participation and involvement. This said, it does not, however, deprive the authorities and all curriculum bodies of the important principle of continuing to encourage and stimulate teacher participation. Tanner and Tanner (1975: 588) remark quite rightly:

> Teachers often get the impression that any inquiries as to why high-level curriculum decisions have been made would be unwelcome. More often than not the impression is well founded. Little wonder, then, that many teachers find it easier not to even ask questions – much less to initiate curriculum change.

The teacher's responsibility with regard to school curriculum development

The school curriculum is, according to Doll (1978: 172), those formal and informal contents and processes which assist learners to acquire knowledge and understanding, to develop skills and attitudes and to acquire values while they are under the control of the school. This therefore comprises the subjects, the more complete, more comprehensive subject curricula and the subject choices offered within the school, as well as co-curricular activities. For the purpose of this publication, however, without disregarding the importance of co-curricular activities, the stress is placed on subject matters. There are virtually no descriptions within the literature of the specific responsibilities at this level, as the role of the teacher is usually described in broad terms.

The misconception may possibly arise that it is the responsibility only of the school principal and persons in promotion posts to see to the planning aspect, as the teacher may also make a contribution at this level in respect of curriculum development. Teacher initiative will probably be dampened if the school principal has created a 'don't rock the boat' atmosphere within the school, as Tanner and Tanner (1975: 588) put it, and this in turn may limit or obstruct professional development in that the latter responsibility is then left to the teachers themselves. Once again, it is the principle of teacher involvement. Doll (1978: 173–174) endeavours to answer the question of how teachers can be professionally involved in the process of school curriculum development as follows:

- Teachers are the core planners, as they know the learners best and have the skills available which may be used during planning of the school curriculum.
- Effective support by subject specialists and subject heads is necessary in order to be able to plan effectively.
- Time should be scheduled to enable teachers to help with this planning.
- The necessary facilities and administrative help are required.
- This teacher participation may contribute to effective personnel development, and therefore efficient opportunities for this purpose should be created.

At this curriculum level, teachers may prosper as agents for change and may make suggestions for extension of the broader school curriculum. This should, however, take place within the broader team context, as the whole school programme may be affected by it, for example where student leadership development is envisaged or where certain culture consciousness programmes are embarked on. Neagley and Evans (1970: 112) link up strongly with the notion of teachers being agents for change:

> Teachers must become partners; they must be involved with their principals in the shaping of school policies, curriculum decisions …!

While this initiative may be dampened if the physical and moral support is lacking, such involvement is necessary for greater personal and professional development.

Franken (1994) describes the principal's role as a curriculum leader and he stresses the importance of teacher involvement. A further responsibility, therefore, is that, if the school principal creates the opportunity for co-planning and involvement, the teachers must react positively to and utilise opportunities for involvement maximally. Only then can maximal satisfaction take place in regard to motivational (growth and recognition) and maintenance (security, work-orientation, status, social, physical and economic) needs. The satisfaction of these needs does not depend only on external influence or persons but also on teachers themselves. Participation is therefore essential.

Teachers may also act as facilitators and initiators with regard to the broad school curriculum. The teacher's responsibility is therefore not limited to subject curriculum development but extends more broadly to the school curriculum. It is, however, an acknowledged fact that the extent of support is determinative, as is the extent of the initiative by the teacher. Weiss (1980: 178) confirms this when he states:

> … [T]he amount of encouragement received … can influence the perceived rewards for this … involvement and possibly deter or encourage further participation.

The extent of teacher involvement and participation with regard to the school curriculum will thus be determined to a great extent by the particular school atmosphere, the existence of opportunities for participation and the level of teacher empowerment. The responsibility of the teacher lies in utilising these opportunities and in participating maximally. This may in turn manifest positively within the classroom, in that instructional learning may now also take place in terms of school objectives (Beauchamp, 1983: 96). This involvement therefore need not only be with regard to subject matters. Kelly (2009: 134–138) sees teachers as being central in any school-based curriculum development. He regards this centrality as the 'crucial feature of school-based curriculum development'.

From the above, it is evident that although it would seem that teachers cannot contribute much to the development of a school curriculum, they should nevertheless be involved therein. The level of involvement is largely determined by the extent to which the school principal creates opportunities for it. Teacher initiative is, however, also of importance, in that teachers, either individually or within a subject group context, should initiate change.

The teacher's responsibility with regard to more comprehensive subject curriculum development

It is especially in the curriculum field of more complete subject curriculum development that the teacher will have particular responsibilities and should be actively involved. More complete subject curriculum development comprises, *inter alia*, further subject planning with a view to giving more content to syllabi. The teacher has the syllabus document in his or her possession and must extend and develop it in various ways. The syllabi are thus developed and extended to a more complete subject curriculum. This extension and development will require various specific responsibilities from the teacher, including the following:

- The selection of suitable and relevant textbooks/curriculum material
- The selection of supplementary textbooks/material
- The interpretation of the syllabus
- The extension of the core and learning content
- The development of a collection of subject reference works in the library
- The building up of an own classroom library
- The identification of community sources
- The collecting or finding of films, posters and video material for utilisation
- The drawing up of own supplementary notes
- The drawing up of a question bank
- Remaining informed of departmental requirements and the execution thereof
- Remaining informed of departmental requirements for examinations and the execution thereof
- The planning for and evaluation/assessment of practical work
- The scheduling, conducting and correcting of tests and examinations/assessment
- Experimentation with media and renewal of teaching methods

There are also more general functions relating to more complete subject curriculum development which include the following: participation in annual planning of a subject group system; planning and holding subject meetings at scheduled times; the class visitation system; arranging or participating in training opportunities (e.g. a day or evening seminar); initiating and/or attending subject-related opportunities at a teachers' centre or on a regional basis; identifying implementation problems and relaying suggestions and proposals to bring about amendments; utilisation of input channels to propose amendments (e.g. teacher associations); and active linking up with and participation in the activities of national or international subject societies.

Ensuring that more complete curriculum development comes into its own usually requires the creation of an effective climate with a view to obtaining greater teacher participation. Doll (1978: 175) mentions that it is necessary to identify specific points where teachers may make a contribution in this connection and that it is also essential to know what each teacher's particular talents and abilities are. There is, however, room for the teacher to make a substantial contribution and, in this way, to promote more effective education. It is clear that more complete subject curriculum/learning programme development is one of the curriculum fields in which the greatest degree of teacher involvement is, or should be, apparent.

The teacher's responsibility with regard to the classroom and micro-curriculum development

It was motivated earlier on in this work that teacher involvement may lead to greater professional development and empowerment, and that this may also be valid with regard to the classroom. From the literature which has been consulted, it appears that the classroom is that level or field in which the teacher may become most actively involved in curriculum development and, more specifically, subject curriculum development. It is the level at which actual implementation takes place, and Weiss (1980: 176) is of the opinion that teachers must have the primary responsibility for what takes place in their classrooms. Doyle and Ponder (1977: 74) also lay particular stress on the key role of the teacher at this level and say: 'They are in fact the ultimate arbiters of class[-]room practice.' Clegg (1973: 30) regards the teacher as the 'heart of the system'.

Writers such as Beauchamp (1983: 96) and Tanner and Tanner (1975) confirm this view, and Della-Dora (1976: 52) lays stress on the fact that teachers will probably conceptualise the curriculum arising from what they themselves do in the classroom. Other factors which may influence this conceptualisation are teacher training, size of classes, school and system regulations or requirements, and extent of stress on cognitive development (Weiss, 1980: 176–177).

From this, another dimension comes to the fore, which is the teacher as developer, initiator, manager, analyser and evaluator of the syllabus, which in turn is recognised by Marks *et al.* (1978: 490) as an important dimension for the teacher's personal professional development, when they say that 'curriculum improvement has been recognized as a chief vehicle of teacher growth'.

Particular curriculum functions

Some particular curriculum actions with regard to the classroom will now be described.

Planning of lessons and lesson units

Within the classroom, the teacher will play a special role, particularly with regard to the planning of lessons and lesson units. To be able to do this, the teacher must be able to identify and formulate objectives; analyse content; plan learning experience opportunities; consider teaching methods and the sequence of constructional learning events; and be able to evaluate them effectively.

In this regard, a thorough knowledge of the relevant curriculum models can assist with meaningful planning. The components of which each model consists offer valuable guidelines with regard to responsibilities, and this may allow the learning events to take place in a systematic and structured manner. The curriculum model may be adapted to particular needs and the goal of the syllabus, and allows a great degree of flexibility should adjustments have to be made.

Through the utilisation of curriculum models, the teacher may plan in finer detail in order to achieve the most positive results from a specific instructional–learning situation. This planning function appears to be a basic function, but this in turn involves other responsibilities. Figure 9.1 depicts a possible process of micro-curriculum planning.

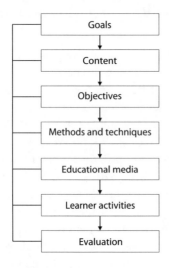

Figure 9.1: Micro-curriculum planning

Implementation of instructional planning

After planning, the next curriculum function would be to apply or implement the lessons which have been planned. Some of these curriculum actions would have a direct connection with instruction, while other actions would have a more indirect link, as indicated in the following:

Direct instructional activities
- Direct transfer of learning content
- Utilisation of educational methods and media

- Evaluation/assessment of effectiveness of the instructional–learning situation
- Evaluation/assessment of suitability of lesson content
- Distribution of homework

Instruction-linked activities
- General organisation of the classroom
- Checking and correcting homework
- Diagnosing learning errors and taking of remedial action
- Revision of additional instruction (e.g. outside normal school hours)
- Evaluation activities, such as drawing up and revising test and examination question papers, and correcting the answers
- Conducting personal self-evaluation

It is during these implementation actions that teachers may make a direct contribution in order to extend and strengthen their particular subject. In implementation, they can experiment with renewing educational methods, apply a variety of media, and implement or test other renewal ideas.

Experimentation

Taba (1962: 464–465) has given strong support to this concept of experimentation, stating the following in this connection:

> Perhaps the greatest need is for protecting experimentation. Teachers need help to try out new and unfamiliar ideas. But, above all, they need to feel free to experiment. They need assurance that the mistakes which occur in the course of experimentation will not be held against them.

If, however, the climate within the school is unfavourable, it may discourage teachers from experimenting with their subjects. To enable it to succeed, instruction leaders and the school principal must give a great deal of support to the teachers.

Teachers often think experimentally without realising it. When, for example, they consider a new method or learning experience, they are actually involved with experimentation. There are, however, various grades of experimental thought, and they vary from daily informal thinking to the adjustment and application of a certain idea, from the solution of a certain problem to the design of a formal experiment and the evaluation of the results (Tanner & Tanner, 1975: 645).

Teachers must be encouraged to think experimentally. Experimental thought is reflected by teacher actions within the classroom, and appears to be an important component of curriculum development and change. A special climate needs to be created, however, to provide sufficient support and opportunities for this to take place.

Classroom research

As developers of the curriculum, teachers should also be involved with research activities. It is sometimes necessary to extend the pool of knowledge by means of classroom research, especially when changes are envisaged. Research may deal with handling slow learners, gifted learners, the relevance of content, educational methods, and working methods, etc. Tanner and Tanner (1975: 613), however, warn that if this classroom research takes place in a haphazard manner and is not accurate and systematic, it is not of much value.

An important question is, naturally, whether teachers are in a position to play a dualistic role of teacher and researcher. Taba (1962: 460) and Kane (1984: 62) mention that teachers do not always have the necessary knowledge and skills to carry out effective research, and that training institutions, such as teacher colleges and universities, have a role to play in this connection. In-service training is, however, also a facet which may be used for this preparation role. Doing research requires of the teacher to study the relevant literature, which, although time consuming, may just help to bridge the gap between theory and practice, and to solve specific problems in the classroom (Tanner & Tanner, 1975: 614).

Kelly (2009: 138–139) is of the view that teachers do need to be researchers as they need to reflect on their work and continuously do self-evaluation. They should get the support to develop these skills as the outcome should be to improve and develop the curriculum.

Marsh (2009: 221) is of the view that action research is a strategy that enables teachers to continually reflect on what they are doing and to improve the curriculum (see 2009: 220–232 for more details). Another close-linked strategy to action research that Marsh (2009: 227–229) mentions, is lesson study.

A very brief description of lesson study is necessary here as the approach is an example of how teachers can on the one hand be involved in curriculum development at classroom level, but on the other hand also play a broader role as curriculum change agents. Lesson study can also make a strong contribution to the professional development of the participants, and can thus be a strategy to enable and empower teachers to be curriculum agents (see Coe, 2009, for a more comprehensive study on lesson study within the South African context; and also Marsh, 2009: 227–231).

Lesson study is described by Coe, Carl and Frick (2010: 207) as 'a systematic approach to the planning, teaching, observing, revising and re-teaching of lessons'. It provides an ideal situation for teachers be collaboratively and actively involved at classroom level in creative curriculum development. Lesson study has been used in Japan for more than five decades and is gaining ground in more countries. Coe *et al.* (2010: 211–213) indicate that the research lesson is the main component of lesson study and that it may consist of a number of steps (the lesson study cycle). These include collaborative goal setting; planning the research lesson; teaching and observing the research lesson; debriefing, revising and re-teaching; and lastly, sharing the results. The authors also stress the value of lesson study as an agent of change in a culture of isolation and that teachers now view 'the improvement of instruction as a collaborative rather than an individual responsibility'. Other benefits include that teachers become comfortable with colleagues observing them, and that there is an increase in teachers' content knowledge. These authors do warn that a great challenge in this whole process is the expectation that teachers must adopt the skills and behaviours of good researchers (Coe *et al.*, 2010: 214). Lesson study is thus an approach and opportunity for teachers to work together as a curriculum team to improve instruction. It does also create the opportunity for teachers to develop their research abilities and play an active and direct role in improving the curriculum for which they are responsible.

Teachers as curriculum leaders

From the previous sections, it becomes clear that teachers are also curriculum leaders in their own right at various levels. An empowered teacher is someone who initiates and leads change. Marsh (2009: 118–119) refers to several change leaders, among whom teachers are as well. One agrees with Ornstein and Hunkins (2009: 25) when they state that teachers have a central role in curriculum development. They form part of a professional team in the school and should be actively involved in the process of curriculum development. In this regard they do have a leadership function.

Brady and Kennedy (2010: 256–266) argue that teachers have a critical role in curriculum change. They are of the view that leadership should be shared and distributed among teachers to optimise teaching and learning and to enhance professional development. They further stress the importance that, in order to lead, teachers understand the complexities and nature of change (2010: 256). Empowered teachers should thus also identify and accept their responsibilities as curriculum leaders to ensure that the curriculum is optimally implemented and that effective teaching and learning occur.

General curriculum functions

There are also some general roles which the teacher may fulfil with regard to curriculum development within the classroom.

Possessor of curriculum competence and knowledge

Being able to make a real contribution to subject curriculum development requires a thorough knowledge of various aspects and the exercise of certain competencies. Cawood (1983: 2) has illustrated some aspects:
* Knowledge and understanding of attitudes towards education
* Philosophies of life
* Educational teaching attitudes

Thorough knowledge of the child and a positive adaptation towards children
* Positive adaptation to education and educational relations
* General curriculum studies
* Knowledge, understanding and critical adaptation with regard to overall school-phase curricula
* Knowledge, understanding and critical adaptation with regard to the particular school's curriculum

Particular subject curriculum studies
* Own subject/learning area specialisation and subject knowledge
* Knowledge, understanding and competence with regard to particular subject curriculum studies

- Knowledge, understanding, competence and critical adaptation with regard to a particular subject curriculum

Didactic knowledge and competence

- Knowledge of and competence in curriculum development at meso- and micro-level
- Knowledge of and competence in goal formulation and goal-orientated teaching
- Knowledge of and competence in content selection and classification
- Knowledge of and competence in educational methods and media
- Knowledge of and competence in evaluation of the child and curricula
- Knowledge of and utilisation of mechanisms/channels to enhance curriculum development
- Knowledge of and utilisation of curriculation development channels/mechanisms
- Support of instructional leaders

The main function of the teacher is not only to instruct but also to facilitate learning. This involves other co-responsibilities for which the above may serve as a basis or point of departure. The teacher who is able to fulfil these functions is the one who will be able to renew and change with a view to bringing subject curriculum development into its own.

Although the following curriculum functions were seen as integral to outcomes-based education, they are still relevant to the current context, and are not restricted to outcomes-based education:

- Teachers must be facilitators and not 'the source of all knowledge'.
- Teachers must encourage discussion and participation in the classroom.
- They should create an atmosphere which will promote critical thinking, discovery of knowledge, debate and reflection.
- They should facilitate relevant learning opportunities that will meet the needs of the learners.
- They must be adaptable and flexible in their teaching.
- They should facilitate learning opportunities that will encourage the development of problem-solving and decision-making skills.
- They must be able to determine learners' needs and their level of competence.
- They should recognise that learning should not be restricted to the classroom, because in reality learning experiences occur outside the classroom as well.
- They should link their teaching with the worlds of work and everyday life.
- They should be able to focus on the portability of one learning experience to another.
- They should take the previous experiences of learners into consideration.
- They should facilitate co-operative learning through their classroom management.

Agents for renewal

As innovator and agent for renewal, the empowered teacher will be expected to play various roles. Karmos and Jacko (1977: 53) and Dull (1981: 204) indicate that teachers must be developers, exercisers and researchers. In order to realise these roles or functions, the teachers must undertake the following sub-functions:

- They must acquire a clear understanding of the envisaged renewal.
- They must communicate preferences and attitudes clearly to all those involved.
- They must make known renewal strategy.
- They must visit other teachers.
- They must utilise sources, such as instructional leaders and other specialists, to supply needs.
- They must evaluate on an ongoing basis and discuss relevant problems.
- They must be patient with renewal and give it a reasonable chance.

Hunkins (1972: 504) mentions a few other roles which arise from being an agent of renewal:

- Motivator
- Negotiator
- Experimenter
- Consultant
- Diagnostician
- Evaluator
- Researcher
- Student
- Analyser

Further functions of renewal agents are the development of curriculum material; the orientation of learners; consultation with colleagues; participation in curriculum development activities; and participation in and planning of in-service training opportunities.

As agents for renewal, teachers therefore have a particular responsibility, as their embracing of the above will also, to a great degree, determine their own professional development, although, once again, the importance of support must be strongly stressed. Linking up with this responsibility, Doyle and Ponder (1977: 80) mention that successful implementation depends largely on the extent to which teachers respond to renewal within the classroom. It is therefore doubtful whether teachers can make a real contribution to subject curriculum development if they do not also reveal an inclination towards renewal. Only then can they truly be empowered curriculum agents.

From the above, it is clear that teachers need not be merely receivers of a syllabus but that they are able to make a particular contribution towards its development and that they have, in fact, many opportunities for doing so. This can, however, only take place if teachers reveal a willingness to utilise their knowledge and competencies in curriculum development and the input mechanisms to the maximum advantage of their subject.

In the whole process, the teacher will probably play a number of roles, but the main ones will be those of developer, experimenter, extender and evaluator. Fulfilling these roles requires enthusiasm, dedication, further studies and utilisation of all possible resources and input channels.

Support by the school principal and other instructional leaders is important, as the degree of support will often determine the degree of involvement and participation, thus affecting greater professional development. As Tanner and Tanner (1975: 582) quite rightly remark, 'if teachers are to be professionals, they must have a role in generating knowledge about the curriculum'.

There can thus be little doubt as to the particular role the teacher has to play with regard to curriculum development. It is, moreover, very clear that the empowered teacher will not merely instruct, but that he or she will also begin to play roles other than that of curriculum developer, but for this purpose, diligence and enthusiasm are important. Hunkins (1972: 506) illustrates the challenge that arises from change as follows – and it is a timeless observation that is valid for every decade:

> New identities, new roles, new attitudes, new organizations, new problems confront us. We are dealing with problems that unless solved can lead to the termination of the world as we currently know it. The school cannot meet the present situations with the same division of labour that served us in the twenties. The challenge is ours.

In the current South African context, the above functions can indeed be seen as being most relevant. The Department of Education (2002a: 9) gives the description of the kind of teacher that is envisaged, a description that portrays all of these functions:

> Educators at all levels are key contributors to the transformation of education in South Africa. Teachers have a particularly important role to play. The National Curriculum Statement envisions teachers who are qualified, competent, dedicated and caring and who will be able to fulfil the various roles outlined in the Norms and Standards for Educators of 2000 (*Government Gazette* No 20844). These see teachers as mediators of learning, interpreters and designers of learning programmes and materials, leaders, administrators and managers, scholars, researchers and lifelong learners, community members, citizens and pastors, assessors and learning area/phase specialists.

Teachers should therefore have a primary responsibility with regard to curriculum development and they should accept this challenge.

9.3 The role of training and other factors in the process of empowerment

Dynamic teacher involvement in curriculum development can make a real contribution to professional development. This can, however, only take place if opportunities for it are created. Taba (1962: 460) states that curriculum development and training must be combined for this purpose. Training is, however, only one instrument in empowering teachers. The ultimate aim is that the process of empowerment should eventually be strongly characterised by self-empowerment.

Aspirant teachers should already, during their original training, receive training in skills enabling them to curriculate, to acquire skills with regard to curriculum planning, and also to acquire greater insights with regard to broader curriculum matters. Skills with regard to research may then already be acquired. Tanner and Tanner (1975: 583–593) see this as a prerequisite for entry to the teaching profession. It is unreasonable and unrealistic to expect teachers to train themselves, as they require the help and support of knowledgeable persons. Many teachers have, however, acquired the necessary skills through their own efforts in the classroom or through one or other form of in-service training programme. Kane (1984: 59) is of the opinion that teachers should be trained as curriculum developers, as they should then be in a position to plan and develop their own work thoroughly. They may then also be more conscious of strategies for change, obtain knowledge of recent curriculum development trends, acquire basic skills in research and be ready to take part in decision making at various levels.

Searle (1972: 523–534) states in connection with initial training that education students should already be involved with curriculum studies during their clinical experience. This may eliminate later curriculum problems. This has important implications for all organisations, such as colleges and universities who are involved with the initial training of teachers, to make provision for this within their training curricula. This aspect should also receive attention during continuing studies and training. Preliminary findings of a research project (Carl, 2010–2011) indicate that the current state of empowering teachers with regard to curriculum studies in faculties of education in South Africa is unfortunately not satisfactory. This seems to be very fragmented and the inclusion and in-depth study of curriculum theory is rare (only a few faculties offer it). The focus is more often on micro-curriculum aspects and not on the deep understanding of the curriculum as a field of study in its own right. To be curriculum agents, teachers need to understand curriculum.

A further important aspect of training is that many teachers enter the profession without having received specific training to deal with curriculum development. In this connection, in-service training plays an important role, as it can contribute to making teachers more competent and to assisting them to master the applicable skills. In-service training may form an integral part of the school's instructional development programme in which use is made of subject meetings, workshops, personnel meetings, and so on. In this regard, the school principal and other training leaders will probably play a dominant role.

In this connection, the strengthening of a subject group approach can be meaningful, as curriculum development may take place on a continuing basis. Class visits, subject group meetings, etc. may then be used as valuable in-service training opportunities. These subject groups could also link up with inspectors/superintendents/subject advisers, as well as with other subject groups. Subject societies may also be established.

It is therefore clear that if the teacher is expected to reveal greater involvement in subject curriculum matters, the necessary support and ongoing training should be supplied, with both initial training and in-service training fulfilling important functions. As mentioned earlier, training is, however, only one factor influencing teacher empowerment. Other factors influencing empowerment are the following:

- Support by instructional leaders
- Opportunities created by facilitators
- How conducive the teaching environment is to involvement and empowerment
- The leadership styles of educational leaders and their own level of empowerment
- Whether structures in schools stimulate empowerment
- The presence of a democratic climate and culture in the school
- Decentralisation
- The presence of channels and opportunities to become involved
- The presence of sources and the availability of time
- The commitment of teachers to self-empowerment and to not being mere receivers of curricula

From the above and from, indeed, the content of this whole publication, it is clear that there are many factors and influences that may stimulate the process of empowerment and self-empowerment of teachers.

9.4   Summary

From the above paragraphs, it is evident that curriculum development may take place at various curriculum levels and in various curriculum fields/sectors:
- The broad community's philosophy of life and therefore also its attitude to education
- Government level through education legislation
- School phase and school type planning
- Syllabus development
- School curriculum
- More complete and comprehensive subject curriculum/programme development
- The classroom (micro-curriculum development)

The responsibilities of the teacher will probably vary from level to level, but there is little doubt that each teacher should have a certain degree of input. With regard to the above hierarchy, the teacher will have a varying degree of involvement and input, i.e. relatively little in respect of the uppermost levels in the hierarchy and a great deal at the lowest levels (more complete subject curriculum development and the classroom). This aspect of varying involvement is represented by Carl (1986: 232) in the model of the inverted pyramids (Figure 9.2).

From the model in Figure 9.2, it is possible to form a clear image of the much greater nature of involvement at the levels of classroom micro-curriculum development and more comprehensive subject curriculum development. The teacher's greatest contribution will, therefore, probably be with regard to subject curriculum development, although this is not a denial of the possibility of making a contribution in respect of the broad curriculum.

Teacher involvement is essential for successful and meaningful curriculum development, as teachers will be the eventual implementers thereof and will experience the problems first hand. By its very nature, curriculum development is an educational process and the teacher should be involved with it. If teachers experience that they also have a share in it, greater professional growth may take place and this may extend to a higher standard of curriculum development. When this teacher involvement is promoted, however, there should be sufficient support, as it is unrealistic to expect that teachers will have the necessary competence and knowledge themselves. Empowerment is of the utmost importance here.

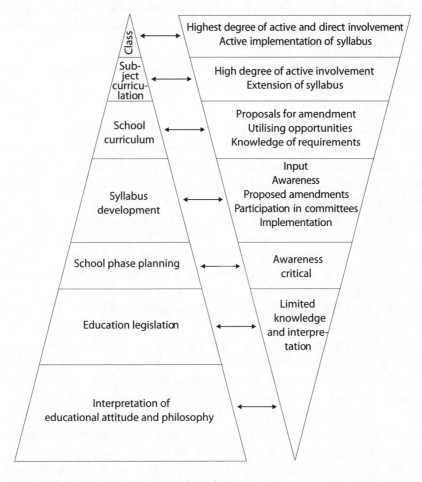

Figure 9.2: Teacher involvement in curriculum development

Besides being necessary for institutional and curriculum development in schools and the curriculum of a country, quality teacher involvement is essential for nurturing the personal and professional growth of the teacher. Teacher participation **can** bring positive results. Sadly enough, this principle is not always fully endorsed, which places the teacher's professional status in jeopardy. Purposeful strategies must therefore be developed in order to integrate the issues of teacher participation and teachers' professional growth effectively. These strategies should take due cognisance of teachers' need to be involved outside the classroom. Teachers do not wish to be viewed as mere recipients who are supposed to implement the curriculum in the classroom. They expect to be included in the initial process of meaningful decision making where their 'voices will be heard' (Carl, 2005: 227–228).

Teachers should therefore not be passive receivers of the curriculum but, as empowered curriculum agents, should show initiative and act as agents for renewal. Through utilisation of the existing and the creation of new input mechanisms, teachers may make a valuable contribution to curriculum development. Tanner and Tanner (1975: 588) also stress the value of teacher involvement in curriculum development for professional development:

> There can be little doubt that being treated as professionals … had a positive impact on … teachers who participated in curriculum revision (and on curriculum improvement processes).

Within the school, the empowered teacher also has a role to play, although the climate within the school and the leadership approach of the school principal will be determinative factors. Teachers may assist in enriching and extending the broad school curriculum by showing a critical adaptation and by liaising with the school's educational leaders. A team approach is essential in order to interrupt and challenge the status quo, and it requires physical and moral support. Teachers may therefore also act as initiators and facilitators at school level, but, as is often the case, if that initiative is dampened, teachers may show resistance to any form of change and renewal. Within the broad school curriculum, the teacher may contribute to more comprehensive subject curriculation which links very closely with curriculum development within the classroom.

It appears from the literature that it is particularly at the micro-level within the classroom that the teacher should show the greatest degree of involvement, i.e. with regard to subject curriculum development. Teachers conceptualise the curriculum in a unique manner within the classroom, perhaps otherwise than as envisaged by the designers, therefore co-operation and involvement in the original design is of cardinal importance. The roles which empowered teachers may play in this regard may be more specific or more general in nature. The successful execution of these functions implies active involvement and can only mean positive results for the particular subject.

The core of the matter therefore appears to be active teacher involvement. Barrow (1984: 269) even contends that teachers must be able to act autonomously and that education must be given back to them. They can only act autonomously if they are empowered. There must be flexibility in order to make teacher participation possible and to develop it. Tanner and Tanner (1975: 589) state this clearly:

> Also deserving of emphasis is the feeling that the teachers who participated in curriculum revision brought a new intelligence to their teaching.

From the above it is clear that the teacher may well have responsibilities with regard to curriculum development at macro- and at meso-level, but that the greatest responsibility will probably lie at micro-level with regard to involvement in subject curriculum development. This responsibility and involvement at micro-level should therefore be the point of departure for curriculum development, as it is from this point that greater involvement at meso-level and eventually at macro-level may be brought about.

Carl (1994: 193) is of the opinion that there are many definitions and views on what empowerment means and what this process encompasses. Some persons are of the view that empowerment is the process of equipping the teacher with certain skills, knowledge and attitudes; in other words, external powers decide what is necessary and the teacher becomes a mere recipient. Empowerment in the truest sense implies that the teacher should play an active role in this process. It does not mean that external powers, factors or influences should be ignored, because it is very often a true leader acting as facilitator that creates opportunities for teacher empowerment.

Empowerment is not the absence of structure, because empowerment often occurs within a certain structure. It is not a process where teachers are left on their own and allowed to do anything they wish, because there is still a lot of emphasis on productivity and the standard of the outcome. Empowerment is the process of development and growth where people are enabled to take decisions independently and in an autonomous way in order to make a contribution to the development of their environment. This process encompasses the development of certain skills, knowledge and attitudes to enable them to contribute to change from within their own power. Factors influencing empowerment would be the presence of a true democratic climate; the role of leadership; the commitment to empowerment itself; a view that regards empowerment not as a threat, but rather as an opportunity; and an openness to allow this process to run its course (Carl, 1994: 193).

It is clear that empowerment is not a simple matter – indeed, it is rather complicated. Empowered teachers must be much more than mere recipients and implementers of curricula and, instead, be curriculum agents in the truest sense. This means that they must be able to develop curricula in a creative way and be involved at a wider level than just the classroom in order to fulfil all the relevant learner needs. This wider level includes areas outside the traditional classroom – for example, the broad school curriculum, syllabus development outside the classroom – as well as more comprehensive subject curriculum or programme development, and even participation at a regional and national level. Teachers must therefore be empowered to be not only subject specialists but also specialists skilled in general curriculum thinking and practices. Only then will they be able to contribute towards changing and developing their environment and to meet the curriculum challenges that face South Africa. Vaughn's (1976: 24) opinion is still very relevant today, when he says:

> All individuals have a role in developing, and sharing accountability for the effective implementation of the educational goals developed. The result … will enhance the educational process and lead to the ultimate goal of quality education for all children.

Empowered teachers will be able to contribute to the achievement of this goal, because true success depends on them.

Empowering teachers through curriculum development therefore does not only require new thinking on relevant curricula, but it also requires new thinking on the changed role of the teacher in this process. The curriculum functions expected from teachers today differ vastly from those assigned in earlier years. Curriculum change should therefore include not only new thinking and action concerning curriculum development but also new thinking about how teachers can be optimally involved in the process, making redundant the outdated focus on the role of teachers as mere recipients (Carl, 2005: 228). Should the teachers' voices be ignored, the outcomes of new thinking on curriculum development may be thwarted, prolonging the dangerous situation that teachers, as potential curriculum agents, simply remain 'voices crying in the wilderness'.

Activities and questions

1. Reflect on each of the following:
   - What teacher involvement in curriculum development means
   - What the nature of this involvement should be
   - What the extent of this involvement should be
   - The relation between involvement and empowerment

2. Evaluate yourself in terms of your own involvement in the respective curriculum areas mentioned in Section 9.2.

3. Identify at least three channels through which syllabus amendments may be forwarded to the appropriate curriculum committees/authorities.

4. Design a strategy (which will be set out in your subject policy) to ensure ongoing teacher participation.

5. What do you think are the most important skills that an empowered teacher should have to enable curriculum development truly to come into its own?

6. With whom does the responsibility lie to make teachers curriculum competent/empowered?

7. What are the most important functions an empowered teacher must carry out in order to make a contribution to relevant and dynamic curriculum development?

8. What do you understand Tanner and Tanner (1975: 589) to mean when they state that 'teachers who participated in curriculum revision brought a new intelligence to their teaching'? What are the implications for teacher empowerment?

9. Identify at least 10 factors that could enhance and stimulate your personal self-empowerment.

10. Formulate your personal mission statement with regard to the process of empowering the teacher.

11. What does the notion of the 'teacher's voice' mean? Do you think that the voice of the teacher is a voice 'crying in the wilderness'? Motivate your response.

12. What does it mean for a teacher to be a curriculum leader?

Bibliography

African National Congress Education Department. 1994. 'A Policy Framework for Education and Training. A draft document'.

Alkin, M C. 1969. 'Evaluation theory development'. *Evaluation Comment*, 2(1).

Babin, P. 1981. *Canadian Curriculum Issues in Perspective (1970–1980)*. Ottawa: University of Ottawa Press.

Bachman, J G & Tannenbaum, A S. 1968. 'The control–satisfaction relationship across varied areas of experience' in *Control in Organizations*, (ed) A S Tannenbaum. New York: McGraw-Hill Book Company.

Barnett, R. 2008. 'Engaging the curriculum'. Workshop. Stellenbosch University.

Barrow, R. 1984. *Giving Teaching Back to Teachers. A Critical Introduction to Curriculum Theory.* Ontario: Wheatsheaf Books.

Beauchamp, G A. 1983. 'Curriculum design'. *Association for Supervision and Curriculum Development Yearbook*, 90–98.

Becher, T, Eraut, M & Knight, J. 1981. *Policies for Educational Accountability.* London: Heinemann.

Becher, T & Maclure, S. 1978. *The Politics of Curriculum Change.* London: Hutchinson of London.

Beets, P A D. 2007. 'Assessering-vir-leer in Geografieklasse in die Verdere-Onderwys-en Opleidingsbaan' (English translation: 'Assessment for learning in Geography classes for the Further Education and Training Band'). PhD thesis. Stellenbosch University.

Benham, J. 1977. 'Thoughts on the failure of curriculum design'. *Educational Leadership*, 35(3), 205–208.

Berman, L & Roderick, J (eds). 1977. *Feeling, Valuing and the Art of Growing: Insights into the Affective.* Washington DC: Association for Supervision and Curriculum Development.

Bernd, M. 1992. 'Shared decision making requires effective instructional leadership'. *NASSP Bulletin*, 76(540), 64–69.

Bernstein, B. 1990. The structuring of pedagogic discourse. *Vol IV: Class, Codes and Control.* London: Routledge.

Bloom, B S (ed). 1956. *Taxonomy of Educational Objectives: Cognitive Domain.* New York: David McKay Company, Inc.

Bloom, B S (ed). 1964. *Taxonomy of Educational Objectives: Affective Domain.* New York: David McKay Company, Inc.

Bobbit, F. 1918. *The Curriculum.* Boston: Houghton Mifflin.

Bogler, R & Somech, A. 2004. 'Influence of teacher empowerment on teachers' organizational commitment, professional commitment and organizational citizenship behavior in schools'. *Teaching and Teacher Education*, 20, 277–289.

Boles, H W & Davenport, J A. 1975. *Introduction to Educational Leadership.* New York: Harper & Row Publishers.

Bradfield, J M & Moredock, H S. 1957. *Measurement and Evaluation in Education*. New York: Macmillan Company, 204; as quoted by Fox, F W. 1965. 'Levels of performance in teaching' in *The Science Teacher*, 32(4), 31–32.

Brady B & Kennedy, K. 2010. *Curriculum Construction*, 4th ed. French Forest NSW: Pearson Australia.

Brandt, R S. 1976. 'Who should be involved in curriculum development?' *Educational Leadership*, 34(1),10–11.

Brandt, R S. 1992. 'On rethinking leadership: A conversation with Tom Sergiovanni'. *Educational Leadership*, 49(5), 46–49.

Brandt, R S & Tyler, R W. 1983. 'Goals and objectives'. *Association for Supervision and Curriculum Development Yearbook*, 40–52.

Bray, A F. 1979. 'Evaluating and selecting programs for gifted, talented students'. *NASSP Bulletin*, 16–20.

Bredeson, P V. 1989. 'Redefining leadership and the roles of school principals: Responses to changes in the professional worklife of teachers'. Paper. Annual meeting of the American Educational Research Association, 27–31 March 1989, San Francisco.

Browder, L H & Singer, A. 1993. 'Resolved: Teacher empowerment is a bad idea if it envisages teachers assuming the paramount formal decision-making role in schools'. *Curriculum Review*, 32(6), 3–8.

Brubaker, D L. 1982. *Curriculum Planning: The Dynamics of Theory and Practice*. Glenview, Illinois: Scott, Foresman & Company.

Bruner, J S. 1960. *The Process of Education*. Cambridge: Harvard University Press.

Calitz, L P, Du Plessis, S J P & Steyn, I N. 1982. *Die Kurrikulum: 'n Handleiding vir Dosente en Onderwysers*. Pretoria: Butterworth.

Carl, A E. 1985. 'Onderwyserbetrokkenheid by kurrikulumontwikkeling: 'n Ondersoek na die stand van onderwyserbetrokkenheid by kurrikulumontwikkeling in Kaaplandse sekondêre skole. 'n Vraelysondersoek geloods onder Kaaplandse sekondêre skole' (Brief translation: 'Questionnaire into the notion of teacher involvement in curriculum development'). Stellenbosch University.

Carl, A E. 1986. 'Onderwyserbetrokkenheid by kurrikulumontwikkeling by sekondêre skole in die RSA' (English translation: 'Teacher involvement in curriculum development in secondary schools in the RSA'). DEd thesis. Stellenbosch University.

Carl, A E. 1987a. 'Onderwyserbetrokkenheid by kurrikulumontwikkeling – 'n mite of 'n feit?' (English translation: Teacher involvement in curriculum development: a myth or fact?). *South African Journal of Education*, 7(2), 113–123.

Carl, A E. 1987b. 'Die onderwyser se rol in kurrikulumontwikkeling – Implementeerder of ontwikkelingsagent?' (English translation: 'The role of the teacher in curriculum development: Implementer or developer?'). *Die Unie*, Part I 83(11), 298–300; Part II 83(12), 339–343.

Carl, A E. 1994. 'Perspektiewe op die proses van bemagtiging (empowerment) van die onderwyser as kurrikulumagent' (English translation: 'Perspectives on the process of empowerment of the teacher as curriculum agent'). *South African Journal of Education*, 14(4), 189–194.

Carl, A E. 2005. 'The "voice" of the teacher in curriculum development: A voice crying in the wilderness?' *South African Journal of Education*, 25(4), 223–228.

Carl, A E. 2007. 'Onderwysers in die Wes-Kaap se persepsies en belewing van huidige onderwysverandering: Vir of teen?' (English translation: 'Teachers in the Western Cape's perceptions and experiences of current educational change: For or against?'). *Acta Academica*, 39(3), 200–223.

Carl, A E. 2008. 'Teachers' experiences of change in South Africa: For or against?' Paper presented at the International Conference on Learning, Chicago, 3–6 June 2008.

Carl, A E. 2009. 'Towards an understanding of "teacher involvement in curriculum development" … an elusive notion'. Paper presented at the International Association for the Advancement of Curriculum Studies, Stellenbosch, South Africa, 7–10 September 2009.

Carl, A E. 2010–2011. 'The state of curriculum studies in faculties of education at South African universities'. Research project funded by Stellenbosch University (Sub-committee A) and the National Research Foundation. Stellenbosch, South Africa.

Carl, A E. 2011a. 'Curriculum Studies as a field of studies within teacher training: The South African case'. Paper presented at the International Conference on Learning, Mauritius, 5–8 July 2011.

Carl, A E. 2011b. 'The state of Curriculum Studies at South African universities'. Paper presented at the London International Conference on Education, London, 7–10 November 2011.

Carl, A E & Park, T. 1998. 'Contemporary educational practices'. BEd Honours class notes. Stellenbosch University.

Carl, A E, Volschenk, A D L, Franken, T, Ehlers, R, Kotze, K, Louw, N & Van der Merwe, C E. 1988. *Curriculum Development in the Primary School: A Modular Approach.* Cape Town: Maskew Miller Longman.

Carlgren, I, Handal, G & Vaage, S. 1994. *Teachers' Minds and Actions: Research on Teachers' Thinking and Practice.* London: The Falmer Press.

Caro, F G. 1977. *Readings in Evaluation Research*, 2nd ed. New York: Russell Sage Foundation.

Carson, A S. 1984. 'Control of the curriculum: A case for teachers'. *Journal for Curriculum Studies*, 16(1), 19–28.

Cawood, J. 1983. 'Die onderwyser as toekomsbouer' (English translation: 'The teacher as builder of the future'). Durban: Congress of the Natal Teachers' Union.

Cawood, J, Carl, A E, Conradie, S M, Hanekom, M & Blanckenberg, J M. 1984. 'Kurrikulering vir hoogsbegaafde leerlinge' (English translation: 'Curriculum development for highly gifted pupils'). Research report for the Human Sciences Research Council.

Cawood, J, Muller, F B & Swartz, J F A (eds). 1982. *Grondbeginsels van die Didaktiek.* Goodwood: Nasou.

Cawood, J, Strydom, A H & Van Loggerenberg, N T. 1980. *Doeltreffende Onderwys.* Goodwood: Nasou.

Centre for Science Education. 1975. 'Curriculum Diffusion Research Project'. Outline report by P J Kelly, University of London.

Cherry, M. 1991. 'School ownership – the essential foundation of restructuring'. *NASSP Bulletin,* 75(537), 33–38.

Christensen, L M. 1991. 'Empowerment of preservice educators through effective mentoring'. University of Alabama. Synopsis in ERIC search.

Clair, N & Adger, C T. 1999. 'Professional development for teachers in culturally diverse schools'. ERIC Digest. EDO-FL-99- 08 [online]. Available from http://www.cal.org/ericcll/digest/profdvpt.html

Clegg, A A. 1973. 'The teacher as "manager" of the curriculum'. *Educational Leadership,* 30(4), 307–309.

Coe, K L. 2009. 'The process of lesson study as strategy for the development of teaching in primary schools: A case study in the Western Cape, South Africa'. PhD thesis, Stellenbosch University.

Coe, K L, Carl, A E & Frick, B L. 2010. Lesson study in continuing teacher professional development: A South African case study. *Acta Academica,* 42(4), 206–230.

Coetzee, J C. 1985. 'Evaluering' (English translation: 'Evaluation'). Class notes. Stellenbosch University.

Coleman, M, Graham-Jolley, M & Middlewood, D. 2003. *Managing the Curriculum in South African Schools.* London: The Commonwealth Secretariat.

Colyn, W. 1991. 'Department of Education and Training Mathematics Education: A preparation for failure'. *Perspectives in Education,* 13(1),108–114.

Committee of Education Department Heads. 1991. ''n Kurrikulummodel vir onderwys in Suid-Afrika. 'n Besprekingsdokument' (English translation: 'A curriculum model for education in South Africa. A discussion document').

Connell, W F. 1955. 'A glossary of curriculum terms'. *The Forum of Education.* Sydney: Teachers' College.

Connelly, F M & Clandinin, D J. 1984. *Teachers as Curriculum Planners: Narratives of Experience.* Ontario: Teachers' College Press.

Connelly, F M, Dukacz, A S & Quinlan, F. 1980. *Curriculum Planning for the Classroom.* Toronto: The Ontario Institute for Studies in Education.

Conradie, S M. 1984. 'Leierskapontwikkeling binne klas- en vakverband by leerlinge in sekondêre skole' (English translation: 'Leadership development within classroom and subject context in secondary schools'). DEd thesis. Stellenbosch University.

Cooley, W W & Lohnes, P R. 1976. *Evaluation Research in Education.* New York: Irvington.

Cornett, J W. 1991. '"Earned powerment" not empowerment of teachers: The role of teachers' systematic reflection in the restructuring of schools'. *Social Science Record,* 28(1), 71–77.

Cortez, C E. 1981. 'The societal curriculum: Implications for multiethnic educations' in *Educations in the 80s. Multiethnic Educations. National Education Association,* (ed) J A Banks. http://www.skatingaheadofthecurve.com/ (accessed on 15 November 2011).

Cremin, L A. 1965. *The Genius of American Education.* New York: Random House Inc.

Cunard, R F. 1990. 'Sharing instructional leadership – a view to strengthening the principal's position'. *Instructional Leadership,* 74(525), 30–34.

Czajkowski, T J & Patterson, J L. 1980. 'Curriculum change and the school'. *Association for Supervision and Curriculum Development Yearbook*, 158– 175.

De Corte, E, Geerligs, C T, Lagerwij, N A J, Peters, J J & Vandenberghe, R. 1981. *Beknopte Didaxologie*, 5th impression. Groningen: Wolters-Noordhoof.

De Lange, E C. 1984. 'Onderwyseraanspreeklikheid in kurrikulumontwikkeling' (English translation: 'Teacher accountability in curriculum development'). MEd thesis. Rand Afrikaans University.

De Villiers, G. 1985. 'Die inspekteur (superintendent) van onderwys as onderrigleier - 'n prioriteitsbepaling, taakanalise en 'n operasionele model vir funksionering' (English translation: 'The inspector (superintendent) of education as instructional leader – a determining of priorities, task analysis and an operational model'). DEd thesis. Stellenbosch University.

Della-Dora, D. 1976. 'Democracy and education: Who owns the curriculum?' *Educational Leadership*, 34(1), 51.

Department of Basic Education. 2011. *National Policy Pertaining to the Programme and Promotion Requirements of the National Curriculum Statements Grades R–12*. Pretoria: Department of Basic Education.

Department of Education. 1997. *Senior Phase. Policy Document (Grades 7–9)*. Pretoria: Department of Education.

Department of Education. 2002a. *Revised National Curriculum Statements Grades R–9 (Schools) Policy. Overview*. Pretoria: Department of Education.

Department of Education. 2002b. *Revised National Curriculum Statements Grades R–9 (Schools) Policy. Life Orientation*. Pretoria: Department of Education.

Department of Education. 2003. *National Curriculum Statement Grades 10–12 (General). Overview*. Pretoria: Department of Education.

Department of Education. 2005. *The National Senior Certificate: A Qualification at Level 4 on the National Qualifications Framework*. Pretoria: Department of Education.

Diamond, R M. 1975. *Instructional Development for Individualized Learning*. New Jersey: Englewood Cliffs.

Doll, R C. 1978. *Curriculum Improvement: Decision Making and Process*, 4th ed. Boston: Allyn & Bacon Inc.

Doll, W E & Gough, N (eds). 2002. *Curriculum Visions*. New York: Peter Lang.

Doyle, W & Ponder, G. 1977. 'The ethic of practicality: Implications for curriculum development'. *Association for Supervision and Curriculum Development Yearbook*, 74–80.

DuFour, R & Eaker, R. September 1987. 'The principal as leader: Two major responsibilities'. *NASSP Bulletin*, 71(500), 80–89.

Dull, L W. 1981. *Supervision: School Leadership Handbook*. Columbus: Charles Merrill Company.

Eisner, E W. 1985. *The Art of Educational Evaluation: A Personal View*. London: The Falmer Press.

Eisner, E W. 1990. 'Creative curriculum development and practice – a development practice'. *Journal of Curriculum and Supervision*, Fall 1990, 6(1), 62–73.

Eisner, E W & Vallance, E (eds). 1974. *Conflicting Conceptions of Curriculum*. Berkeley: McCutchan.

Elbaz, F. 1991. 'Teachers' participation in curriculum development' in *The International Encyclopedia of Curriculum*, (ed) A Lewy, 365–367. Oxford: Pergamon Press.

English, F W & Kaufman, R A. 1975. *Needs Assessment: A Focus for Curriculum Development*. Washington DC: Association for Supervision and Curriculum Development.

Eraut, M. 1990. 'Approaches to curriculum design' in *Handbook of Educational Ideas and Practices*, (ed) N Entwhistle. London: Routledge.

Fay, C. 1990. 'Teaching and leading: In the teacher's voice'. Paper. Annual meeting of the American Educational Research Association, 17–20 April 1990, Boston.

Firestone, W A & Wilson, B L. 1984. 'Culture of school is a key to more effective instruction'. *NASSP Bulletin*, 68(476), 7–11.

Foshay, A E. 1975. 'Towards a humane curriculum' in *Essays on Curriculum*. New York: Teachers' College Press.

Foster, K. 1990. 'Small steps on the way to teacher empowerment'. *Educational Leadership*, 47(8), 38–40.

Frame, J. 2003. 'Theorising curriculum' in *Managing the Curriculum in South African Schools*, (eds) M Coleman, M Graham-Jolley & D Middlewood. London: The Commonwealth Secretariat.

Franken, M J. 1994. 'Die leierskapsrol van die skoolhoof ten opsigte van kurrikulum-ontwikkeling' (English translation: 'The leadership role of the principal with regard to curriculum development'). MEd thesis. Stellenbosch University.

Freeman, H E & Sherwood, C C. 1965. 'Research in large-scale intervention programs'. *The Journal of Social Issues*, 21(1), 11–28.

Fullan, M G. 1991. *The New Meaning of Educational Change*, 2nd ed. New York: Teachers' College Press.

Fullan, M G. 1993. 'Why teachers must become change agents'. *Educational Leadership*, 12–17.

Fullan, M G. 2001. *The New Meaning of Educational Change*. New York: Teachers' College Press.

Fullan, M G & Hargreaves, A. 1992. *Teacher Development and Educational Change*. London: The Falmer Press.

Fullan, M G & Pomfret, A. 1977. 'Research on curriculum and instruction implementation'. *Review of Educational Research*, 47, 335–397.

Gabashane, I & Taylor, N (NEPI co-ordinators). 1992. National Education Policy Investigation (NEPI). Summarized Briefing Papers.

Gagne, R M. 1977. *The Conditions of Learning*. New York: Holt, Rinehart & Winston.

Gagne, R M & Briggs, L J. 1974. *Principles of Instructional Design*. New York: Holt, Rinehart & Winston.

Gay, G. 1980. 'Conceptual models of the curriculum – planning process' in *Considered Action for Curriculum Improvement*, (ed) A W Foshay. Alexandria: Association for Supervision and Curriculum Development.

Georgiades, W. 1980. 'A time to do or die: Curriculum change. What are the ingredients?' *NASSP Bulletin*, 70–75.

Glatthorn, A A. 1987a. 'Teacher autonomy vs curricular anarchy'. *NASSP Bulletin*, 71(498), 77–84.

Glatthorn, A A. 1987b. *Curriculum Leadership*. London: Scott, Foresman & Company.

Goodlad, J I and Associates. 1979. *Curriculum Inquiry: The Study of the Curriculum Practice*. New York: McGraw-Hill Book Company.

Gore, J M. 1989. 'Agency, structure and the rhetoric of teacher empowerment'. Paper. Annual meeting of the American Educational Research Association, 27–31 March 1989, San Francisco.

Gorton, R A. 1976. *School Administration: Challenge and Opportunity for Leadership*. Dubuque: WMC Brown Company Publishers.

Gow, D T & Casey, T W. 1983. 'Selecting learning activities'. *Association for Supervision and Curriculum Development Yearbook*, 112–125.

Goyne, J, Padgett, D, Rowicki, M & Triplitt, T. 1999. 'The journey to teacher empowerment'. Report. ERIC Record details ED434384 (accessed on 18 October 2011).

Grafft, W D. 1993. 'Teaming for excellence'. *Thrust for Educational Leadership*, 18–22.

Greene, M. 1989. 'Educational philosophy and teacher empowerment' in *Proceedings of the National Forum of the Association of Independent Liberal Arts Colleges for Teacher Education*. Synopsis of ERIC search.

Guilford, J P. 1956. 'The structures of intellect'. *Phychological Bulletin*, 53, 267–293.

Haberman, M. 1992. 'The role of the classroom teacher as a curriculum leader'. *NASSP Bulletin*, 76(547), 11–19.

Hall, G E. 1979. 'The concerns-based approach to facilitating change'. *Educational Horizons*, 57(4), 202–208.

Hattingh, C R. 1989. 'Kurrikulumdisseminasie as 'n kritiese fase binne effektiewe kurrikulumontwikkeling' (English translation: 'Curriculum dissemination as a critical phase in effective curriculum development'). MEd thesis. Stellenbosch University.

Havelock, R G. 1973. *Planning for Innovation through Dissemination and Utilization for Knowledge*. Michigan: Institute for Social Research.

Havelock, R G. 1982. 'The utilization of educational research' in *Challenge and Change in the Curriculum*, (eds) T Horton & P Raggatt. London: Hodder & Stoughton.

Hecht, E W D, Higgerson, M L, Gmelch, W H & Tucker, A. 1999. *The Department Chair as Academic Leader*. Phoenix, Arizona: American Council on Education Oryx Press.

Heller, G S. 1993. 'Teacher empowerment – sharing the challenge: A guide to implementation and success'. *NASSP Bulletin*, 77(550), 94–103.

Hill, J S. 1974. 'Kriteria vir die seleksie en ordening van kurrikuluminhoud' (English translation: 'Criteria for the selection and organising of curriulum content'). DEd dissertation. Pretoria University.

Hill, J S. 1977. 'Beginsels en prosedures vir die praktyk van kurrikulumontwikkeling' (English translation: 'Principles and procedures for the practice of curriculum development'). Paper. Annual meeting in Pretoria of the Transvaal Teachers Association's Interest Group.

Hill, J S. 1989. 'Kurrikulering vir relevante onderwys' (English translation: 'Curriculum development for relevant education'). Internal seminar on relevant teaching. Administration, House of Assembly.

Hooper, R (ed). 1971. *The Curriculum: Context, Design & Development*. Edinburgh: Oliver & Boyd.

Hord, S M, Rutherford, W L, Huling-Austin, L & Hall, G E. 1987. *Taking Charge of Change*. Alexandria: Association for Supervision and Curriculum Development.

Houston, P D. 1993. 'Wanted: Transformational leaders'. *Thrust for Educational Leadership*, 10–12.

Howes, B J & Quinn, R E. 1978. 'Implementing change: From research to a prescriptive framework'. *Group and Organization Studies*, 3(1), 38–51.

Huddlestone, J, Claspell, M & Killion, J. 1991. 'Teacher empowerment: Participative decision making can capitalize on teacher expertise'. *NASSP Bulletin*, 75(534), 80–88.

Human, P G. 1987. 'Manifestations of the curriculum'. Presentation at a seminar. Stellenbosch University.

Human, P G, Taylor, C A, Steyn, I N & Jansen, C P. 1986. 'Strukture vir die uitvoering van kurrikulumnavorsing en -ontwikkeling in die Republiek van Suid-Afrika' (English translation: 'Structures for the execution of curriculum research and development in South Africa'). *Sub-report of the Working Committee of the Human Sciences Research Council*, 1–23.

Human, R T (ed). 1973. *Approaches in Curriculum*. Englewood Cliffs: Prentice Hall.

Human Sciences Research Council. 1981. 'Ondersoek na die onderwys: Verslag van die Werkkomitee insake Kurrikulering' (English translation: 'Investigation into education: Report of the Working Committee on Curriculum Development'). Pretoria.

Human Sciences Research Council. 1984. 'Report of the Committee: Part 1. Curriculum development for highly gifted pupils'. (Project team: Cawood, J (project leader), Carl, A E, Hanekom, M & Blanckenberg, J M).

Hunkins, F P. 1972. 'New identities for new tasks'. *Educational Leadership*, 29(6), 503–506.

Imber, M & Neidt, W A. 1990. 'Teacher participation in school decision making' in *Teachers and their workplace: Commitment, performance and productivity*, (ed) P Reyes. London: SAGE.

Independent Examination Board. 1996. *Understanding the National Qualifications Framework: A Guide to Lifelong Learning*. Johannesburg: Heinemann Educational Publishers.

Jacobs, M, Gawe, N & Vakalisa, N C G. 2000. *Teaching–Learning Dynamics. A Participative Approach for OBE*, 2nd ed. Johannesburg: Heinemann.

Jordaan, V. 1989. 'Kurrikulumontwikkeling vir onderwyseropleiding aan Kaaplandse onderwyserskolleges' (English translation: 'Curriculum development for teacher training at Cape Teacher Training Colleges'). DEd thesis. Stellenbosch University.

Kane, J. 1984. 'Educational innovation in physical education and sport'. Paper. Annual conference of the South African Association for Sport, Science, Physical Education and Recreation, 2 October 1984, Stellenbosch.

Karmos, J S & Jacko, C M. 1977. 'Innovations: A note of caution'. *NASSP Bulletin*, 61(411), 47– 56.

Kavina, G & Tanaka, W. October 1991. 'Does empowerment affect administrators?' *NASSP Bulletin*, 75(537), 115–119.

Keiser, N & Shen, J. 2000. 'Principals' and teachers' perceptions of teacher empowerment'. *The Journal of Leadership Studies*, 7(3), 115–121. Available from http://leadershipcenter.osu.edu/publications/L_discoveries/LD_2002/Teacher%20empowerment.doc

Kelly, A V. 1977. *The Curriculum: Theory and Practice.* London: Harper &Row.

Kelly, A V. 2009. *The Curriculum: Theory and Practice,* 6th ed London: SAGE.

Kelly, P. 1980. 'From innovation to adaptability: The changing perspective of curriculum development' in *Curriculum Change: The Lessons of a Decade,* (ed) M Galton. Leicester: University Press.

Kent, T H *et al.* 1974. 'College-wide development of educational objectives for a medical curriculum'. *Journal of Medical Education,* 49, 750–751.

Killen, R. 1996. 'Outcomes-based education: Rethinking teaching'. Paper. University of South Africa, 15 October 1996, Pretoria.

Killen, R. 2007. *Teaching Strategies for Outcomes-based Education,* 2nd ed. Wetton, Cape Town: Juta.

Kirk, D & Macdonald, D. 2001. 'Teacher voice and ownership of curriculum change'. *Journal of Curriculum Studies,* 33(5), 551–567

Kissock, C. 1981. *Curriculum Planning for Social Studies Teaching.* New York: John Wiley & Sons.

Knaub, R F. 1979. 'Three principals discuss the principal's leadership role: Shared decision-making a must'. *Educational Leadership,* 36(6), 406.

Knoetze, F L. 1978. 'Die leierskaprol van die inspekteur van onderwys ten opsigte van primêre onderwys in Kaaplandse skole: 'n Onderwysadministratiewe studie van bepaalde aspekte met die klem op supervisie (kontrole en toesig) en professionele leiding' (English translation: 'The leadership role of the inspector of education with regard to primary schools in the Cape: An educational administrative study of certain aspects with regard to supervision (control) and professional guidance'). MEd thesis. Stellenbosch University.

Koerner, T. 1988. 'In search of excellence – a talk with Tom Peters about the principalship'. *NASSP Bulletin,* 72(12), 36–45.

Krüger, R A. 1980. *Beginsels en Kriteria vir Kurrikulumontwerp.* Pretoria: HAUM.

Kruse, S D & Louis, K S. 1998. 'Creating the conditions of empowerment: Resilient teachers and resilient students'. *Centre for Applied Research and Educational Improvement,* 6(1). University of Minnesota, College of Education. Available from http://cehd.umn.edu/carei/reports/rpractice/fall98/empowerment.html

Lagana, J F. 1989. 'Managing change and school improvement effectively'. *NASSP Bulletin,* 73(518), 52–55.

Lawton, D. 1982. 'The politics of curriculum evaluation' in *Curriculum Evaluation in Schools,* (eds) R McCormick & J May, 1983. London: Croom Helm.

Levine, M P. 1987. 'For educational excellence academic leaders need a purpose'. *NASSP Bulletin,* 71(498), 43–48.

Lewy, A (ed). 1991. *The International Encyclopedia of Curriculum.* Oxford: Pergamon Press.

Lichtenstein, G, McLaughlin, M & Knudsen, J. 1991. 'Teacher empowerment and professional knowledge'. Consortium for Policy Research in Education. Washington DC. Synopsis of ERIC search.

Lintner, J D. 2008. 'The relationship between perceived teacher empowerment and principal use of power'. DEd dissertation. Auburn University. http://gradworks.umi.com/33/17/3317329.html (accessed on 18 October 2011).

Little, J W & McLaughlin, M W. 1993. *Teachers' Work: Individuals, Colleagues and Contexts.* New York: Teachers' College Press.

Londoner, C A. 1972. 'The systems approach as an administrative and programming planning tool for continuing education'. *Educational Technology*, 12, 25.

Loucks, S F & Lieberman, A. 1983. 'Curriculum implementation'. *Association for Supervision and Curriculum Development Yearbook,* 126–141.

MacDonald, B *et al.* 1982. *Bread and Dreams.* Norwich: University of East Anglia.

Marks, J R, Stoops, E & King-Stoops, J. 1978. *Handbook of Educational Supervision: A Guide for the Practitioner,* 2nd ed. Boston: Allyn & Bacon.

Marsh, C J. 2009. *Key Concepts for Understanding Curriculum,* 4th ed. London: Routledge.

Martin, O L. 1990. 'Instructional leadership behaviors that empower teacher effectiveness'. Paper. Annual meeting of the Mid-South Educational Research Association, 14–16 November 1990, New Orleans. ERIC search.

McKernan, J. 2008. *Curriculum and Imagination – Process Theory, Pedagogy and Action Research.* London: Routledge-Taylor & Francis Group.

McCarty, B J & Davis, K. 1992. 'Alternative assessment: A constructivist approach'. *Personal narratives* [online]. Available from http://www.coe.uga.edu/quig/proce… uig92_Proceedings/mccarty.92.html

McCormick, R & May, J. 1983. *Curriculum Evaluation in Schools.* London: Croom Helm.

McCoy, S & Shreve, G R. 1983. 'Principals – why are some more successful than others in implementing change?' *NASSP Bulletin,* 67(464), 96–103.

McElrath, R L. 1988. 'Will empowerment of teachers remove barriers to educational reform?' Paper. National Council of States on In-service Education, 18–22 November 1988, New Orleans.

McNeil, J. 1977. *Curriculum: A Comprehensive Introduction.* Toronto: Little, Brown.

Melenyzer, B J. 1990. 'Teacher empowerment: The discourse, meanings and social actions of teachers'. Paper. Annual meeting of the National Council of States on In-service Education, 16–20 November 1990, Orlando, Florida. Synopsis of ERIC search.

Melenyzer, B J. 1991. 'Empowering the school community: Meeting the challenge through intra-university and university–school district collaboratives'. Paper presented at the annual National Conference of the National Council of States on In-Service education, 22–26 November 1991, Houston, Texas. Synopsis of ERIC search.

Miller, J P. 1983. *The Educational Spectrum: Orientations to Curriculum.* New York: Longman.

Moon, B. 1990. 'Implementing the Curriculum' in *Handbook of Educational Ideas and Practices,* (gen ed) N Entwistle, 1990. London: Routledge.

Mostert, J M. 1986a. 'Riglyne vir Kurrikulumontwikkeling. 'n Kort verslag' (English translation: 'Guidelines for curriculum development: A short report'). Pretoria: Insto-Print.

Mostert, J M. 1986b. ''n Model vir prosedures in kurrikulumnavorsing en ontwikkeling vir die RSA' (English translation: 'A model for procedures in curriculum research and development in the RSA'). Project Report: Human Sciences Research Council.

National Education Policy Investigation (NEPI). 1992. (See Gabashane & Taylor, 1992)

Nasionale Opleidingsraad (National Training Council). 1994. 'Bestuursopsomming: 'n Besprekingsdokument oor 'n nasionale opleidingstrategie-inisiatief' (English translation: 'Executive summary: A discussion document on a national training strategy'). Pretoria.

Nasstrom, B P. 1974. 'Teacher authority over the curriculum'. *Educational Leadership*, 31(8), 713–715.

Neagley, R S & Evans, N D. 1970. *Handbook for Effective Supervision of Instruction*, 2nd ed. New Jersey: Prentice Hall, Inc.

Newmann, F M. 1991. 'What is a "restructured" school? A framework to clarify end and means'. *Issue Report #1, Centre on Organization of Schools and by the National Association of Secondary School Principals.* Madison, Wl: University of Wisconsin.

Nicholls, A & Nicholls, H. 1972. *Developing a Curriculum: A Practical Guide.* London: George Allen & Unwin.

Nieto, S. 2003. *What Keeps Teachers Going?* New York: Teachers' College Press.

Nihlen, A S. 1992. 'Schools as centers for reflection and inquiry: Research for reacher empowerment'. Paper. Annual meeting of the American Educational Research Association, 20–24 April 1992. Synopsis of ERIC search.

Norlander-Case, K A, Reagan, T G & Case, C W. 1999. *The Professional Teacher. The Preparation and Nurturance of the Reflective Practitioner*, vol. 4. San Francisco: Jossey-Bass Publishers.

Oliva, P F. 1988. *Developing the Curriculum*, 2nd ed. Boston: Scott, Foresman & Company.

Orlosky, D E & Smith, B. 1978. *Curriculum Development: Issues and Insights.* Chicago: Rand McNally.

Ornstein, A C. 1982. 'Curriculum contracts: A historical overview'. *Phi Delta Kappan*, 404–408.

Ornstein, A C. & Hunkins, F P. 1988. 'Implementing curriculum change – guidelines for principals'. *NASSP Bulletin*, 72(511), 67–71.

Ornstein, A C & Hunkins, F P. 2009. *Curriculum – Foundations, Principles, and Issues*, 5th ed. Boston: Pearson.

Park, T. 1980. 'Didaktiese analise van vakhoofleiding aan groot Kaaplandse sekondêre skole' (English translation: 'Didactical analysis of subject head leadership in large secondary schools in the Cape'). MEd thesis. Stellenbosch University.

Park, T. 1981. 'Die vakhoof en onderwysvernuwing' (English translation: 'The subject head and educational innovation'). *Die Unie*, 271–274.

Parker, J C & Rubin, L. 1966. *Process as Content: Curriculum Design and the Application of Knowledge.* Chicago: Rand McNally.

Passow, A H. 1962. *Curriculum Crossroads.* New York: Teachers' College Press.

Peters, T & Waterman, R H. 1982. *In Search of Excellence: Lessons from America's Best-run Companies*. New York: Harper Business Essentials.

Phenix, P H. 1962. *The Uses of Disciplines as Curriculum Content*. The Education Forum.

Phenix, P H. 1964. *Realms of Meaning*. New York: McGraw-Hill.

Pinar, W F, Reynoldts, W M, Slattery, P & Taubman, P M. 1995. *Understanding Curriculum. An Introduction to the Study of Historical and Contemporary Curriculum Discourse*. New York: Peter Lang.

Posner, G J & Rudnitsky, A N. 1982. *Course Design: A Guide for Curriculum Development for Teachers*, 2nd ed. New York: Longman Inc.

Pratt, D. 1980. *Curriculum: Design and Development*. New York: Harcourt Brace Jovanovich Inc.

Prawat, R S. 1992. 'Teachers' beliefs about teaching and learning: A constructivist perspective'. *American Journal of Education*. 100(3), 354–395.

Prescott, W. 1976. 'Issues in curriculum innovation' in *Innovation: Problems and Possibilities*. London: The Open University Press.

Raubenheimer, C D. 1992/1993. 'An emerging approach to teacher development: Who drives the bus?' *Perspectives in Education*, 14(1), 67–80.

Reddy, C P S. 2000. 'Leadership in curriculum transformation'. MPhil Leadership in Education: Unit 3. Course material. Stellenbosch University.

Reep, B B & Grier, T B. 1992. 'Teacher empowerment: Strategies for success'. *NASSP Bulletin*, 76(546), 90–96.

Richmond, W. 1971. *The School Curriculum*. London: Methuen.

Rodgers, F A. 1983. 'Curriculum research and evaluation'. *Association for Supervision and Curriculum Development Yearbook*, 142–153.

Rogers, C A. 1962. 'Towards becoming a fully functioning person' in *Perceiving Behaving Becoming: A New Focus for Education*. Washington DC: Association for Supervision and Curriculum Development.

Rogers, E M. 1983. *Diffusion of Innovation*. New York: The Free Press.

Romanish, B. 1991. 'Teacher empowerment: The litmus test of school restructuring'. *Social Science Record*, 28(1), 55–69.

Romiszowski, A J. 1981. *Designing Instructional Systems*. London: Kogan Page.

Ross, E W. 1990. 'Teacher empowerment and the ideology of professionalism'. Paper presented at the Annual Convention of the New York State Council for Social Studies, April 1990. ERIC Record details ED 323198.

Rowley, S R. 1991. 'A new mindset for restructuring schools'. *NASSP Bulletin*, 75(537).

Rowntree, D. 1978. *Educational Technology in Curriculum Development*. London: Harper & Row.

Ruddock, J & Kelly, P. 1976. *The Dissemination of Curriculum Development: Current Trends*. London: NFER Publishing Company Ltd.

Saylor, J, Alexander, W M & Lewis, A J. 1981. *Curriculum Planning for Better Teaching and Learning*, 4th ed. New York: Holt, Rinehart & Winston.

Schiro, M. 1978. *Curriculum for Better Schools: The Great Ideological Debate*. New Jersey: Educational Technology Publications.

Schon, T A. 1971. *Beyond the Stable State*. London: Temple Smith.

Schreuder, D R, Blanckenberg, J M & Reddy, C P S. 2000. 'Leadership in curriculum transformation'. MPhil Leadership in Education: Unit 3. Course material. Stellenbosch University.

Schubert, W H. 1986. *Curriculum – Perspective, Paradigm and Possibility.* New York: Macmillan.

Schwartz, A T. 1980. 'Problems in evaluating planned change efforts in schools' in *Schools Conflict and Change,* (ed) M M Milstein. New York: Teachers' College Press.

Scriven, M. 1972. 'Pros and cons about goal-free evaluation'. *Evaluation Comment,* 3, 1–4.

Searle, H A. 1972. 'Student teachers need experience in curriculum development'. *Educational Leadership,* 29(6), 523–534.

Sergiovanni, T J. 1974. 'Synergistic evaluation'. *Teachers College Record,* 75(4), 540–552.

Sergiovanni, T J. 1990. 'Adding value to leadership gets extraordinary results'. *Educational Leadership,* 47(8), 23–27.

Short, P M. 1992. 'Dimensions of teacher empowerment'. Report. Pennsylvania State University. 16 pp. ERIC Record details ED 368701.

Short, P M. 1994. 'Defining teacher empowerment'. Education, 114. Short abstract: http://www.questa.com/googlescholar/ (accessed on 18 October 2011).

Short, P M & Rinehart, J S. 1992. 'Teacher empowerment and school climate'. Paper. Annual meeting of the American Educational Research Association, 20–24 April 1992.

Sidani-Tabbaa, A & Davis, N T. 1991. 'Teacher empowerment through change: A case study of a Biology teacher'. Paper. Annual meeting of the Association of Teacher Educators, 16–20 February 1991, New Orleans, Los Angeles.

Singh, V D. 2003. 'Pedagogy for empowerment'. *The Hindu.* [Online edition of India's national newspaper, June 10]. Available from http://www.hindionnet.com/thehindu/2003/06/10/stories/2003061000030200.htm

Sleeter, C E (ed). 1991. *Empowerment through multicultural education.* Albany, NY: State University of New York Press.

Smith, E E. 1924. *The Heart of the Curriculum.* Garden City, New York: The Country Life Press.

Smith, J M. 1984. 'Taking Humpty Dumpty out of the curriculum'. *National Association for School Principals Bulletin,* 68(476), 103–107.

Snyman, C. 1992. 'Kurrikulumontwikkeling in spesiale sekondêre skole vir verstandelik gestremde leerlinge in Kaapland' (English translation: 'Curriculum development in secondary special schools for the mentally handicapped in the Cape Province'). DEd thesis. Stellenbosch University.

Sönghe, W F. 1977. 'Die probleem van grondslagdenke in die kurrikulumbesinning'. *Educare,* 38. University of South Africa.

South Africa. 1967. Education Policy Act, Act 39 of 1967.

South Africa. 1983. *White Paper on the Provision of Education in the Republic of South Africa.* 23 November 1983. Pretoria: Government Printer.

South Africa. 1995. South African Qualifications Authority Act, Act 58 of 1995.

South Africa. 1995. *White Paper on Education and Training in a Democratic South Africa: First Steps to Develop a New System.* February. Pretoria: Government Printer.

South Africa. 2000. 'Norms and Standards for Educators. National Education Policy Act, 1996'. *Government Gazette*, 415(20844), 4 February 2000.

South African Qualifications Authority. 1997. *South African Authority Bulletin*, 1(1), 1–20.

South Africa. 12 September 2011. National Education Policy Act, 1996 (Act 27 of 1996), *Government Gazette*, 555 (34600). Approval of the National Curriculum Statements Grades R–12 as National Education Policy.

Stake, R E. 1967. 'The countenance of educational evaluation'. *Teacher College Record* 68(7), 523–540.

Stenhouse, L. 1976. *An Introduction to Curriculum Research and Development*. London: Heinemann Educational Books Ltd.

Stevens, M P. 1990. 'School climate and staff development: Keys to school reform'. *NASSP Bulletin*, 74(529), 66–70.

Steyn, I N. 1982. *Onderrig-leer en Wyse van Opvoeding*. Pretoria: Butterworth.

Stone, S J. 1995. 'Empowering teachers, empowering children'. *Association for Childhood Education*. Available from http://findarticles.com/p/articles/

Stratemeyer, F *et al*. 1957. *Developing a Curriculum for Modern Living*, 2nd ed. New York: Teachers' College Press.

Suchman, E. 1967. *Evaluative Research*. New York: Russell Sage Foundation.

Taba, H. 1962. *Curriculum Development: Theory and Practice*. New York: Harcourt, Brace & World Inc.

Tanner, D & Tanner, L. 1975. *Curriculum Development: Theory into Practice*. New York: Macmillan.

Taylor, C A. 1981. 'Die evaluering van die makro-inhoud van 'n kurrikulum' (English translation: 'The evaluation of the macro-content of a curriculum'). *South African Journal of Education*, 1(3/4), 128–132.

Taylor, N. 1997. 'Focus on the education debate: Curriculum 2005'. *Joint Education Trust Bulletin*, 7: 1–16.

Terry, P M. (n.d.). 'Empowering teachers as leaders'. *National Forum Journals*. Memphis: University of Memphis. Available from http://www.nationalforum.com/ Electronic%20Journal%20Volumes/Terry,%20paul%20M.%20Empowering %20Teachers%20As%20Leaders.pdf/ Google

Trousdale, A M & Henkin, R L. 1991. 'Reflection on negotiating curriculum: Praxis in the language arts class-room'. *Teaching Education*, 4(1), 175–180.

Tunmer, R. 1981. 'The curriculum in the decade of the "eighties"'. Paper. SAVBO Congress, 132–136. Pretoria; and *South African Journal for Education*, 1(1/2), 30–39.

Tyler, R W. 1949. *Basic Principles of Curriculum and Instruction*. Chicago: University of Chicago Press.

Tyler, R W. 1977. 'Curriculum development'. *The Education Digest*, XLII (6), 11.

University of South Africa (Unisa). 1997. Edufac-N/301/97. Study letter.

University of Stellenbosch. 1983. 'Curriculum model'. Department of Didactics, Stellenbosch University.

Vallance, E. 1982. 'The practical uses of curriculum theory'. *Theory into Practice*, 25(1), 24–30.

Vallance, E. 1991. 'Hidden curriculum' in *The International Encyclopedia of Curriculum*, (ed) A Lewy. Oxford: Pergamon Press, 40–42.

Van der Merwe, C R. 1997. 'Kurrikulumkonsultasie in Suid-Afrikaanse primêre skole' (English translation: 'Curriculum consultation in South African primary schools'). DEd thesis. Stellenbosch University.

Van Rensburg, D J J. 1992. 'Education must relate to work'. *Academic Standard*, 1(3), 5.

Van Wyk, M L. 2006. 'Die leerderportefeulje as 'n assesseringsinstrument in die Leerarea, Sosiale Wetenskappe in die Intermediêre Fase (Grade 4–6)' (English translation: 'The learner portfolio as an assessment instrument in the Learning Area, Social Sciences in the Intermediate Phase (Grades 4–6)). Stellenbosch University.

Vaughn, J B. 1976. 'The expanding role of teachers in negotiating curriculum'. *Educational Leadership*, 34(1), 21–23.

Vavrus, M. 1989. 'Alienation as the conceptual foundation for incorporating teacher empowerment into the teacher education knowledge base'. Proceedings of the National Forum of the Independent Liberal Arts Colleges for Teacher Education, 2– 4 June, Indianapolis.

Verduin, J R. 1967. *Co-operative Curriculum Improvement*. Englewood Cliffs: Prentice Hall.

Walker, D F & Schaffarzick, J. 1974. 'Comparing curricula'. *Review of Educational Research*, 44(1), 83–110.

Walker, W. 1978. 'Education's new movement – privatism'. *Educational Leadership*, 35(6), 472.

Walters, S W. 1978. 'The design of a theoretical model for the construction of a curriculum for Physical Science'. PhD thesis. University of Cape Town.

Walters, S W. 1985. 'Die ontwikkeling van kurrikulering op internasionale en nasionale vlak' (English translation: 'Curriculum development at international and national level'). MEd class notes. Stellenbosch University.

Warnich, P G. 2008. 'Uitkomsgebaseerde assessering van Geskiedenis in Graad 10' (English translation: 'Outcomes-based assessment of History for Grade 10'). PhD thesis. North-West University.

Weiss, J. 1980. 'The realities of curriculum work: The class-room level'. *Association for Supervision and Curriculum Development Yearbook*, 176–795.

Wheeler, D K. 1976. *Curriculum Process*, 7th printing (10th printing of 1967 ed). London: Hodder & Stoughton Ltd.

White, J P. 1971. 'The concept of curriculum evaluation'. *Journal of Curriculum Studies*, 3(2), 101–112 in *Curriculum Design*, (eds) M Golby, J Greenwald & R West, 1982, 387–389. London: The Open University Press.

Whitehead, D J. 1980. *The Dissemination of Educational Innovations in Britain*. London: Hodder & Stoughton Ltd.

Whitehead, R. 1992. 'A Masters course on curriculum design'. 1–22 July 1992. Faculty of Education, University of Ottawa, Canada.

Wiles, J & Bondi, J L. 1984. *Curriculum Development: A Guide to Practice*, 2nd ed. Columbus: Charles E. Merrill.

Wilson, L & Cuban, L. (n.d.). 'Types of curriculum'. http://coefaculty.valdosta.edu/stgrubbs/definitions%20%of%20curriculum.htm (accessed on 18 October 2011).

Zeichner, K M. 1991. 'Contradictions and tensions in the professionalization of teaching and the democratization of schools'. *Teacher's College Record Review*, 92(3), 363–379.

Index

Page numbers in *italics* refer to figures and tables.